International Banking for a New Century

This new textbook provides an up-to-date overview of international banking as the second decade of the twenty-first century unfolds. Integrating geo-economic, operational, institutional, and regulatory changes in the financial sector, the volume's methodology incorporates specific case studies and research, combining theory with practical examples to illustrate the impact and consequences of past and present financial crises.

The volume considers the core aspects of international banking, including its structural and technical features, historical context, institutional evolution in core markets, and wholesale, retail, investment, and private banking. It uses specific examples from past and present literature, post-2008 case studies and histories, and research materials, offering a fully updated overview of how international banks respond to global crises, the origin, efficacy and evolution of financial markets, and the regulatory framework within which they function.

One chapter is devoted to the evolution and potential of new markets, including the financial sectors of the BRICS and other emerging economies. Each chapter examines background, causes, impact, and resolution, focusing on specific cases and their broader implications for the sector.

This textbook is a guide to the new, and at times uncharted, landscape to be navigated by large domestic, cross-regional, and global banks, and will be invaluable reading for students of finance, business, and economics, as well as for those in the financial sector.

Irene Finel-Honigman is Adjunct Professor in banking and European economic history at Columbia University's School of International and Public Affairs (SIPA), USA.

Fernando B. Sotelino is Adjunct Professor in banking and finance at Columbia University's School of International and Public Affairs (SIPA), USA.

D1331397

PO40201 8037/5
KNOW
13/2/19

International Banking for a New Century

**Irene Finel-Honigman and
Fernando B. Sotelino**

Routledge
Taylor & Francis Group

LONDON AND NEW YORK

First published 2015
by Routledge
2 Park Square, Milton Park, Abingdon, Oxon OX14 4RN

and by Routledge
711 Third Avenue, New York, NY 10017

Routledge is an imprint of the Taylor & Francis Group, an informa business.

© 2015 Irene Finel-Honigman and Fernando B. Sotelino

British Library Cataloguing in Publication Data
A catalogue record for this book is available from the British Library.

Library of Congress Cataloging in Publication Data
Finel-Honigman, Irene.
International banking / Irene Finel-Honigman and Fernando Sotelino.
pages cm
1. Banks and banking, International–History. 2. International finance–History. I. Sotelino, Fernando. II. Title.
HG3881.F4394 2015
332.1'5–dc23
2014047700

ISBN: 978-0-415-68132-2 (hbk)
ISBN: 978-0-415-68133-9 (pbk)
ISBN: 978-1-315-72317-4 (ebk)

Typeset in Times New Roman
by Cenveo Publisher Services

MIX
Paper from
responsible sources
FSC
www.fsc.org   FSC® C013604

Printed and bound by CPI Group (UK) Ltd, Croydon, CR0 4YY

Contents

Illustrations

Boxes

Acknowledgments

We are extremely grateful to Provost John Coatsworth (Columbia University) and Dean Merit Janow (Columbia SIPA) for their generous support for this project.

Our colleagues at Columbia SIPA, Columbia Business School, and Columbia Law School have offered invaluable advice, inspiration, and encouragement, in particular Associate Dean Dan McIntyre and Professors Georges Ugeux, Volker Berghahn, Albert Fishlow, Richard Robb, Richard Goldberg, and Alessia Lefebure.

We have benefitted greatly from the lectures of and discussions with friends in the corporate world, media, and academia including Mordecai Kreinin, Bernard Shull, Albert Eckes, Lucio Vinhas de Souza, Marc Chandler, Kathleen Hays, Thomas Trebat, Lisa Schineller, Robert Albertson, Rodrigo Gonzalez, Markus Jaeger and many others with whom we have shared our professional lives.

Finally, we want to express our deep appreciation to Geraldine McAllister at Columbia University whose knowledge and editorial skill brought this book to fruition.

Introduction

Since 2007, we have taught the core international banking course in the Master of International Affairs Program (International Finance and Economic Policy Concentration), at Columbia University's School of International and Public Affairs (SIPA). Coming from complementary backgrounds in economics, finance, bank management, and intellectual history, we have sought to offer our students a comprehensive perspective of the evolution of international banking, including economic, geopolitical, and cultural determinants.

In 2010, Routledge invited us to develop a textbook in international banking encompassing the financial crisis of 2008 and its implications for banks and banking systems globally. We were excited by this opportunity, if slightly daunted by the enormity of the task. Yet, we could not have foreseen the extent to which events such as the EU sovereign debt crises, the gradual (but still incomplete) convergence of new banking regulations, the expanded supervisory roles of central banks, and too-big-to-fail legislation would necessitate rewrites and updates.

Banks have shown extraordinary resilience, aided in part by innovative programs introduced by governments during the worst of the crisis to make funds available to financial institutions, but we have witnessed an important erosion of the trust of society at large in these institutions. Our challenge has been to address the critical elements of this process, while the identity and culture of banks, and the fundamental role played by them, continue to be questioned and redefined.

Methodology

This volume is organized into nine chapters. In Chapter 1, we present an historical overview from the origins of international banking through the first decades of the twenty-first century. We explore the evolution of banks from domestic to global institutions; from separate deposit, savings, investment, and custody functions to the universal banking model; and from institutions bound by national jurisdiction to globally-interconnected institutions. The individual cases that we examine in this chapter include institutions once instrumental in domestic and cross-border economic development, but which, since the early 1990s, have been dissolved or have undertaken a much-reduced scope of activities (Barings, Rothschild, and Crédit Lyonnais), as well as institutions that have achieved global predominance since their inception, despite challenges and setbacks (HSBC, Citibank, JPMorgan, Deutsche Bank).

In Chapter 2, we consider international wholesale banking, and examine how, between the late 1980s and early 2000s, international banks redefined themselves in order to compete effectively for the business of their institutional clients – corporations, governments, and other financial institutions. We begin by exploring why and how major commercial banks around the world have engaged in investment banking, and then describe the corporate commercial and investment banking product offerings of international wholesale banks.

In Chapter 3, we consider international personal banking, retail and private. We explore how some of those same forces that led to the reinvention of corporate banking, and the enforcement of legislation to prevent tax evasion and money laundering globally, have influenced banks in their pursuit of international personal banking activities, private banking, and consumer banking. We begin by exploring the common aspects and the distinctive features of the provision of personal banking services to high net worth individuals versus the public at large, and then examine alternative strategies adopted by financial institutions in their pursuit of private banking and consumer banking activities abroad.

In Chapter 4, we examine the causes, ramifications, and resolution of specific bank failures, systemic crises, and country and regional banking crises, from the U.S. Savings and Loan crisis (mid 1980s), Nordic banking crisis (1991–1993), Japanese banking crisis (1995–1998), to the U.S. financial crisis and global credit crunch of 2008. We explore the case of Iceland, where the collapse of the banking sector brought about a near-default on sovereign debt, and that of Ireland, where the failures of Irish banks induced near financial collapse.

In Chapter 5, we consider sovereign risk, exploring the causes of, build-up to, and resolution of sovereign debt crises, and the implications for banks. We examine a number of sovereign debt crises that have resulted in major regulatory reform and/or institutional changes, in addition to offering valuable risk management lessons to creditors, borrowers, and the International Monetary Fund (IMF). We study the Latin American debt crisis of the 1980s that preceded the Basel I Accord; the Asian crisis of 1997 and Russian crises of 1998 (the latter causing the collapse of Long Term Capital Management) that preceded the Basel II Accord; the Argentine crisis of 2002, a unilateral default still unresolved as of mid 2014; and the Economic and Monetary Union (EMU) debt crises of the European Union (EU) that preceded important institutional reforms, including the establishment of the EU Banking Union.

In Chapter 6, we begin by reviewing the rationale for bank regulation. We then examine the domestic regulatory regime of Canada, and the evolution in form and substance of the international bank regulation accords, Basel I (1988), Basel II (2004), and Basel III (2010). We discuss briefly measures aimed at protecting the stability of domestic and global financial systems beyond the Basel III guidelines, including restrictions to banks' proprietary trading activities, and the evolving debate around regulation of non-bank financial institutions, often bundled under the label of shadow banks.

In Chapter 7, we examine how domestic macroeconomic conditions, internal political forces, and major external economic events have combined to shape the structure of the banking industries of eight selected emerging economies, in particular the resulting dynamics of competition among public sector, domestic private sector, and foreign banks. The countries selected – all G-20 nations and as such members of the Basel Committee on Bank Supervision – are from Latin America (Mexico and Brazil); Asia (China, India, and Indonesia); and Europe, the Middle East, and Africa (Russia, Turkey, and South Africa).

In Chapter 8, we examine a series of situations in which international banks have failed to comply with domestic and international laws or regulations, resulting in significant penalties and severe reputational damage. The situations selected include the Securities and Exchange Act violations of Madoff and Enron; the activities of rogue traders at UBS, Société Générale, and JPMorgan (London Whale); money laundering violations at BCCI, Vatican Bank, Standard Chartered, and BNP Paribas; tax evasion violations at UBS and Credit Suisse; and manipulation of the London Interbank Offered Rate (LIBOR).

In Chapter 9, we review in brief the forces that resulted in the internationalization of leading OECD banks between the late 1980s and 2008 (see Chapters 2, 3, and 7). We examine the consequences of government responses to the US subprime crisis and global credit crunch (see Chapters 4, 5, and 6), and explore the political and cultural consequences of those cases of financial fraud examined in Chapter 8. We conclude Chapter 9 with a discussion of a conceptual framework for decision making by major international banks, regarding the scope of their international activities, and taking into consideration the challenges faced by their boards of directors and management in rebuilding and maintaining the trust of clients, investors, and society at large.

1 History of international banking

International banks (almost)
never die

Introduction

This chapter presents a historical overview of the origins of international banking through the first decades of the twenty-first century. It examines the evolution from domestic to global institutions; from separate deposit, savings, investment, and custodial functions to the universal banking model (or financial supermarket); from institutions bound and limited by national jurisdiction to globally interconnected institutions, subject to cross-border regulation.

Equally important to note is what this chapter does not cover. A history of banking and money would encompass a broader geographic and geo-economic spectrum, including the development of merchant societies in the Levant from the Byzantine to the Ottoman Empire; the rise of commercial banks in eighteenth and nineteenth century India and China; and the beginning of transactional trade and deposit activities in Africa and Latin America.

However, the concept of international banks defined as financial institutions, which offer retail, wholesale (corporate and investment banking), and insurance services, establish branches, subsidiaries, and conduct business across borders, is much more limited in geo-historic scope. Our focus, therefore, will be on its origins in Europe and the United States, moving from Italy northward through Amsterdam to London and, from 1905, to New York.

International banking was contingent on a strong central bank, a stable currency, and the growth of a retail client base, which entrusted financial institutions with deposits and savings, and a corporate client base, which needed credit lines to further expand domestic and, in time, its international operations.

Nineteenth century economic expansion and wealth generation was fueled by industrial innovation, a new economically active middle class, and the rise of colonial empires. The surge in global trade required British and French banks to extend their reach across Africa, the Indian subcontinent and South-East Asia.

London was the epicenter of banking and the markets in stock, bonds, and currency, with the pound sterling the sole globally convertible currency from the late seventeenth-century to the twentieth century, followed by the French franc after 1865 and the US dollar after 1905.

The historic resilience of European banks (including those of Britain and Switzerland) and American banks is illustrated by the 2014 list of global systemically important banks (G-SIBs) in Table 1.1.

International banks in Europe, Japan, the United States, and Canada have a long history of survival despite internal and external shocks, including acquisitions and mergers, restructurings, wars, and economic crises. The financial crisis of 2008 first spelled the near death of Royal Bank of Scotland (United Kingdom), ING (Netherlands), Commerzbank (Germany), UBS (Switzerland), and Citibank

Table 1.1 Global systemically important banks (G-SIBs) as of November 2013 allocated to buckets corresponding to required level of additional loss absorbency

Bucket[1]	G-SIBs in alphabetical order within each bucket
5 (3.5%)	(Empty)
4 (2.5%)	HSBC JP Morgan Chase
3 (2.0%)	Barclays BNP Paribas Citigroup Deutsche Bank
2 (1.5%)	Bank of America Credit Suisse Goldman Sachs Group Crédit Agricole Mitsubishi UFJ FG Morgan Stanley Royal Bank of Scotland UBS
1 (1.0%)	Bank of China Bank of New York Mellon BBVA Groupe BPCE Industrial and Commercial Bank of China ING Bank Mizuho FG Nordea Santander Société Générale Standard Chartered State Street Sumitomo Mitsui FG Unicredit Group Wells Fargo

Source: Financial Stability Board, 2013 (available at http://www.financialstabilityboard.org/wp-content/uploads/r_131111.pdf).

[1]"The bucket approach is defined in Table 2 of the Basel Committee document *Global Systemically Important Banks: Updated Assessment Methodology and the Higher Loss Absorbency Requirement*, July 2013. The numbers in parentheses are the required level of additional common equity loss absorbency as a percentage of risk-weighted assets that will apply to G-SIBs identified in November 2014, with phase-in starting in January 2016" (Financial Stability Board, 2013: 3).

(United States), but government assistance, and partial takeovers or restructuring enabled these institutions to remain in business, and most returned to profitability.

On the French CAC 40, German DAX 30, and London FTSE 100 stock indexes, over one third of the listed companies were created before World War I. The financial institutions listed on these exchanges include Société Générale, BNP Paribas, Crédit Agricole, Commerzbank, Deutsche Bank, Postbank, Standard Chartered, HSBC, Barclays, Lloyds, and Royal Bank of Scotland. On the Japanese Nikkei 225, the eleven banks listed include Sumitomo Mitsui, Mizuho Trust, Resona Holdings, and Mitsubishi Financial, which originated in the period of bank–industry conglomerates of the 1880s to 1900.

In the last decades of the twentieth century, banks such as Deutsche Bank (Germany), UBS (Switzerland), HSBC (United Kingdom), UniCredit (Italy), and Citibank (United States) evolved from powerful domestic brands with global presence to multinational and multiregional, universal institutions, their profitability often dependent more on host country investment and corporate arms than on home country retail operations. International bank interconnectivity has increased as transactions have come to depend increasingly on political and economic conditions of more than one nation, and on the stability and effectiveness of more than one system of laws and financial mores.

This chapter is organized into four sections as follows:

1. The evolution of cross-border and cross-regional banking from the Middle Ages to the 1600s.
2. The history of central banking from the 1600s to the 1800s.
3. The maturation and expansion of international banking from the 1800s to World War II.
4. Financial institutions, multilaterals, and international banks post-World War II.

The evolution of cross-border and cross-regional banking from the Middle Ages to the 1600s

The concept of international banking developed in Europe in concert with almost a thousand years of cross-border wars, cross-regional trade, and currency transactions, as money lenders, money changers, and merchants were needed to provide funds, lend, and create instruments for expansionary wars.[1]

Great natural resources did not automatically generate domestic or regional economic development. Empires rich in commodities, mineral wealth and human capital such as the Mamluks in Egypt or the Ottoman Empire, remained entrenched in autocratic and theological structures, which often hindered the development of independent financial systems and institutions. Although these dynasties fostered merchant classes, urban commercial centers, and monetary transactions, banking remained extremely limited as rulers maintained absolute control over state and private wealth, constricting capital mobility and the development of financial instruments and services.

Across Europe, development of a merchant and financial class was far from even. From the Renaissance period onwards, key players in international banking were small geographic entities in need of trade and international monetary transactions to increase productivity and exert power. These included the Italian city states of Genoa, Florence and Venice, as well as the Netherlands and England. These latter thrived due to parliamentary and republican regimes, few Church-led constrictions and relatively tolerant open societies, which fostered wealth generation and industrial activity. Hampered by church interdictions, repression of minorities and lack of economic control, the Holy Roman Empire, encompassing Spain, Portugal, and parts of Germany, never became a banking or financial center, despite vast maritime power and movement of currencies.[2]

Origins of cross-border banking

From the fall of the Roman Empire (456) until the Crusades (1095–1270), banking was limited within domestic borders. Under the Carolingian Empire (800–888), silver coinage circulated over an area almost the size of the present day European Union (EU), but trade did not extend beyond limited perimeters. By the eleventh century, seasonal markets, fairs, and the greater concentration of urban centers helped propagate acceptance of coins and specie. Yet barter economies remained the norm in isolated rural communities. From 1095 to 1270 the expeditions of the Crusades, instigated by the Vatican, led thousands toward the Holy Land. All routes from Europe passed to and from Italy, requiring complex financial dealings and activating commodity and currency markets. Italian merchants took on international banking functions, serving as intermediaries between monarchies, lending and extending credit to finance wars and trade. In 1338, there were more than eighty banking houses in Florence. The Bardi, Peruzzi, and Datini families, with branches in England, lent to the British Crown until Edward III's massive debts at the start of the Hundred Years' War provoked the first city state bankruptcy in 1345 to 1347. By 1470, the House of Medici had branches in Avignon and Lyon (France), Bruges (Belgium), and London (England), where accounts were kept in florins, the official gold coin minted in Florence and convertible throughout Europe. In fourteenth century Florence there were clear distinctions between moneychangers and bankers who dealt in international trade and coordinated government and papal loans.

Cross-border trade and exchanges

Cross-border trade transacted by dynastic merchant families generated immense profits and wealth. As merchants required the freedom to conduct trade year round and travel without restrictions new instruments were created, which did not require carrying large amounts of specie, including bills of acceptance, endorsed checks, bank notes, and promissory notes. A merchant in Florence could purchase goods from a merchant in Bruges, and pay for them by buying a bill of exchange drawn by a third party in Seville. The concept of one-month, three-month, and six-month or year-long maturities stems from the period assigned to payment based on geographic distance. The 1596 records of the Besançon fair describe the proceedings of wealthy merchants, government emissaries, brokers and important moneychangers who came from Genoa, Seville, and Florence to establish a syndicate to regulate rates of exchange by decree. From 60 to 200 men paid a membership fee of 3,000 gold ecus for the privilege of deciding rates and closing deals worth 30–40 million ecus: "Four times a year it was the scene of decisive but discreet meetings, something like the International Bank of Basel in our day" (Braudel Vol. 1, 1979: 91). During the reign of Francois I of France (1517–47), and under the Spanish-led Holy Roman Empire (1519–1608), large merchant houses no longer limited or beholden to their community, thrived wherever money could be generated and reinvested in different regions or countries.

The Age of Discovery, from the sixteenth to the mid seventeenth century, transformed trade and currency transactions as new markets in Asia and the Americas fueled a surge in trade in gold and silver from the Americas to Seville, Lisbon, and on to Amsterdam and London.[3] Unregulated, exploitative, and extremely profitable, trading houses functioned as centers of exchange, finance, and multinational transactions. The Dutch East India Company, chartered in Amsterdam in 1601, dominated trade between Europe and Asia through the seventeenth and eighteenth centuries as the world's largest import–export company. Declaring annual dividends for its stockholders, it offered "longer terms of credit, low prices, forswearing of freight and related charges, offers of full insurance, substantial advances, new arrangements for pay involving half bill and half bond: such became the stock in trade for merchants eager to acquire a piece of the growing India traffic" (Hancock 2002: 164).

The history of central banking from the 1600s to the 1800s

Public finance and independent central banks first developed in the Netherlands, Sweden, and England. These parliamentary monarchies or republics relinquished total control over state finances and promoted interdependency between fledgling markets, merchants, and financiers. By the end of the seventeenth century, bankers in Amsterdam and London no longer served the monarch solely, but rather invested in the interests of a community or nation.[4] At the end of the Wars of Religion (1524–1598), Protestantism helped further promote economic development in Northern Europe, freeing commercial activity from theological restrictions and enabling the rise of an empowered merchant class.

After almost two generations of wars and the Revolution of 1688, England achieved fiscal harmonization, putting into practice the use of bank notes and deposits, a century before Continental Europe. The creation of the Bank of England in 1694, the monetary reforms of 1699, and increased Parliamentary control of state finances allowed British merchant and trading houses, including the Royal Bank of Scotland and Barclays, to evolve organically into joint stock companies.

Central banking: political and economic evolution

The evolution of government guaranteed financial institutions[5] established to foster international trade, finance the government, and function as national commercial and deposit banks represented a major shift from autocratic to oligarchic control of a nation's finances. The creation of the Bank of England under the aegis of Parliament in 1694 marked a major evolution away from Crown control of money issuance, to a separate institution granted the power to set monetary policy through its monopoly right to print fiat money with legal tender. "Independence of central banks is itself not a measurable variable, but it usually goes hand in hand with institutional settings such as the nomination of members of the monetary policy board for defined terms, the protection of board members from political interference, and the independence of central banks' budgets within the confines of applicable public sector guidelines" (Standard and Poor's 2011). In addition to "[t]he truly unique power of a central bank ... the power to create money ..." (Deane and Pringle 1994: viii), each central bank was entrusted with custodial, transactional and settlement powers.

As central banks in the European Union, Japan, and the United States expanded the scope of their activities and responsibilities in the wake of the 2008 financial crisis, it is important to distinguish between (i) central banks established organically as economies evolved from private to public finance, which called for harmonization of minting and note issuance, government guaranteed trading and credit facilities, unified monetary policy, and supervision of financial institutions; and (ii) central banks that were created in times of crisis as a means of stabilizing and restructuring economies. The former include the German Reichsbank (1875), Bank of Japan (1882), Bank of Canada (1934), Imperial Bank of Russia (1866), and the Federal Reserve System (1913). The latter include the Bank of France (1801), Deutsche Bundesbank (1957), Bank of Russia (1991, 1998), and Bank of China (1949). The role and responsibilities of these institutions evolved over time, in response to events both at home and abroad.

The Bank of Amsterdam, established in 1609 "...under the city's guarantee [...] took in a merchant's coinage, assessed the valid metal and [...] gave him credit on its books and stored the metal away" (Deane and Pringle 1994: 34). It acted as a custodial and deposit entity, but high risk loans to the Dutch East Indian Company brought about its demise in 1819.

The Bank of Stockholm was established by royal charter in 1656 as both a lending and exchange bank, combining commercial and deposit functions. Over-lending and inadequate collateral provoked a run and the Bank collapsed in 1664. In 1668, Parliament created the Bank of the Estates (Riksens Ständers Bank) as a government lending bank, which only "advanced money against six month interest bearing deposits or tangible assets" (Deane and Pringle 1994: 35). Renamed Sveriges Riksbank in 1867, it assumed all private banks' right of issuance and was granted monopoly over note issuance in the early twentieth century.

The Bank of England was chartered in 1694 when merchant financier William Patterson, backed by a powerful group of London merchants, provided a

£1.2 million loan to the government at 8 percent return. "The subscribers to the loan were to be incorporated as the Governor and Company of the Bank of England, the first joint stock bank in the country" (Deane and Pringle 1994: 38). Once approved by Parliament, the Bank was granted a "monopoly of joint stock banking, the handling of the government's account, the right to deal in bullion, to discount approved bills of exchange ... and to issue notes" (Deane and Pringle 1994: 39). Established in Threadneedle Street in 1734, the Bank of England has never ceased operations nor changed location in nearly 300 years. The Bank received a monopoly over all banking activity until 1800, when a new charter began to "permit joint stock banks of deposit in London or within 65 miles thereof" (Bank of England Charter of 1800). "With the government's promise to pay behind it, the Bank could issue notes to match the sum lent to the government" (Deane and Pringle 1994: 39), the Bank would also become the bankers' bank, where other commercial banks used accounts with it to settle claims between themselves and kept their reserves. Oversight power over all financial institutions was further reinforced in the aftermath of the South Sea Bubble in 1720 (see Chapter 4).

Reforms were enacted under Sir Robert Peel's Bank Charter Act of 1844. The note-issue department was separated from its commercial banking operations in an attempt to mitigate the inherent conflict of interest between the ability to print fiat money and the temptation to lend, for either profit or power. Furthermore, oversight of commercial and merchant banking was enhanced as the Bank balanced its various responsibilities: "a political duty to attend to the government's financial needs [...]; a statutory duty to maintain the convertibility of banknotes into gold" and a commercial duty to pay dividends to its shareholders (Ferguson 2001: 179). Finally, in the 1870s, the Bank of England assumed the role of lender of last resort to the banking system as a whole.

The Gold Standard

The decisions to unilaterally peg the pound sterling to gold occurred in stages over the course of the nineteenth century from the creation of the universal Gold Standard of 1880 to 1914. During the period 1815 to 1860, England's flexible gold standard and France's bimetallism worked in concert to assure cooperation on currency fluctuations, especially in the volatile period following the American Gold Rush of 1849 and the Australian Gold Rush of 1851. As gold production rose dramatically, destabilizing currency markets and contributing to the Crash of 1857, the Bank of England and the Bank of France coordinated efforts to maintain stability in the inflows and price of gold.

Despite currency destabilization and realignments in the wake of World War I, the United Kingdom remained on the Gold Standard until 1931. Yet, France and England experienced economic crises provoked by their inability to coordinate and stabilize monetary policies, exacerbated by delayed and ineffective responses to German hyperinflation in the period 1921 to 1922, and the failure of the Bank of England, the Bank of France and the Federal Reserve to act as lenders of last resort. Following World War II, the Bank of England was nationalized on March 1, 1946.

The next major challenge to the Bank of England's authority and role came with the signing of the Maastricht Treaty (Treaty on European Union) in 1991–2, with an opt-out clause for the United Kingdom regarding economic and monetary union. British Prime Minister Margaret Thatcher rejected the concept of an independent super-banking structure: "We do not accept that a European system of central banks or Eurofed should be wholly independent" (Smith 1990). In 1992, the United Kingdom, Denmark and, in 1995, Sweden were granted opt-out clauses, allowing them membership of the European Union without the requirement to participate in the European Monetary Union. They would retain their domestic currencies, and their monetary and regulatory policies would remain under the control of their central banks. In conclusion, the Bank of England retained full autonomy and, in 1997, following the edicts of the Maastricht Treaty, the Bank gained operational independence in setting monetary policy. EU Banking Union (2014–15) will be discussed in Chapter 6.

The Bank of France

The Charter of the Bank of France, signed by Napoleon Bonaparte and the Minister of Finance, stated that "as inevitable result of the French Revolution and a long and expensive war, the nation needed to establish a bank that would reestablish commercial credit, movement of capital in order to foster the recovery of public and private entities" (Charter of the Bank of France, 13 February 1800). The founding shareholders were Napoleon Bonaparte, members of his family, and Consuls of the Republic. It was created with state funds and private capital of 30 million francs, in the form of metal alloy (as France was devoid of gold or silver), and divided into 30,000 shares.

The Bank of France was subject to the policies of the state in coordination with the Ministry of Finance, with the Governor of the Bank appointed by the state. The Bank would be entrusted to honor the obligations of the newly created French Republic. Its mandate was to discount bills of exchange, and to extend credit and payment to the extent permitted by its reserves. The Bank enjoyed a monopoly over issuance of the new French franc (1801), power of decision over monetary policy, and the sole authority to open branches or subsidiaries.

From 1840, the Bank could offer lending facilities, bank branching, and serve as a vehicle for the government's industrial and monetary policy. And in 1866, special decree extended its authority over monetary policy and currency issuance in Algeria, and throughout the French colonial Empire of French Indochina (1898), Tunisia (1902), and Morocco (1907).

The Reichsbank

Until unification in 1871, German banking was dominated by independent merchant banks in Bremen, Frankfurt, and Cologne. There were divergent currency standards: The Prussian thaler and Austrian gulden were linked to silver, while Bremen was on the gold standard. Paper money was neither readily accepted nor trusted, as different principalities issued non-convertible notes. By the mid 1860s, bankers and industrialists called for a new currency, the mark, and the introduction of the gold standard, to link the German currency to the pound sterling. Following unification under Bismarck, Germany accepted the Gold Standard in the Coinage Act of December 4, 1871. The Banking Act of March 14, 1875 established the Reichsbank, modeled on the Bank of England. The Banking Act named the Reich's Chancellor as head of the Reichsbank, giving Bismarck unsurpassed power over financial and political institutions.

Post-world War I banking crisis and hyperinflation

In the aftermath of World War I, the burden of reparations imposed on defeated Germany severely destabilized the European balance of power. While the Allies could raise capital in the United States, German assets were expropriated under the Trading with the Enemy Act of October 1917 (Kobrak 2008). Between 1919 and spring 1921, the exchange rate of the German mark to the US dollar remained steady until the Allies delivered the ultimatum to Germany requiring 121 billion gold marks in reparations by October 1921. Hyperinflation took hold, and the rate of the mark to the dollar spiked from 275 in May 1922, to 370 in June 1922, to 400 in July 1922, 2000 by August 1922, reaching 7000 by November of that year. The Reichsbank continued to print money in higher and higher denominations until by the end of 1923, the exchange rate reached 12 trillion marks to one US dollar on the black market. The crisis was partially staunched when Hjalmar Schacht, President of the Reichsbank, created a new currency, the Rentenmark. In June 1931, the Federal Reserve, Bank of England, Bank of France, and the newly formed Bank for International Settlements (BIS) organized to lend the failing Reichsbank US$100 million, but it was too little, too late. Political and social chaos ensued and in the wake of economic disaster in 1933 the Nazi regime came to power. The Bank was nationalized and served as finance vehicle for the Third Reich's war efforts and their appropriation of capital and assets from occupied countries.

World War II and reconstruction

Under Allied Occupation following its defeat in World War II, Germany was forbidden from recreating an independent banking system. German banking was reconstructed in 1948, allowing regional banks, Landesbanken, to be established as note issuing banks. In order to control immediately rampant inflation, a new currency was created in June 1948: the Deutsche mark.

The Bundesbank

Germany's new central bank was created under the Bundesbank Act of 1957, under which the eleven Landesbanken became regional headquarters of the Bundesbank.

The Bundesbank enjoyed a monopoly over note issuance, clearing house, and supervision of all German banks. It acted as the state's banker and manager of currency reserves. Far more importantly, the Bundesbank Charter "designates the safe guarding of the currency as the bank's prime responsibility" (Bernanke and Mihov 1996: 2). Based in Frankfurt, the bank was declared absolutely independent of the German government in Bonn. With the collapse of the Soviet Union in 1991, and the reunification of East and West Germany, Chancellor Kohl required the Bundesbank (over the objections of its Governor, Otto Pohl) to establish immediate parity of 1:1 between the near worthless ost mark and powerful Deutsche Mark. With the signing of the Maastricht Treaty, the Bundesbank and the Bank of France coordinated policies to maintain the structure of the European Monetary System (the Snake fixed parity bands of the 12 EU currencies). Bundesbank monetary policy would become the model for the new European Central Bank in 1998.

Bank of Japan

The Edo reign of the Shogunate era, where financial activity was limited to merchant banks was replaced by the Meiji Restoration in 1871 to 1882. Japan established the yen under the New Currency Act of 1871, and the Bank of Japan under the Bank of Japan Act in June 1882. In 1884, the Bank abolished regional (former feudal fiefdoms) rights to open private banks and print money, establishing monopoly of the money supply. The period from the 1880s to 1905 saw the modernization of market and banking practices and institutions. Following the German model of industrial-financial interdependency with emphasis on heavy industry, military expenditures, large industrial groups (zaibatsu) established their own in-house banks: Mitsui, Mitsubishi, Sumitomo, and Yasuda.

During World War II, the Bank of Japan was reorganized under ward powers in 1942 to help finance the military. Following its defeat and under U.S. occupation (1945 to 1949) the functions of the Bank of Japan (as was the case with the Reichsbank) were suspended. The Bank of Japan reopened in 1949, the same year that the American Dodge Plan was put into effect, based on the model of the Marshall Plan. American funded reconstruction required Japan to have a balanced budget, reduced inflation, and a fixed exchange rate pegged to the US dollar of US$1=360 yen. Although General McArthur abolished the industrial monopolies (keiretsu) in order to force diversification and transparency, the Japanese Diet amended the Anti-Monopoly Law in 1953, allowing major corporations to resume the practice of cross shareholdings and interlocking directorates. Mitsui, Mitsubishi, Sumitomo, and Dai-ichi-Kangyo reorganized into "horizontal keiretsu comprised of several dozen members including a main bank, large financial institutions, the largest manufacturing firms and a large general trading company" (Pyle 1996: 250). Between 1950 and 1973, "74.1% of all external financial sources raised by Japanese corporations were provided through banks (the corresponding number for the Federal Republic of Germany was 66.6%, and only 28% for the U.S.)" (Schaede 1996: 5). A strong recovery was fueled by capital accumulation (savings rate reached 27 percent in 1970), and export driven industrial growth financed by public and private banks.

The Ministry of International Trade and Industry (MITI), the Ministry of Finance, and the Bank of Japan set industrial policy and interest rate policy aimed at export growth and innovation. Companies could borrow massively from state approved banks with lax oversight. In case of default there would be "bailouts by mother banks of troubled industrial entities" (Schaede 1996: 4). Following the economic collapse of 1995 to 1998, a number of reforms were implemented, with independence and transparency included in the Bank of Japan's new charter under the Japanese bank reform edicts of June 1997 (see Chapter 4).

The Federal Reserve system

In the United States, the U.S. Government sought to establish a central bank in 1792 and again in 1816. Yet both the First and Second Bank of the United States were rejected by Congress as infringements of state rights and federally imposed regulation. Only following the Knickerbocker Bank crash of 1907, and a series of scandals that exposed the level of corruption and unregulated activity in stocks, bonds and interlocking directorates, did the House Committee on Banking and Currency call for hearings to establish a central bank with supervisory and oversight functions. The United States Congress was under pressure to establish a central bank within the Treasury, but a consortium of bankers proposed the alternate Aldrich Plan to maintain central bank independence. The Federal Reserve Act of 1913 was a compromise between the Wilson Administration and the Aldrich Plan. "The Federal Reserve, then was a regionally diversified joint venture [...] that affiliated the banking community with the federal government" (Shull 2005: 57), with one member elected from each district for its Reserve Board.

The Federal Reserve assumed responsibility for monetary policy, as monopoly issuer of fiat money with legal tender, and as lender of last resort. The prosperity and expansion of the U.S. economy until 1927 seemed to validate Federal Reserve monetary policy, which encouraged the expansion of consumer credit, and stock market speculation often on margin calls.

Post-1935, the Charter of the Federal Reserve was expanded to include "formulating and executing monetary policy; Supervising and regulating depository institutions; Providing an elastic currency; Assisting the Federal Government's financing operations and; Serving as the banker for the U.S. Government" (Federal Reserve Bank of New York). Following the financial crisis of 2008, the powers of the Federal Reserve were expanded once again, and this will be examined in more detail in Chapters 4 and 6.

Following the stock market crash of October 1929, the values of all stocks and investment trusts declined dramatically. Bank deposits were not protected and in December 1929, when the New York City-based Bank of the United States was closed, 400,000 depositors were affected. The Federal Reserve and New York State banking authorities did not intervene to save the bank.

Between 1932 and 1937, a number of significant banking reforms were introduced. In 1932, the first Glass-Steagall Act addressed issues of giving the Federal Reserve more leeway in lending to banks. Although bank reserves increased in 1932, this did not "stem the continued decrease in bank loans and investments or in the money supply" (Shull 2005: 99). Between 1930 and 1932, over 5,000 banks failed: "Most banks had both liquidity and solvency problems resulting from declines in the value of their assets" (Shull 2005: 99). In February 1933, on the eve of Franklin D. Roosevelt's inauguration, groups of banks began to suspend payments. In March 1933, President Roosevelt declared a four-day banking holiday and, under Proclamation 2039, prohibited "any transactions in foreign exchange and the export, hoarding, melting, or earmarkings of gold or silver coin or bullion or currency."

Congress enacted the Securities Act of 1933 and the Securities Exchange Act of 1934, giving the newly-created U.S. Securities and Exchange Commission (SEC) supervisory responsibility for all U.S. broker dealers, trading, and investment firms. Full disclosure was required on new security issues. Inside operations and short selling were outlawed. The Federal Reserve Board was granted authority to fix margin requirements, and, under the Glass-Steagall Act of 1934, commercial banks were divorced from their securities affiliates.

Title 1 of the Banking Act of 1935 established Federal Deposit Insurance "on a permanent basis under the auspices of the Federal Deposit Insurance Corporation" (Shull 2005: 115). Furthermore, The Banking Act of 1935 increased the powers of the Board of Governors of the Federal Reserve, making it "an independent agency of the federal government, removed from political consideration" (Shull 2005: 117).

Although the Federal Reserve Act codified the function of "examination and supervision of member banks" in its charter, major banks could choose whether they would be regulated by state charters or by a national charter with oversight by the Office of the Comptroller of the Currency (OCC) (see Chapters 4 and 7 on the JPMorgan London Whale trading losses, which revealed both a lack of compliance with OCC regulations and the inability of the OCC to monitor U.S. global bank subsidiaries).

The Federal Reserve Bank of New York, has powers in addition to those of the other Reserve Banks. These additional powers include "conducting open market operations; intervening in foreign exchange markets, storing monetary gold for foreign central banks and international agencies" (Federal Reserve Bank of New York). The New York Fed's functions include responsibility for the regulation and supervision of international operations of the banks under its charter. Supervisory powers are complemented by the New York State Banking Department on the oversight of the largest U.S. global banks, including Citi and JPMorgan Chase. The New York Clearing House Interbank Payments System (CHIPS), was established in 1953 (and restructured in 1970), as a computerized funds transfer system for international dollar payments linking major U.S. and foreign banks with offices in New York. Since 1981, settlements occur at the end of each day with the final settlement through adjustments in the special accounts balance at the Federal Reserve Bank of New York. The role of the Federal Reserve in the 2008 financial crisis is discussed in Chapter 4; and its expanded regulatory powers under the Dodd–Frank Wall Street Reform and Consumer Protection Act (2010) (Dodd-Frank Act) are presented in Chapter 6.

European Central Bank

The creation of the European Central Bank on January 1, 1998 was a unique phenomenon. For the first time in financial history, a central bank was established to set monetary policy for a regional bloc rather than one sovereign nation and one currency zone. The Maastricht Treaty mandated as of January 1993 that:

> When exercising the powers and carrying out the tasks and duties conferred upon them by this Treaty and the Statute of the ESCB,[6] neither the ECB, nor a national central bank, nor any member of their decision-making bodies shall seek or take instruction from Community institutions or bodies, from any government of a Member State or from any other body.
>
> (Treaty on European Union, The Maastricht Treaty, Article 107, 1993:221)

Functions

Under the provisions of the Maastricht Treaty, all central banks of the European member countries had to renounce sovereignty and become part of a new entity, the European Central Bank. "The prime objective of the ESCB shall be to maintain price stability" (Article 105: 218). This mandate respected the legacy of the Bundesbank which had served as the anchor for European monetary policy. (The European Central Bank will be examined in greater depth in subsequent chapters.)

The gradual convergence in the functions of central banks is illustrated in Table 1.2.

Maturation and expansion of international banking from the 1800s to post-world War II

Great Britain and France: Bankers to the World

By 1800, as banker to Europe, London functioned as "clearing house to foreign countries" (Bagehot 1897: 33) with its financial center on Lombard Street serving as intermediary between international commerce and British finance. England was the world's largest lender: "because she possesses an unequalled fund of floating money, which will help in a moment any merchant who sees a great prospect of new profit" (Bagehot 1897: 15).

From the 1850s, Britain and France established vast industrial financial networks spread across Africa, India, and most of South East Asia, while maintaining trade connections in the Americas, Canada and Russia through railroad financing.

Table 1.2 Monetary policy frameworks

	Bank of England	Eurosystem	Federal Reserve System	Bank of Japan
Established/Made independent	1694/1998	1998	1914	1882/1998
Monetary policy decision-making body	Monetary Policy Committee	Governing Council, comprising 22 members: the ECB Executive Board (6 members) and the Governors of the 16 NCBs of the Eurosystem	Federal Open Market Committee (FOMC), 12 members: 7 Board Governors, President of the New York Fed, and 4 of the 11 other reserve banks Fed Presidents on rotating basis; 19 participants	Policy Board, 9 members
Appointment of policy makers	Nine members: the Governor, the three Deputy Governors for Monetary Policy, Financial Stability and Markets & Banking, the Bank's Chief Economist and four external members appointed directly by the Chancellor	President and Governing Council members appointed for 8 years by national governments; ratified by European Parliament	Governors (14-year terms)/ Chairman (4-year term) appointed by the President and approved by the Congress; Bank Presidents selected by Bank directors (largely local banking/ business community)	Board members appointed for 5 years by the cabinet; parliamentary ratification required
Independence from political influence	Yes. Enshrined in the 1998 Bank of England Act	Yes. Enshrined in the Maastricht Treaty	Yes. Fed is a "creature of the Congress" and must report regularly, but enjoys substantial independence by long-standing tradition	Yes. Established in the 1998 BoJ law, but (at times) not well respected by the political establishment

	Bank of England	ECB	Federal Reserve	Bank of Japan
Monetary policy objective(s)/ Mandate	Monetary stability: stable prices and confidence in the currency. Stable prices are defined by the Government's inflation target, which the Bank seeks to meet through the decisions taken by the Monetary Policy Committee	Price stability is the primary objective as set in the Maastricht Treaty. The ECB has quantified this as medium-term inflation goal of below but close to 2%	Multiple objectives: to promote maximum employment, price stability, and moderate long-term interest rates. Price stability not defined, but widely viewed as 1–2% comfort zone (skewed toward upper portion) for core PCE inflation	Multiple objectives: price stability and the stability of the financial system. Price stability objective is set in qualitative terms in the 1998 law and policy board has quantified this as a range of 0% to 2% inflation in the medium term
Monetary policy strategy	The MPC intends ... to maintain the present highly stimulative stance of monetary policy until economic slack has been substantially reduced, provided this does not entail material risks to price stability or financial stability	Two pillar strategy. First pillar focuses on shorter-term economic and price developments ("economic pillar"); second pillar focuses on longer-term inflation outlook based on monetary analysis	Focus on economic forecasts; rates adjusted to optimise expected outcomes and minimise risks of deviating from those outcomes (factoring in costs of those deviations). Preference for gradualism unless risks dictate more aggressive action	Two perspectives strategy, the first focusing on short-term inflation developments and the second on economic and inflation developments as well as financial stability in a longer-term perspective
Decision-making style	By majority vote	Consensual, with the President assuming the role of moderator; dissents are rare	Consensual (less so under Bernanke than Greenspan), with Chairman clearly first among equals. Dissents are infrequent, multiple dissents are very rare	By majority vote; dissents are frequent (55% of decisions since the BoJ law was enacted were taken with at least one dissenter); Governor is generally opinion leader
Role of monetary aggregates and asset prices	Both play a significant role	Both play a significant role	Neither plays a significant role independent of their effects on growth and inflation	Both play a significant role

(Continued)

Table 1.2 Monetary policy frameworks (Continued)

	Bank of England	Eurosystem	Federal Reserve System	Bank of Japan
Established/Made independent	1694/1998	1998	1914	1882/1998
Accountability and transparency	a. The decisions on interest rates are announced at 12 noon immediately following the Thursday meeting	a. Immediate press conference after Council meetings with introductory statement and Q&A (2:30 pm local time)	a. Immediate announcement following the FOMC, with voting record (2:15 pm local time)	a. Immediate announcement after monetary policy meetings (around 12 noon local time) with voting record, followed by Governor's press conference (3:30 pm local time)
	b. Minutes are published two weeks after meeting, detailing members' votes	b. Annual Report to EU institutions and presentations to the European Parliament	b. Meeting minutes three weeks later	b. Minutes (generally a month later, three days after next monetary policy meeting)
	c. Members can be called to answer questions before Parliament	c. Monthly Bulletin published	c. Full transcripts of meetings five years later	c. Monthly Report of the Policy Board 34–40 days after meetings
		d. Speeches	d. Frequent speeches by FOMC participants	d. Speeches
			e. Semi-annual monetary policy report to Congress; other hearings	e. Semi-annual report to the Diet

Source: Gerdesmeier et al. 2007, with author's additions from the Bank of England website.

British and French banks established branches, representative offices, and subsidiaries in their respective colonial holdings to finance railroads, mining, diamonds, and trade in agricultural commodities. Standard Bank of British South Africa financed diamond fields and gold mining in Johannesburg. The Charter Bank had offices in Bombay, Calcutta, Shanghai, Hong Kong, and Singapore.[7]

From 1850 to 1900, merchant banking shifted into specialized investment houses, and large domestic institutions were established based on universal banking, mixed banking, house banking, and overseas and colonial banking (Bonin 2009).

Hong Kong Shanghai Bank (HSBC) was founded in 1865 by Thomas Sutherland, Hong Kong Superintendent of the largest British navigation company. He envisaged the need to create a separate bank to help finance the growing trade between China and Europe, and new opportunities for China–United States trade, opening the first branch of a British bank in San Francisco in 1865. Instrumental in railroad financing in India and China, within a decade the bank also opened branches in Yokohama and Kobe (Japan), and Shanghai (China). In 1889, HSBC took a stake in Imperial Bank of Persia. The Commonwealth Bank Corporation, founded in Australia in 1912, extended the presence of the Commonwealth through the Pacific Islands.

In India, Charter Bank established subsidiaries in Bombay and Calcutta in 1853, followed by HSBC which was to dominate the banking market in India after 1870. After independence in 1947, there were 1,100 small banks across India, which combined insurance and commercial activities. The evolution of the Indian banking sector from nationalization (1969), to the consolidation of public sector banks (1991), to the slow privatization and creation of new private banks from (1993 to 2014) will be examined in Chapter 8 on emerging markets).

In North Africa and Indochina, the French Banque Suez and Banque IndoChine (1875) functioned as political vehicles for the interests of the French State and as conduits for trade and investment.

International investment banks

The Barings and Rothschild banking dynasties led their respective sectors from the domestic to the global market. Both families began as merchant houses in London and Frankfurt in the 1760s, and had expanded by the mid nineteenth century into bond issuance, advising governments, and acting as intermediaries in cross-regional financial transactions. Beyond Europe, Barings led in the Americas and Rothschild in Russia and the Ottoman Empire. Barings, according to an anecdote circulated as early as 1817, was perceived as the sixth great power in Europe following England, France, Prussia, Austria, and Russia (Fay 1996). Rothschild, and to a lesser degree Barings, bridged the gap between being banker to the Crown, banker to the state, and partner or guarantor to other banks.

The Second Empire (1852 to 70) pursued pro-business policies and legislative measures, which allowed corporate and regional deposit banks to flourish. The challenge was to catch up rapidly with British finance and to mobilize "'sleeping funds' (hoarded, liquid, or savings) … to support the growth of industry and

Box 1.1 Barings banking dynasty

Francis Baring founded Barings bank in 1762, lending to the Crown during the American Revolutionary War of 1776. During the Napoleonic Wars of 1801 to 1815, Alexander Baring transformed the bank into a major international house. In the railroad boom of the 1840s, Barings speculated on its own account in French and Russian bonds, Austrian stocks, and American railroad shares. Barings partnered in syndicated loans and bond issues across Europe, with Rothschild, Bischoffsheim, Cassel, and Oppenheimer Banks, and in New York and Boston with Kidder Peabody and JPMorgan, becoming America's lead correspondent banker. Its reputation was undisputed until the near-fatal decision to invest in the volatile Argentinian market in 1890, when the bank disastrously opted to underwrite a share issue for Buenos Aires Water Supply and Drainage Company. Once the market collapsed amid political chaos in South America, the shares became worthless, leaving Barings heavily overcommitted. The resolution to the crisis was the first multinational bailout of an international bank. In November 1890, Barings was rescued by a consortium established by the Bank of England, the Bank of France, the Imperial Bank of Russia, and Rothschild. After World War I, Barings functioned as banker to the monarchy. Expanding in the 1970s and, following the transformation of British investment banking in 1986 (known as Big Bang), it engaged in corporate finance and trading activities. By the late 1980s, once again under family ownership, the bank turned from traditional banking to high risk foreign exchange (FOREX) transactions, concentrated in its overseas subsidiaries, falling victim to and unwitting participant in a massive rogue trader fraud (See Chapter 4). Barings lost over US$1.8 billion in 1995. The bank collapsed and was taken over by the Netherland bank ING for the price of US$1.

Box 1.2 The house of Rothschild

The Rothschild family originated in Frankfurt as textile and commodities traders dealing in bills of acceptance in the late 1780s. During the Napoleonic Wars, Nathan Rothschild arrived in London and made a fortune buying gold bullion and selling it to the British government. By 1815, established in Paris, Frankfurt, and London, the family set up information networks, alliances, and cross linkages with German, Austrian, and French banking houses and governments, including the establishment of Credit-Anstalt in Vienna in 1855. Instrumental through the 1850s in the underwriting of railroad bonds throughout Europe, their interests later turned to copper, rubber, and oil. Railroads required government–private sector cooperation and joint financing.

Governments had to sell or lease land, and private engineering, construction, design and industrial companies had to build the tracks, trains, and stations which created immediate need for cross-border bonds and massive long-term investment and guarantees. In 1852, at the start of the Second Empire (1852 to 1870), the French branch of the Rothschild's, wanting to emulate British joint stock banks, helped fund the first French investment bank, Société Générale du Crédit Mobilier in direct competition with the Bank of France. Following the Franco-Prussian War of 1870, the bank played a key role in the first French war reparation bond issue. Returning to France after being forced out during World War II, the bank was briefly nationalized in 1981 under President Mitterrand's socialist government. In the early 2000s, the French and British houses of the Rothschild bank merged.

services growth ... [and] to accelerate economic history" (Bonin 2009: 3). In 1863, a new law was passed on the creation of joint stock companies, no longer under the aegis of the Bank of France and its branches. Crédit Lyonnais, Société Générale, and Crédit du Nord were established in competition, but also in cooperation with the Banque de France. These commercial banks established universal banking, defined as "the overlap between retail and corporate banking, on one hand, and investment banking on the other—that is, the convergence of lending activities and the management of payment type on one side, and issuing securities, underwriting and brokerage activities, and structured finance (long-term lending, financial engineering, project financing) on the other" (Bonin 2009: 3).

These institutions evolved into international banks in three separate and intersecting venues: deposit-taking and corporate commercial banking, cross regional investment banking, and colonial banks. In the first category, Crédit Lyonnais (1863) and Société Générale (1864) established branches and offices abroad, opening the first foreign branch of a French credit facility in London in 1870. By 1875, Crédit Lyonnais had branches in Cairo and Alexandria to finance cotton, in Constantinople to serve wheat trade from Ukraine, and in Smyrna, Jerusalem, and Jaffa. Branches were opened in Russia from 1878, extending credit facilities between Russia and the Ottoman Empire. Yet Crédit Lyonnais was closed out of two major markets: India due to British hegemony, and the United States due to protectionist tariffs against foreign banks, state banking laws, and British competition led by Barings.

German Hausbank: from domestic to international banking

Universal banking remained the European model until the 1890s, when Germany developed a new concept of industry–bank interdependency. Based on cross-shareholdings, which allowed banks to promote industrial policy, the hausbank model was created. Following German unification in 1871, and the creation of the Reichsbank in 1875, Deutsche Bank, Commerz, Dresdner and Disconto were established.

Deutsche Bank was created as a joint-stock company in 1870 by George Siemens of Siemens and Halske "for the purpose of representing German financial interests on international markets ... to clear transactions, absorb foreign debt, and take positions in foreign firms" (Kobrak 2008: 5). From 1876 to 1899, Deutsche Bank, like Crédit Lyonnais, expanded activities outside the country with offices in Bremen, Hamburg, and London, followed by holdings in France, New York, and branch offices in Shanghai and Yokohama. As British banks were dominant in Asia, Germany decided to focus on South America and the United States, working closely with Morgan, Warburg, and Speyer, as well as the Rockefellers. Deutsche Bank's business expanded significantly: "from 1870 to 1913 business volume grew from 239.3 million mark to 129.2 billion mark" (Kobrak 2008: 19). Forced out of American markets in World War I, as an enemy agent institution, and branded with collaborating with the Third Reich during World War II, Deutsche Bank and other German banks reconstituted in the late 1950s, kept a low profile and did not return to the United States until the 1970s.

Swiss banks

Swiss banking focused on small private banks, founded from the 1760s, to represent French interests through Geneva, and German Austrian interests through Zurich and Basel, with domestic offices in Geneva, Zurich, Basel, and Lugano, and international offices in Luxembourg, London, and New York. Post-1848, the creation of the Swiss franc and the neutrality of Switzerland made it a safe haven.

Adopting the French universal banking model, Credit Suisse was founded in 1856, the Swiss Bank Corporation in 1872, and Union des Banques Suisses in 1912. After World War I, Swiss banks offered discrete wealth management services with the added advantage of political neutrality through the 1930s. The Swiss Banking Act of 1934 assured total confidentiality on numbered accounts. The evolution of Swiss international private banking and expansion into international investment banking is discussed in Chapter 3. The ramifications of the 2008 crisis are discussed in Chapters 4 and 7.

The first Pan-European investment bank: Paribas

Paribas, chartered in 1872 in the aftermath of the Franco-Prussian war, became the leading international investment bank in Europe, under French home office and directorship. It was a unique model of cross-border cooperation: "to German signatures were added French, Swiss, Belgian, Dutch, and Danish signatures; Jewish signatures next to Catholic and Protestant signatures; Paris is associated to London, Brussels, Amsterdam and Geneva" (Bussière 1992: 28). The founding German Bischoffsheim family opened a small private bank in Brussels after Belgium's independence in 1830, and a bank in Paris during the July Monarchy (1830–1848). In 1869, they set up the third major deposit bank in France, Banque de Paris. By 1877, Paribas became lead bank in Russia and Sweden, and established connections to Barings and the Americas. With branches in Amsterdam,

Brussels, and Geneva, Paribas participated in the creation of the Russo-Chinese Bank in 1896, to help finance railroad and mining projects in Siberia and Manchuria (Bussière 1992: 51). Rival and partner in international syndications with Crédit Lyonnais and Société Générale, the bank remained the leading French investment bank through the twentieth century. Briefly nationalized from 1983 to 1986, it merged with BNP in 1999 to become France's largest universal bank.

Russia: imperial bank to the Trans-Siberian railroad

Russia under Tsar Alexander II opened to the modern economic world with the creation of the Imperial Bank of Russia in 1860, modeled on the Bank of England. However, as in previous (and future) periods of economic and social reform, the momentum was short-lived and impacted only a small segment of the urban population. Although the Imperial Bank in the 1890s had the largest reserves of gold and was an active partner in transcontinental transactions, its economic progress remained sporadic and barely extended beyond Moscow and St Petersburg. Russia never created independent banks and depended on vast investments and bond issues from French and American investors to finance the Trans-Siberian railroad, completed in 1905. Defeat in the Russo-Japanese War (1904 to 1905), with a newly militarized Japan and the beginnings of popular rebellion in 1905, further limited Russia's fledgling entry into the modern economic age.

In 1917, during the Russian Revolution, the revolutionary leader Lenin appropriated and nationalized all foreign holdings in the Imperial Bank of Russia, closing the door to international investment. Crédit Lyonnais, the largest bank in St Petersburg in 1917, lost all assets invested in railroad bonds. U.S. National City's office in Petrograd (formerly St Petersburg) was forced to close on December 14, 1917, when all banking assets were appropriated by the State, losing almost US$26 million.

Under the Soviet Union (1917 to 1991), Russian banking consisted of four state-owned banks: Gosbank, the USSR state bank, which presided over credit allocation; Vneshtorgbank for foreign trading operations; Stroibank for long term capital investment; and Sberbank, the only deposit savings bank for Soviet citizens, with all deposits backed by a government guarantee.

The fall of the Soviet Union and transition period: 1991–1998

In 1991, individuals were given the right to create banks, which, "led to a huge increase in the number of small banks from less than one hundred in 1988 to nearly 2,500 at the end of 1995" (Fitch Ratings Report 2007). Sberbank was privatized, but volatility and changes in the leadership of the Central Bank, in conjunction with large-scale privatization of over 250,000 state and municipal enterprises, created a period of confusion and a need for emergency funds. Although the policies of the Central Bank stabilized in 1994, the privatization process remained opaque and prone to corruption, setting the stage for the oligarchs' takeover of the former government-owned commodity and oil and gas sectors. The Russian ruble crises and the international consequences will be examined in Chapter 4.

By 2000, a second wave of foreign bank penetration into Russia had begun, led by Citi, HSBC, Société Générale, Unicredit, Raiffeisen, and Goldman Sachs.

United States: global banker

After the American Revolution in 1787, currencies began to flow toward the United States, with Holland the largest subscriber to overseas loans. Banking remained a state-by-state endeavor with little interest in international transactions outside of New York, Boston, and San Francisco – following the gold rush of 1849. French and Dutch bond issues helped finance the railroads until the 1857 financial crises on Wall Street and the Paris Stock Exchange briefly curtailed the flow of capital to the United States. The first foreign bank, Bank of Montreal, opened in 1859, followed by the Hong Kong Shanghai Banking Corporation.

Prior to the American Civil War (1861 to 1865), banks proliferated, and were largely unregulated. In the West, wildcat banks were issuing close to 7,000 different kind of notes, many totally worthless, with no proof that they were backed by gold or silver. By 1860, there were about 1,600 banks with capital of more than US$400 million, and bank note circulation of more than US$200 million. In 1863, during the American Civil War, President Lincoln established the Office of the Comptroller of the Currency (OCC) under the auspices of the Treasury Department, which would serve as the sole chartering, supervisory, and monitoring bank regulator until the creation of the Federal Reserve in 1913. The OCC's function was to regulate, supervise, and charter agencies of foreign banks, and to guarantee "the safety and soundness of the national banking system" (Office of the Comptroller of the Currency 2007: 11).

Throughout the nineteenth century, state restrictions required foreign banks to go through London for transactions denominated in foreign currency, and for commercial transactions with European counterparts (Wilkins 1989). These limitations created opportunities for Barclays and Barings, which established partnerships with U.S. investment houses, including Morgan, and Kidder Peabody. An American bankers' conference, in 1901, emphasized the need to combat "American banking provincialism" and hoped to persuade Washington that "authorizing the establishment of international banks with headquarters to be in New York" would facilitate international trade and benefit the U.S. economy ("Bankers Discuss Far Eastern Commerce." *The New York Times*, 1901). However, despite interest from American bankers in 1904 to set up a Russo-Chinese bank for Far Eastern commerce, and in 1910 to create a Russo-American bank to facilitate investment in the Russian fleet, French and British banks dominated global financial markets right up to World War I.

In the late 1890s, retail banks opened in urban immigrant communities to serve ethnic communities, with businesses focused on facilitating remittances back to the home country: Bank of America began as Bank of Italy in San Francisco in 1904, to cater to the Italian small-businesses community.

National City Bank of New York (Citibank): first American international bank

Foreign exchange operations opened in First National Bank of Chicago in 1873, in Bank of New York in 1893, and in National City Bank in New York in 1897. National City Bank, which represented the interests of Rockefeller and Standard Oil, was the first major U.S. bank to establish branches abroad. By 1905, National City directors were on the boards of railroad and insurance companies, as well as Western Telegraph, and utility companies engaged in foreign investment.

During World War I, the United States, a major supplier of grain, steel, and arms, also became the world's leading provider of capital as Wall Street financed the war with foreign loans and war bonds. By 1919, "the country shifted from its former net debtor position and became a net creditor to the world" (Myers 1970: 270). Foreign holdings of American securities declined from US$5.4 billion in 1914 to US$1.6 billion in 1919. "When their securities had been liquidated, the Allies had to borrow and by the end of 1920, Great Britain owed the United States 4.2 billion dollars, France owed 3 billion and Italy 1.6 billion" (Myers 1970: 270).

The Edge Act of 1919 allowed corporations to carry on commercial banking activities abroad and issue foreign securities. Between 1914 and 1916, American banks led by National City Bank opened branches in Buenos Aires, Rio de Janeiro, Santiago, and Havana. In 1927, National City Bank had branches across China, with the largest amount of loans, assets, and overdrafts in Shanghai, totaling US$8.7 million. Between 1920 and 1929, "the total of American foreign investment, direct and portfolio, increased from US$7 to 17 billion" (Myers 1970: 96). By 1930, "European firms and governments were far and away the largest borrowers under-written by National City" (Miller 1993), and in 1933, National City Bank was present in twenty countries with seventy-six branches (Annual Reports of the Comptroller of the Currency 1927–29). After World War II, First National City Bank and Chase Manhattan led the return of U.S. financial firms to international markets. In 1961, First City Overseas Investment Corporation was created for new U.S.-based subsidiaries and affiliates. In 1966, the newly named Citibank introduced Dollar Certificates of Deposit in London and a year later, the first international credit card, which would later become MasterCard. Under the leadership of Walter Wriston (President and Chairman from 1967 to 1984), Citi began to aggressively expand abroad its corporate and retail operations. Once the Soviet Union fell, Citibank became one of the first foreign-owned banks in Russia and returned to China in 1995. After the merger with Travelers in 1998, under the guidance of Sandy Weil, Citi's presence in over 100 countries began to suffer setbacks. Foreign retail operations were cut back in the 2003–7 period, after legal and risk management problems in Italy, Japan, Australia, and India. (For more details of the post-2008 period, see Chapters 2 and 4).

JP Morgan: the first U.S. lender of last resort

JP Morgan opened JP Morgan & Company in 1861. Willing to invest in new scientific and industrial ventures in the late 1870s, he funded the work of both

Thomas Edison and Andrew Carnegie. In the crash of 1873, Morgan orchestrated a compromise between the battling railway interests, establishing himself as the mediator in financial rescues. In 1893, in order to calm the markets during the bimetallism currency crisis, President Cleveland called on Morgan to rescue the Treasury's gold supply by setting up a special bond issuance, guaranteed by JP Morgan & Company. Assuming the mantle of central banker, "Morgan spent most of the decade reorganizing bankrupt railroad and industrial companies. When the government all but ran out of gold in 1895, he raised 65 million dollars and made sure it stayed in the Treasury's coffers" (Strouse 1999: 66). In 1907, without interstate or federal regulations in place, banks functioned haphazardly across the country with processing and clearing house operations in New York. As a result of failed commodity ventures in October 1907, New York-based Knickerbocker Trust could not meet its obligations with US$60 million dollars on deposit, and only US$10 million in cash. With no national central bank, the Government called on Morgan to bring together the heads of all major New York banks to arrange a loan to Knickerbocker Trust in order to calm markets and stem the flight of gold from New York, staunching a potential crisis in London and Paris.

The creation of the Federal Reserve and U.S. income tax: 1913

The Stock Market Crash of October 1929 and period of the Great Depression happened against all expectations. Irving Fischer, respected U.S. economist had stated only a few months before that "stock prices have reached what looks like a permanently high plateau" (Shull 2005: 96). "Tuesday, 29 October, was the most devastating day in the history of the New York stock market" until October 19, 1987, and September 15, 2008 (Galbraith 1988: 133). New York banks increased loans in order to avert a money panic, as banks outside New York reacted "by calling home over two billions" (Galbraith 1988: 136).

The two major New York banks with international operations, National City and Chase National, suffered huge losses of money, prestige, and credibility. Charles Mitchell, head of National City was arrested on tax evasion in 1933, accused of stock manipulation and insider trading. The repercussions of the Great Crash and the subsequent reforms are discussed in Chapters 4 and 6.

From the end of World War II until the 1980s, U.S. banks consolidated, with investment banks focused on traditional underwriting and advisory services. Through the early 1990s, American banks began to merge, starting at the regional level.[8] The 1994 repeal of the McFadden Act of 1927, which had prohibited interstate branching by commercial banks, precipitated a surge of acquisitions. The announcement of the Travelers–Citibank merger in 1998 brought about the repeal of the Glass-Steagall Act (1934), which had established the separation between commercial banking and securities underwriting activities, including insurance. Following the enactment of the Gramm-Leach-Bliley Act in 1999, most major U.S. corporate commercial lenders began to engage in investment banking (see Chapter 2).

The Eurodollar and Eurobond market

Eurodollars was the term for dollars on deposit outside of the United States, "an international money market focused on short term credit flows, while the Eurobond market is an international capital market dealing with long term bonds (debt)" (Hughes and McDonald 2002). In 1948, under the Marshall Plan (European Recovery Program), the United States provided US$13 billion in aid to help rebuild the infrastructure and industrial base of war-torn Europe. Within a decade, American corporations such as IBM, General Motors, and General Electric expanded into Europe, generating vast flows of US dollars. This phenomenon coincided with a weakening of British trade hegemony following the 1956 Suez Canal crisis, and the recovery and gradual return of Germany to the international financial market after 1957, increasing the need for US dollar-based instruments. The first international transactions between the United States and the European Economic Community were in the Eurobond market, and took place between European investors who owned dollars and European borrowers who wanted dollars. SG Warburg of London (who created the market in 1963 with a US$15 million issue for the Italian State Highway Authority) competed with Credit Suisse for the first 1.8 billion Eurobond issue by the European Economic Community. "About $4.8 billion of Eurobonds were issued from 1963 through 1967, rising to $17.5 billion in the five years through 1972" (Glover 2013).

The establishment of the London Interbank Offered Rate (LIBOR), in 1963, set the criteria for the euro currency interbank market, channeling flows of capital between international banks. (The Libor scandal on manipulation of rates between 2008 and 2012 will be discussed in Chapter 7). President Nixon's decision to decouple gold and the US dollar in August 1971, and the 1973 oil crisis, generated a flood of petrodollars (oil was denominated in US dollars) recycled in U.S. and British banks. Between 1973 and 1988, euro deposits increased from $300 billion to $1.2 trillion, the result of the flow of petrodollars and the resurgence of Asian economies. As international banks used the euro bond market as a safe haven for placing surplus funds short term, it created a need for new clearinghouses and oversight mechanisms.

In 1973, Society for Worldwide Interbank Financial Telecommunications (SWIFT) was created in Brussels, with 239 banks in 15 countries to establish common standards for financial transactions and standardization of financial messages. In 2009, it expanded to centers in Switzerland, the Netherlands and the United States. (Global syndicated loans and fixed income securities markets are examined in Chapter 2.)

Financial expansion and reciprocity in foreign markets

U.S. bank presence abroad

In 1960, only nine U.S. banks had overseas offices, led by First National City Bank, Bank of America, and Chase Manhattan. By 1970, the number increased to 80 banks with 540, increasing to over 900 by the 1990s. In the early 1970s, U.S. banks held 30 percent of the world's banking assets (by contrast, in May 1990 they held less than 10 percent). By the end of 1974, U.S. banks (with Bank of America, Citicorp, and Chase Manhattan) were in the top five global banks by total assets. As U.S. bankers sought access to the recovering economies in Europe and Asia, there began a demand for reciprocity by foreign banks entering the U.S. market, led by French, Swiss, and British banks and followed after 1878 by German and Japanese banks.

Foreign corporate banks seeking to expand into new markets, took advantage of more flexible regulation in the United States, which allowed foreign banks to open interstate branches or subsidiaries. After the Crash of 1987, Alan Greenspan, Chairman of the Federal Reserve, endorsed efforts by large industrial corporations to acquire banks, creating vast pools of capital which favored large mergers. The U.S. Treasury decided that "the Government should encourage creation of very large banks that could better compete with financial institutions in Japan and Europe" (Nash 1987). In 1991, after the fall of the Soviet Union and the opening of new markets across Central and Eastern European countries, U.S. and European banks competed for market share in emerging markets across Asia, Latin America and the former Eastern Europe. However, following the Asian and Russian currency crisis of 1997 to 1998, 65 to 80 percent of the banking sector of the Central and Eastern European countries came under foreign ownership, led by Austrian (Raiffeisen, Ernst), Swedish (Swedbanken, Nordea), Italian (Unicredit), and French (Société Générale) banks. For political and cultural reasons, Germany did not pursue buyouts in these countries or in the former Soviet Union. Deutsche Bank expanded its U.S. and Asian operations, while Spain's Santander expanded into Latin America.

The Bank for International Settlements

The Bank for International Settlements (BIS) "is an international institution, founded in 1930 with the goal of resolving the reparations problems that arose following World War I" (Yago xvi). However, in May 1931 when Austria's largest bank, Credit-Anstalt, collapsed, when called upon to help engineer a bailout, the BIS did not have the power to intervene (see Chapter 4). In 1938 it was suggested that the BIS serve as a clearing house or common fund to help finance trade and stabilize economies, as volatility in exchange rates increased, but this plan failed. The BIS came under severe attack after World War II, when it was revealed to have violated neutrality and served as conduit for Third Reich confiscated gold, which allowed the Nazi regime to purchase raw materials and equipment. At Bretton Woods in 1944, the American contingent represented by Harry Dexter White and Treasury Secretary Robert Morgenthau asked that the BIS be liquidated and replaced by the IMF (Steil 2013). The BIS survived and, following the Smithsonian Agreements in the 1970s, the BIS took on new advisory and regulatory functions with the establishment in 1974 of the Basel Committee on Banking Supervision.

Following the Crisis of 1987, the Basel Committee set out recommendations on capital adequacy requirements, which became Basel I. Basel II was set out in 2003, and in 2010 the framework for Basel III was established (see Chapter 6).

Post-World War II financial institutions, multilaterals and international banking

Bretton Woods

The Bretton Woods meeting in July 1944 at Mount Washington hotel in Bretton Woods, New Hampshire, brought together delegates from 44 countries to create a global financial framework under the aegis of the United States. In a near-completely devastated world, it established a system of fixed exchange rates with one percent parity bands pegged to the US dollar, with the US dollar acting as reserve currency, overseen by the International Monetary Fund (IMF), and the International Bank of Reconstruction (World Bank). Following John Maynard Keynes' and Harry Dexter White's blueprint, it established the United States as guarantor of economic security. Until August 1971, when President Nixon expediently decided to decouple the US dollar from gold and freed foreign exchange markets (formalized in the December 1971 Smithsonian Agreements), the conditions set out in Bretton Woods guided all global financial decisions.

The International Monetary Fund

The International Monetary Fund (IMF), established in 1944 in the framework of Bretton Woods, was to provide international coordination of monetary policy; coordination of inflation criteria; and coordination and oversight of trade balances, in order to protect against the devastating post-World War I consequences of hyperinflation, severe trade imbalances, and adversarial and disjointed monetary policy.

This was accomplished by "making general resources of the Fund temporarily available ... under adequate safeguards" (IMF 2014) in order to allow nations to correct balance of payments, stabilize currencies and regain market credibility. *De facto*, after 1960 the IMF assumed the function of global lender of last resort to sovereign governments, expanding from 30 members in 1947 to 103 in 1966, and 187 in 2011.

Starting in the 1960s, the IMF increased in size and scope, its mandate enlarged to include: technical assistance; consultative monitoring to new countries (Africa); increased collaboration with the World Bank, the General Agreement on Tariffs and Trade (GATT), and the Organisation for Economic Co-operation and Development (OECD); and the creation of Special Drawing Rights facility (SDR). With the fall of the Soviet Union, the IMF assumed a larger role in emerging economies: monitoring inflation, growth, and productivity as preconditions to assistance (Article IV consultation). In the Asian and Russian crises of 1997–8, the IMF began to demand greater scrutiny of countries' banking and financial supervision, and regulatory soundness.

After 1998, the IMF worked in closer coordination with BIS, central banks, and the World Bank to prevent as well as resolve banking crises. (See Chapter 5 on the Turkish crisis of 2001; see Chapters 4 and 5 on the global financial crisis of 2008 and the EU sovereign debt crisis.)

The World Bank group

The World Bank and in particular the International Bank for Reconstruction and Development was established in 1946 to provide long-term financing for the reconstruction of Europe's destroyed infrastructure. Its functions include the promotion of economic development, with specific emphasis on the financing of infrastructure investments, business and social development initiatives. Under the presidency of Robert McNamara (1968 to 1981), driven by the emergence of new nations across Africa, the World Bank expanded its role in non-OECD countries.

The interrelationship between the World Bank and international finance developed in the 1950s to promote closer cooperation between private business investment and joint public private endeavors in developing countries. The International Finance Corporation (IFC) was established in 1956 as a member of the World Bank Group, its function to be a multilateral source of loans for the private sector in emerging markets. The first investment in 1958 was a US$1 million loan to help finance Siemens' projects in Brazil. The objectives of the IFC are financing private sector projects in the developing world, helping private companies mobilize capital, and providing technical assistance and advisory services to help build financial markets.

European international banking: consolidation and mergers pre- and post-Maastricht

The fall of the Soviet Union, and the creation of the European Union following the currency crisis of 1992 to 1993 was accompanied by a series of financial shocks, reversals, and major restructuring. Over the course of the decade and a half from 1992 to 2007, Europe underwent privatization, reform, consolidation, and deregulation.

The 1989 Single Banking Market Program, implemented in the 1993 Second Banking Directive, established the single banking passport, which provided any bank licensed to do business in one European Union member state reciprocal rights to do business in all other European Union states. The goal was to establish pan-European banks and to facilitate the creation of bank branches and subsidiaries across the European Union. Domestic consolidation (see chart below) began in the 1990s through privatization, deregulation, and liberalization prompted by increased competitiveness, led by the United States. After the 1995 bailout of Crédit Lyonnais, the largest French state-owned bank, the European Commission had to address the issues of privatization, limits on state subsidies and the rights of foreign banks to acquire any other EU member country banks (see also Chapter 4). Under the provisions of the European Commission on Competitiveness decision of July 1995 on state subsidies and privatization of state banks, any bank in a European Union member state could set up a branch, subsidiary, merge or acquire any bank in another member state.

Between 1997 and 2005, the European Union, and in particular Germany and France remained heavily overbanked. Despite domestic mergers, cross-border deals (outside of the Nordic region) rarely occurred, nor were encouraged.[9] Cross-border mergers worked more smoothly in countries with long traditions of financial and commercial cross-border interactions and interdependencies, such as was the case with Finland's Merita Bank, Sweden's Nordbanken, and in the Belgian-Dutch merger of Banque Brussels Lambert and ING.

Germany

Despite becoming Europe's economic powerhouse, German banking remained averse to consolidation. In 1997, Germany's major merger occurred between Bayrische Vereinsbank and Bayrische Hypotheken und Wechsel bank to create a "bank of regions" with an emphasis on retail banking seeking to emulate the United States approach to "super regional" banks (Dermine 2006). Deutsche Bank initiated the first large scale US–EU merger with Bankers Trust in 1998. However, despite powerful corporate and industrial cross-shareholdings and international name recognition, German international banks represent only a small share (about 35 percent) of the domestic market, which was dominated by the State-subsidized Landesbanken until 2005 and savings institutions (see also Chapter 4). Failed attempts at mergers between Deutsche Bank and Commerz Bank, and Deutsche Bank and Dresdner in 2000 were symptomatic of the internal fragmentation and lack of efficiency. Only in summer 2008, Commerz and Dresdner were merged to create a new German mega bank.

France

From 1950 to 1980, France benefited from three decades of steady recovery and growth in domestic retail and corporate banking. The largest banks (BNP, Crédit Lyonnais and Société Générale) as well as the Bank of France and large segments of the industrial base remained under Government majority owner-ship. In 1981, a Socialist government under President Mitterrand imposed nationalization of all private and semi-private banks with assets of over one billion francs. As the economy faltered these measures were reversed by 1983, following the British and U.S. model in favor of modified capitalism promoting growth and an aggressive push for investment abroad. From the mid 1980s to 1993, corporations and banks were denationalized: Paribas in 1984, Société Générale privatized in 1987, and BNP in 1993. Crédit Lyonnais was privatized in 1999 and merged with Crédit Agricole in 2003. In 1999, BNP merged with Paribas, rapidly diversifying from traditional commercial activities and corporate banking into investment banking, underwriting, proprietary trading, and mergers and acquisition activity.

Italy

Italian banks, weakened by fragmentation, inefficiency, and close to 80 percent public sector control, underwent an aggressive turnaround in the 1990s. Bank ownership was further complicated by federal, regional, and municipal holdings as well as century-old foundation and church holdings. Consolidation reduced the number of banks from nearly 1,200 to about 900. In 2000, only about 15 percent of the sector remained under state control. Five large international banking groups dominated, further reduced to three, Unicredito, Intesa and Capitalia, by 2010.

United Kingdom

After two decades of post-war economic stagnation under heavy government regulation, the U.K. economy surged under Prime Minister Margaret Thatcher's pro-privatization, pro-business, pro-market policies. The London euro dollar market attracted global capital and new opportunities for U.S. investment banks, led by Solomon and Morgan Stanley. The U.K. bank model of separation of merchant bankers, stockbrokers, and jobbers under fixed commissions began to unravel under intense U.S. competition. By 1984, merchant bankers began to buy stakes in brokers and jobbers, and foreign banks led by SG Warburg and Morgan Stanley were allowed to participate in the privatization of British Telecom. These reforms culminated in the October 27, 1986 deregulation of the financial merchant banking structures known as Big Bang.

U.K. banks concentrated on the United States, Far East, and emerging markets, largely bypassing the European Union. Although U.K. banks were judged more profitable and better run than their competitors, by 2007 after the failure and government bailout of Northern Rock, the situation had deteriorated drastically (see also Chapters 4 and 5).

Spain

After the acquisition of Banco Banesto in 1994, Santander began a process of growth through mergers and acquisitions in Latin America and the United Kingdom. Santander was the EU leader in successful cross-border mergers and acquisitions, with the acquisition of Abbey National in 2004, and the Santander–Royal Bank of Scotland–Fortis buyout of ABN Ambro in 2007 (which subsequently collapsed in 2008). Santander and BBVA, the leading Spanish corporate banks, emerged relatively unscathed from the 2008 crisis until the failure of the Spanish savings and thrift sector and the collapse of Bankia in 2012, requiring massive EU bailouts (see Chapter 4).

Through 2013, cross-border banking mergers have been limited as each member state maintained its own banking regime and internal regulatory structures, coupled with economic patriotism policies: France, Germany, Italy, and Spain avoided rigorously foreign buyouts of major domestic banks.

Central and Eastern Europe and former Soviet Union

Between 1991 and 1993, the countries of Central and Eastern Europe and the former Soviet Union established central banks, reinstated domestic currencies, and sought to create and restructure their banking sectors. The European Commission's 1995 White Paper, "Preparation of the Associated Countries of Central and Eastern Europe for Integration into the Internal Market of the Union" described a number of major impediments including a lack of trained management, supervisory bodies, appropriate legislation, and credit worthiness. The World Bank IFC *Emerging Markets Yearbook* (1997) and the Fink et al. paper (1998) found the sectors extremely weak due to: residual inefficient state ownership; ineffective supervision due to lack of funding and training; excessive corruption due to cronyism and lack of accountability and information.[10] In the aftermath of the 1998 ruble crisis, all Central and Eastern European banks had to be recapitalized (see also Chapter 5).

Between 1998 and 2003, between 65 and 80 percent of these banking sectors were foreign bought or acquired by the core EU banks: Unicredit, Raiffeisen, Swedebank, Nordea, and Société Générale. Despite these economic challenges, under the Accession Clauses of the Treaty of Nice, Poland, Latvia, Lithuania, Hungary, the Czech Republic, Estonia, Slovenia, and Slovakia (as well as Cyprus and Malta) became new members of the European Union in 2004, followed by Romania and Bulgaria in 2007, and Croatia in 2013.

Global consolidation in banking

From the end of World War II until the 2008 U.S. subprime meltdown crisis, through country and regional financial crises and bank failures (discussed in Chapters 4 and 5), the world marched inexorably toward globalization, through the increased liberalization of the flows of goods and factors of production (including capital, although not labor) and the resulting expansion of the international reach of business enterprises.

As amply discussed in the previous sections of this chapter, the internationalization of banking activities can be traced to the early 1200s, and has never ceased to expand. But until the early 1980s, it had rested fundamentally in green field type initiatives by banks, such as the opening of representative offices and/or branches overseas to explore trade financing opportunities, provide credit in foreign currency to large institutional borrowers and/or capture personal savings of individual customers in the host country.

It is only toward the end of the 1980s that a process of financial liberalization that increasingly lowered the barriers to entry to foreign banks in most jurisdictions around the world (see Chapter 2) and greater harmonization of banking regulations among sovereign jurisdictions (see Chapter 6) created the conditions for their more aggressive allocation of capital in the establishment of commercial and investment banking operations overseas

Table 1.3 at the end of this chapter illustrates this trend. It presents a list of major domestic and international acquisitions and mergers involving OECD banks around the world between 1989 and 2008. For the purpose of this table, "major" is defined as either a merger between two of the top five competitors of any particular jurisdiction (a country or, in the case of the United States, a state) or an acquisition where the institution being acquired is one of the top five competitors in its home jurisdiction.

A few observations to be more thoroughly explored throughout this book already emerge from the examination of Table 1.3.

First, the establishment of national champions – defined as clear domestic market leaders – tended to precede major cross-border acquisitions.

Second, U.S. and Japanese national champions, formed only around the turn of the century, showed significantly less aggressiveness toward major cross-border acquisitions than their European counterparts, formed during the early 1990s.

Third, German and Swiss banks – the former facing domestic cultural barriers to further domestic consolidation in commercial banking as a result of the relative strength of state-owned *Landesbanks* and the latter already internationally well-established in wealth management – were the ones that engaged in the most important acquisitions of investment banks overseas.

This long period of market-driven expansion of geographic reach and broadening of the scope of activities by leading banks around the world came to a halt in 2008. The U.S. subprime meltdown crisis and global credit crunch forced governments to come to the rescue of many of their major financial institutions, a process that included financial support for bank mergers without much regard for potentially excessive concentration of market power.

Examples of such transactions were: the Commerzbank–Dresdner and Lloyds–HBOS mergers in Germany and the United Kingdom, respectively; the absorptions of Bear Stearns and Washington Mutual by JPMorgan Chase, of Countrywide and Merrill Lynch by Bank of America, and of Wachovia by Wells Fargo in the United States; and the acquisition of Fortis by BNP Paribas.

The crisis also brought about a thorough re-examination of bank regulation globally, which resulted in significantly tighter standards of minimum capital adequacy, minimum liquidity, and transparency and disclosure requirements, in addition to expanded supervision and intervention power to bank regulators.

Faced with the need for immediate replenishment of capital cushions, international banks began to divest from non-core operations, many of them overseas businesses sold to home banks.

Examples of such transactions were the acquisitions by Capital One (United States) of HSBC's credit card operations and of ING-Direct in the United States; the purchase by Itau Unibanco (Brazil) of Citibank's Credicard subsidiary in Brazil; and of Barclays (United Kingdom) of ING-Direct in the United Kingdom.

Table 1.3 Major mergers and acquisitions involving OECD banks, 1986–2008

Country[1]	Domestic[2]	International[3]
France	Crédit Agricole-Indosuez, 1996 Crédit Agricole-C. Lyonnais, 2003 -> **Crédit Agricole** BNP-Paribas, 1999 -> **BNP Paribas**	
Germany		**Deutsche**: M. Grenfell (UK), 1989; B. Trust (US) 1999 **Dresdner**: K. Benson (UK), 1995
	Bayerische Vereins-B. Hypotheken, 1998 -> **HVB**	**HVB**: Bank Austria, 2000; Credit Anstalt, 2003 (Austria)
Italy	C.Romagnolo-C.Italiano, 1995 -> **UniCredito** Ambroveneto-Cariplo, 1997 -> **INTESA** Sanpaolo-IMI-B.Napoli,1999 -> **Sanpaolo IMI** INTESA-Sanpaolo, IMI, 2006 -> **Intesa Sanpaolo**	**UniCredito**: HVB (Germany, Austria, C. Europe), 2005
Netherlands	ABN-Amro, 1990 -> **ABN Amro** NMB Postbank-ING, 1991 -> **ING**	**ABN Amro**: Real (Br), 1998; Antonveneta (It), 2005 **ING**: Barings (UK), 1995
Spain	B.Vizcaya-B.Bilbao, 1988 (BBV) BBV-Argentaria, 1999 -> **BBVA** B.Central-B.Hispano, 1992 (BCH) Santander-Banesto, 1994 Santander-BCH, 1999 -> **Santander**	**BBVA**: Continental (Peru), 1995; Francez (Arg), 1996; Bancomer (Mex), 2000 **Santander**: Rio (Arg), 1997; Serfin (Mex), 2000; Banespa, 2000 and ABN Real, 2007 (Br); Totta, (Portugal),1999; Abbey (UK), 2004; Sovereign (US), 2005
United Kingdom	Britain HSBC(HK)-Midland (UK), 1992 -> **HSBC**	**HSBC**: Marine Midland (US),1980; Roberts (Arg), 1997 Bamerindus (Br), 1997; Bital (Mex), 2002; Household International, 2003 (US)

Source: Authors
[1]Country or state of acquirer's headquarters
[2]Name of acquirer first; name of resulting financial group in bold at the end
[3]Name of acquirer in bold; country of acquired in parentheses

However, as the global economy in 2014 continued to heal from the great recession and the international framework of bank regulation across multiple jurisdictions to evolve, important challenges remained for the boards of directors and the management of banks around the world to navigate their companies toward growth, and less volatile profitability, while also collectively contributing to the restoration of society's faith in the financial system.

Notes

1. These wars of conquest, religion and expansion included the Crusades; the Hundred Years War (1347–1453); Dutch–Spanish and Anglo Dutch Wars (1558–1674); American War of Independence (1775–1776); Napoleonic Wars (1799–1815); Revolutions of 1848; Franco Prussian War of 1870; World Wars I and II.
2. In spite of its political and military power, France never achieved a corresponding level of economic power. This is explained by the power the absolute monarchy retained over the State Treasury, and their refusal to transfer minting privileges to a central bank to reform a corrupt and exploitative tax system or to establish independent oversight of State finances.
3. Despite being leaders in international maritime trade, German and Nordic city states of the Hanseatic League remained wary of banking and credit-based activities.
4. This was contrary to the situation in the Austro-Hungarian, Russian, Mongol and Ottoman Empires.
5. The term central bank does not appear until the mid 1800s.
6. European System of Central Banks
7. Standard Chartered was created by the 1969 merger of these institutions.
8. In the north east, Bank of America acquired Bank of Boston and Bank of New England (1985); Wells Fargo expanded throughout the west, acquiring Signet Banking Corporation, Crocker National Bank, First Fidelity Bancorp (1986–7), and Core States Financial Corp (1990). In New York, Bank of New York and Irving Trust merged into Bank of New York Mellon (1988); and Chemical, Manufactures Hanover Trust merged with Chase Manhattan (1996). JPMorgan and Chase merged in 2000.
9. "For continental Europeans recent takeover battles and mergers constitute a radical departure. But it will be pointless radicalism if politicians and bankers are unwilling to permit a genuine efficient economic outcome. The arrival of the Euro will not in itself, create competitive European financial markets" ("Shaking Up Europe's Banks", *Financial Times*, 24 August 1999).
10. The assets of the eight countries of Central and Eastern Europe totaled only US$188 billion, with disproportionately high liquid assets and bad loans.

2   International wholesale banking

Introduction

In this chapter we examine the process of adjustment and re-invention engaged in by international banks over recent decades in order to compete effectively for the business of their *institutional* clients – corporations, financial institutions, and government entities.

We begin by exploring *why* most major *commercial banks* around the world have chosen to engage in *investment banking* activities, and *how* they have sought to achieve this goal and become fully-fledged *wholesale banking* (corporate commercial plus investment banking) franchises.

We explore next the typical corporate commercial and investment banking product offerings of international wholesale banks. We conclude each examination with examples drawn from publicly available information on the wholesale banking activities of two major international banks, Citibank and Deutsche Bank.

The concept of wholesale banking

The 1990s were a period of rapid expansion and reinvention for the banking industry globally. Three main factors affecting the fundamentals of financial intermediation contributed to this expansion: significant regulatory changes; an extraordinary acceleration in the use of digital technology; and the explosive growth of securities markets.

On the regulatory front, substantial changes in response to a trend toward financial liberalization came about almost simultaneously on both sides of the Atlantic. In Europe, the Financial Services Action Plan (1999) formalized a series of measures toward a single wholesale financial market and a more open retail market in the European Union (EU), completing a process of gradual reduction of barriers to cross-border financial intermediation initiated ten years previously, with the EU Second Banking Directive (Dermine 2002).

In the United States, over six decades of regulations around both interstate banking and universal banking were removed. In 1994, the Riegle-Neal Interstate Banking and Branching Efficiency Act revoked restrictions on interstate banking and mergers among banks, first introduced in 1927 under the McFadden Act.

The Gramm-Leach-Bliley Act of 1999 completed the elimination of regulatory constraints on securities underwriting activities by commercial banks set in place originally by the Glass-Steagall Act of 1933.

On the technological front, rapid acceleration of the paper-to-digital trend revolutionized the ways in which financial information could be consolidated and disseminated, contractual obligations established and monitored, and trades conducted and settled.

Finally, and facilitated by the technological evolution mentioned above, there was a huge increase in the volumes of savings managed outside the banking sector, from insurance companies and pension and mutual funds to a myriad of independent asset managers. As recorded by the working group commissioned by the Bank for International Settlements' (BIS) Committee on the Global Financial System in 2007, financial assets managed by institutional investors had more than doubled in most countries between 1995 and 2005: from US$321 billion to US$1.507 trillion in Australia; from US$556 billion to US$1.432 trillion in Canada; from US$1.176 trillion to US$3.008 trillion in France; from US$1.057 trillion to US$2.152 trillion in Germany; from US$1.759 trillion to US$4.014 trillion in the United Kingdom; and from US$10.546 trillion to US$21.811 trillion in the United States (www.bis.org/publ/cgfs27.pdf).

Other things being equal, increased competition for a particular asset class in any given market results in downward pressure on the credit risk spreads associated with that asset class. As investment opportunities in one country became increasingly available to savers from another country, credit spreads tended to narrow further. The extraordinary reduction in the costs associated with bridging the information asymmetry between savers and borrowers that resulted from this technological change and financial liberalization, regardless of their geography, had the effect of substantially reducing the financial margins banks could charge for top credit risks. The most traditional core source of revenues for a commercial bank – carrying businesses' credit risk on its balance sheet – became less and less financially rewarding.

The natural response of most leading commercial banks was to expand the scope of their corporate banking activities into securities underwriting and corporate finance advisory services, such as project finance mergers and acquisitions advice. The strategies adopted varied from building from within, acquiring independent investment banks, and/or a combination of both. Nevertheless, once their investment banking capabilities became institutionally well-rooted, most banks proceeded to combine the offerings of corporate commercial and investment banking platforms under a single major organizational structure, the *wholesale bank*.

A selected list of well-known broker-dealers and/or investment banks acquired by commercial banks, such as the acquisition of Morgan Grenfell by Deutsche Bank (1990), prior to the global financial crisis triggered by the U.S. subprime meltdown in 2008 is presented in Table 2.1.

As a final observation, government entities and other financial institutions demand most of the same financial services offered by banks to large corporations. For this reason, while choosing different denominations (e.g. *Institutional Clients Group*, at Citicorp; *Corporate Banking and Securities*, at Deutsche Bank), most

Table 2.1 Commercial banks' acquisitions of investment banks, 1989–2006

Year	Acquirer	Country of Origin	Target	Country of Origin
1989	Deutsche Bank	Germany	Morgan Grenfell	United Kingdom
1995	Dresdner Bank	Germany	Kleinwort Benson	United Kingdom
1995	ING	Netherlands	Barings	United Kingdom
1996	Credit Suisse	Switzerland	First Boston	United States
1997	Nations Bank	United States	Montgomery Secs.	United States
1997	BancBoston	United States	R. Stephenson	United States
1997	Bankers Trust	United States	Alex Brown	United States
1998	SBC	Switzerland	Warburg D. Read	United Kingdom
1998	Credit Suisse	Switzerland	Banco Garantia	Brazil
1999	Chase Manhattan	United States	Hambrecht & Quist	United States
1999	Deutsche Bank	Germany	Bankers Trust	United States
2000	BNP	France	Paribas	France
2000	Citigroup	United States	Schroder	United Kingdom
2000	Credit Suisse	Switzerland	DLJ	United States
2000	UBS	Switzerland	Paine Webber	United States
2001	SunTrust	United States	Robinson Humphrey	United States
2003	Chase Bank	United States	R. Flemings	United States
2003	Wachovia	United States	Prudential	United States
2006	Wachovia	United States	A.G. Edwards	United States
2006	UBS	Switzerland	Banco Pactual	Brazil
2006	Wells Fargo	United States	Barrington Assoc.	United States

Source: Authors

banks have converged to place the full spectrum of their corporate banking, capital markets, and financial advisory services to institutional clients (large companies, government entities, and financial institutions) under a single organizational umbrella, a full service wholesale bank.

International corporate commercial banking

An international (or cross-border) loan is a credit obligation between a borrower established in one national jurisdiction and a lender from a second national jurisdiction. A cross-border loan can be structured as a funded (e.g. a cash advance by the lender to finance the exports of a borrower) or unfunded credit facility (e.g. a bank guarantee made to an exporter on behalf of an importer); it can be provided directly to a company, or take the form of credit support to another bank which, in turn, takes the credit risk of that company; it can be secured (e.g. backed by some sort of collateral such as inventory, receivables, a contracted flow of exports) or unsecured; it can be short-term or long-term; it can be made by one bank alone, a small group of banks (club deal), or a large number of banks with various roles and taking different levels of risk (loan syndicate); and, finally, it can be extended with full recourse to a particular borrower or with limited recourse to the borrower, with different third parties taking the responsibility for specific risks (project finance).

International trade finance and correspondent banking

As suggested by Beard and Thomas (2006), the settlement of an international commercial transaction can range from a cash payment in advance (risky for the importer, riskless for the exporter) to a deferred payment until final sale of goods with ability to return unsold merchandise by the importer (risky for the exporter, riskless for the importer). Banks step into the middle of this push-pull of risk between exporter and importer to provide the type of financial settlement and credit support solution which best meets the objectives and constraints of both parties.

The confirmed import letter of credit (import LC) is the most common and effective financial instrument utilized by banks from different countries to pair-up efficiently and with great attention to detail, and make possible an international trade, which might not, otherwise, materialize.

Let us assume a cutlery manufacturer in Germany wants to export specialty knives with a total price of €1 million to a retailer in Argentina. While the German cutlery manufacturer may have a positive perception of the Argentine retailer's commercial record, (s)he cannot be certain of payment in full and on schedule. The import LC resolves this dilemma. Bank A, an Argentine bank that knows the Argentine retailer well and can assess its credit risk, issues an LC in favor of the importer guaranteeing that if the Argentine retailer fails to make the payment in full and on schedule, the Argentine bank will do so on their behalf. Nevertheless, as the German cutlery manufacturer cannot properly assess the creditworthiness of the Argentine bank, it becomes necessary for another bank, in this case most likely a German bank, Bank G, to provide advice on the authenticity of the documentation and to confirm to the German manufacturer that it guarantees the performance of the LC issued by Bank A on behalf of the Argentine importer. Bank G collects from Bank A an LC advice and confirmation fee. Bank A charges the Argentine retailer an import LC fee, which covers the cost of Bank G's LC advice and confirmation fee plus compensation for the credit risk taken by Bank A.

Upfront payment to the German manufacturer upon the contracting of the sale or the shipment of the goods to the Argentine retailer could have been also arranged through a cash advance from the German bank, based on its assessment of the export transaction. In this case, the German bank would also be providing export financing to the German manufacturer.

A major contributor to the cost efficiency of this process has been the continuous development over the past three centuries of international correspondent banking networks. It should be noted that correspondent banking, the cooperative interaction between two banks to work together under pre-agreed conditions to meet the financial needs of clients in locations not served by one of them, is not specific to the international arena, as insightfully described below:

> Before the existence of the Federal Reserve System, many of its functions were performed for the smaller banks by the larger correspondent banks in

the principal financial centers... The correspondent banking system is an entirely informal arrangement whereby the small banks in towns and villages maintain deposits with larger banks in nearby cities and look to them for a variety of services and assistance. The city banks, in turn, keep correspondent balances with still larger banks in the principal money centers... Thus, correspondent banks provided liquidity and credit fluidity to a diverse economy... Correspondent banks are still active in the collection of checks and still supply credit to the smaller banks in consideration of the balances the latter maintain. In addition, correspondent banks perform many services that would otherwise be unobtainable to the smaller banks and their customers. They give investment advice, hold customers' securities, arrange international financial transactions, trade in Federal funds, participate in loans too large for the small banks, sell participations in large loans to small banks with surplus funds, and provide a wide range of other services.

(Crosse and Hempel 1973: 14)

Commercial banks understood early on that the support of international trade should be a central element of the offering to be provided to corporate customers. As a result, they have sought to establish and maintain a network of stable international correspondent banking relationships to ensure effective facilitation of credit for, and reliable settlement of, their customers' cross-border trades.

A correspondent banking relationship is, by nature, bilateral as it typically encompasses a pre-approved line of credit and a pre-agreed rate structure for standardized transactions (revised annually), so that individual transactions between customers of the two banks can flow seamlessly and securely through the two organizations. The juxtaposition of the multitude of bilateral correspondent banking relationships among financial institutions from every corner of the world results in the creation of a global correspondent banking network of credit and settlement services, crucial for the smooth functioning and continued development of international trade.

Given that significant economies of scale can be achieved in the highly capital-intensive payments and collections services industry, it is natural that international money center banks would choose to pursue aggressively leadership in global payments and custody services, as we shall examine.

Term lending and bank syndicates

Credit risk increases not only as a function of the amount of the exposure a bank has to a customer, but also as a function of the tenure of the loan. It is, therefore, unsurprising that banks should seek ways in which to combine efforts to accommodate the larger and longer-term loan demands of their customers.

A syndicated loan is defined as a credit extended to a borrower by two or more banks under the same loan agreement. The most visible and profitable role for the bank is to be the arranger (or book runner), the bank that negotiates the facility with the borrower and syndicates the loan to the other banks. The arranger is also typically the leading underwriter, the bank committing to the highest level of risk participation in the hierarchy of the loan syndicate. The agent of a loan syndicate is the bank responsible for the administration of the credit facility, which includes collecting fees, interest, and principal payments from the borrower for distribution to all participants and monitoring the borrower's adherence to the conditions of the loan agreement. Frequently, the arranger is also the agent for the syndicate. Box 2.1 provides a simple hypothetical example of the hierarchy of roles and corresponding returns for credit risk taken in a major loan syndicate.

Column 6 of Box 2.1 shows the average annual return on risk assets (RORA) of the transaction for each bank. As can be observed, the average annual RORA

Box 2.1 International steel loan syndicate

Borrower: International Steel
Amount: US$700 million, fully disbursed upon loan signing
Maturity: six years, semi-annual interest payments, bullet repayment of principal
Repayment of Principal: Bullet (one single principal repayment), at the end of six years from initial disbursement
Underwriting conditions: Full commitment (as opposed to best efforts) by lead arranger(s) and underwriter(s)
Interest rate: six-month LIBOR plus 2%
Arrangement fees: 50bps on the total amount of the transaction upon disbursement
Participation fees, upon disbursement: 0.60% for US$50 million, 0.40% for US$30 million, 0.25% for U$20 million

Syndicate structure and compensation (per bank)

Role	(1) No. of banks	(2) Amount	(3) Total fee + interest income	(4) Avg. annual rev.	(5) Avg. RORA
Arranger	1	$50m	0.50% x $700m + 0.60% x $50m + 2% x $50m x 6 = $9.8m	$1.63m	3.26%
Lead Manager	4	$50m	0.60% x $50m + 2% x $50m x 6 = $6.30m	$1.05m	2.10%
Manager	6	$30m	0.40% x $30m + 2% x $30m x 6 = $3.72m	$0.62m	2.06%
Co-Manager	10	$20m	0.25% x $20m + 2% x $20m x 6 = $2.45m	$0.41m	2.04%

Source: Author

increases with the amount of underwritten commitment, but is significantly higher for the top position, the arranger and book runner. Furthermore, the relative attractiveness of higher levels of participation is, in fact, even more pronounced than is suggested in the calculations in Box 2.1, as upfront fees are typically treated as income in the moment they occur. In other words, for the arranger of this particular example the RORA would have been ten percent (US$5m/US$50m) for the first year, and two percent thereafter, while still 3.26 percent per annum, on average. In addition, the arranger is also often agent, further reinforcing its profitability as a result of the additional annual stream of fee income for the service of administering the credit facility until final maturity.

Competing successfully for lead arranger positions requires not only access to key decision makers and an understanding of the needs of major borrowers and the business risks but, also, strong distribution (or syndication) capacity. While major international banks have these capabilities in place and consistently seek the lead arranger role, they can also be found in senior secondary positions in major transactions for their target clients. Two principal reasons explain this acceptance of secondary roles: first, it is often better tactically to remain close to an important customer, even at a lower but still acceptable level of return; and, second, syndicated lending is a two-way street, the ability of a bank to step into the leading role and obtain from others the level of balance sheet commitments necessary at the higher levels of a loan syndicate is also dependent on its willingness to cooperate with peers and accept a lower role in other transactions.

Not uncommon when speed is of the essence – and/or credit conditions are tight – are club deals where arrangement and underwriting fees are shared equally by a small group of co-lead arrangers and underwriters to fully subscribe a credit facility for later distribution to other banks. These types of transactions, which had become popular in the late 1980s, in the aftermath of the Latin American debt crisis when stricter minimum capital requirements imposed by Basel I inhibited wider distribution of non-OECD sovereign credit risk (Hughes and MacDonald 2002: 100), are, today, a not uncommon financing solution for major acquisitions by corporations as well as private equity funds.

Global syndicated lending

The consolidation of the Eurodollar market in London in the 1960s was a fundamental stepping stone for the development of the global syndicated loan market (Rhodes 2011: 2–16) as it allowed for London branches of foreign banks to fund themselves at the London Interbank Offered Rate (LIBOR) to provide medium term LIBOR-based credit facilities to major corporations and governments around the world. Recycling by international banks of petrodollars – fast growing U.S. dollar surpluses accumulated by oil exporting nations during the 1970s – gave the international loan syndication market another major boost, in great part concentrated on private and public sector Latin American debt.

By the mid 1980s, the Latin American debt crisis – and its resolution – had pushed sovereign borrowers away from the syndicated loan market toward the fixed income securities market. By then, however, the U.S. domestic loan syndication market had become a major source of financing for leveraged buy-outs (LBOs) and management buy-outs (MBOs). While this type of highly leveraged financing would not immediately take off outside the United States, the international syndicated loan market would, in short order, present itself as a preferred source of financing for large private sector borrowers engaging in major strategic moves where expediency was of the essence. By 1997, global syndicated loan borrowings had reached US$1.8 trillion (up from US$500 billion in 1992), and acquisition finance had become the most important segment of the syndicated loan market globally (Fight 2004: 5).

Figure 2.1 shows the evolution of global syndicated loan issuance since 1997. As can be observed, total volume dropped from US$1.8 trillion in 1997 to under US$1.5 trillion in 1998, reflecting the effects of the Asian (1997) and Russian (1998) debt crises. It resurged to almost US$2 trillion in 2000, but sank back to below 1997 volume in 2002 (approximately US$1.6 trillion), as the world absorbed the impacts of the Enron debacle and corporate governance crisis (late 2000), Argentina's sovereign default (2001), and the September 11, 2001 terrorist attacks. Total syndicated loan issuances returned to dramatic growth in 2004, benefitting from perceived robust global economic growth and unusual levels of monetary liquidity, before declining sharply US$4 trillion in 2007 to approximately US$1.6 trillion in 2009, as a result of the international financial crisis following the U.S. subprime mortgage meltdown. By 2010, total volume was back to approximately US$2.6 trillion, a modest gain on 2004 levels, and a demonstration of the resilience and importance of this capital market for corporations around the world.

A fundamental characteristic of the syndicate loan business is that it demands both financial structuring and distribution capacity (typically perceived as investment

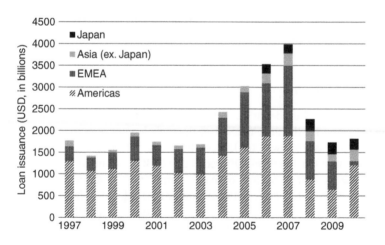

Figure 2.1 Global loan new issuance by region

Source: Thomson Reuters LPC (2011)

banking skills), as well as the ability and willingness to underwrite and often retain (for a significant period of time, if not to maturity) credit risk, a traditional core competency of corporate commercial lenders. This notion is clearly reflected in Table 2.2, which ranks the top 25 lead-managers of syndicated loans globally.

As can be observed, the first four positions were occupied by U.S. universal banks with long histories in corporate commercial lending: JPMorgan, Bank of America, Citicorp, and Wells Fargo. Former investment banks and since 2008 bank holding companies, Goldman Sachs and Morgan Stanley, ranked 12th and 16th respectively, still among the top 20, but not the top ten.

The rest of the list is composed of universal banks with long traditions in medium-term international corporate commercial lending from other developed economies (such as Mizuho, Mitsubishi, and Sumitomo of Japan; Deutsche Bank and Commerzbank of Germany; Barclays, HSBC, and RBS of the United Kingdom; BNP Paribas, Crédit Agricole, and Société Générale of France; RBC, CIBC, Scotiabank, and TD of Canada; Credit Suisse and UBS of Switzerland), in addition

Table 2.2 Global syndicated loans, 1Q 2014

Rank	Book Runner	Proceeds Amount (US$ Million)	Mkt. Share	Number of Issues
1	JP Morgan	84,328.58	10.0	316
2	Bank of America Merrill Lynch	72,094.01	8.6	301
3	Citi	43,687.96	5.2	147
4	Wells Fargo & Co	38,938.06	4.6	205
5	Deutsche Bank	36,907.42	4.4	141
6	Mitsubishi UFJ Financial Group	35,979.37	4.3	309
7	Mizuho Financial Group	35,036.81	4.2	241
8	Barclays	31,632.61	3.8	117
9	Sumitomo Mitsui Finl Grp Inc	27,260.07	3.2	237
10	RBC Capital Markets	25,626.53	3.0	107
11	Credit Suisse	25,324.74	3.0	101
12	Goldman Sachs & Co	24,656.70	2.9	96
13	BNP Paribas SA	20,999.65	2.5	83
14	HSBC Holdings PLC	19,035.51	2.3	86
15	State Bank of India	18,558.92	2.2	40
16	Morgan Stanley	18,349.90	2.2	69
17	RBS	16,674.98	2.0	85
18	Crédit Agricole CIB	14,373.24	1.7	57
19	US Bancorp	12,264.70	1.5	89
20	UBS	11,840.34	1.4	52
21	BMO Capital Markets	9,791.59	1.2	70
22	PNC Financial Services Group	8,233.99	1.0	76
23	TD Securities Inc	7,025.55	0.8	23
24	Societe Generale	6,615.39	0.8	36
25	Commerzbank AG	6,584.74	0.8	31
	Subtotal with Book Runner	842,681.08	100.0	2171
	Subtotal without Book Runner	-	0.0	0
	Industry Total	842,681.08	100.0	2171

Source: Thomson Reuters Date: 2014-05-24 04:58:16 EDT

to a number of leading U.S. regional franchises (such as US Bancorp and PNC), and one emerging market lender (State Bank of India (SBI), the latter due, primarily, to a strong presence in their domestic markets.

Secondary markets for syndicated loans

Contractual arrangements have always made possible the transfer – at a premium, par or discount – of a loan from one bank's balance sheet to another's. In December 1995, in an effort to establish standard operational and settlement procedures for greater efficiency in loan trading, a group of banks decided to create the Loan Syndications and Trading Association (LSTA), with headquarters in New York. This initiative preceded the establishment in London of the Loan Market Association (LMA), formed in mid 1996 by leading financial institutions operating in Europe with the specific purpose of developing a more efficient secondary loan market.

The market response was immediate. Between 1995 and 2000, annual secondary loan trading volumes quadrupled from US$30 billion to US$120 billion (Fight 2004: 146–57). The development of the secondary loan market had the effect, also, of transforming an exclusively bank-based loan trading activity into a broader investment market, further stimulated by the introduction of external credit ratings to syndicated loans in the late 1990s.

The 1998 Basel II Accord (see Chapter 6) provided an additional boost to a market craving credit ratings. By formally allowing external credit ratings to materially affect the minimum capital requirements imposed on banks by regulators, Basel II helped make them a critical ingredient for successful distribution of the largest transactions. By 2001, syndicated loan issuances benefitting from external credit ratings already accounted for 67 percent of total syndicated loan issuances and 90 percent of those of US$750 million and above.

Nonetheless, the time urgency toward closing that characterizes major acquisition-type situations and/or the sheer complexity of certain credit situations (such as more complex project financing structures, and private-public partnership endeavors) has continued to demand from bank syndicates the ability and willingness to underwrite significant amounts of credit risk with the assumption of long-term carry of such positions in participant banks' balance sheets.

Project finance

The fundamental difference between *project finance* and conventional long-term corporate lending is that in project finance the borrower is not a corporation with a financial history and significant assets of its own, but a newly-formed company created for the specific purpose (*special purpose company* (SPC)) of engaging in a capital intensive and very specific economic mission (e.g. energy, transportation, telecommunications, mining, and real estate projects).

From the project sponsors' standpoint, the benefit of the project finance structure is its *limited recourse* nature: failure by the SPC to meet debt obligations would have either no impact on the project sponsors' balance sheet or affect it only to the extent of the limited credit support (or guarantee) provided by them to the SPC. For the lender, this requires careful assessment of creditworthiness based on sensitivity analysis of the future cash flows of the project under different scenarios, in light of which additional specific credit support from the project sponsors may be demanded to mitigate clearly identified and well-quantified risks. In-depth understanding by lenders of a project's specific risks, with the resulting appropriate allocation of these risks to the parties better qualified to 'bank' them, allows for project finance structures to offer longer repayment periods than traditional corporate loans (Sotelino and Gustafson, 1985).

A typical project finance structure brings together participants with different objectives: equity investors, service providers, and project lenders (Weber and Alfen, 2010). The equity investors are the project's principal sponsor(s) – the party (or parties) with the primary interest in the exploration of the particular economic activity – plus other, possibly unsecured, passive financial investors willing to be rewarded exclusively from a share of the venture's cash flow, following payments to service providers and lenders. The service providers are the different parties hired by the SPC to perform well-defined and specific tasks such as construction and operation of the facilities, supply of critical inputs to the production process, and/or marketing of output. The obligations of service providers are established in task specific agreements, which also contemplate penalties for failure to perform as contracted as well as guarantees, provided by them to lenders. It is not uncommon for service providers, such as large engineering contractors, to act also as project sponsors in infrastructure-type ventures such as transportation (e.g. ports, airports, and highway concessions), and alternative energy (e.g. wind farms, waste-to-energy, etc.).

The project lenders are the banks and other financial institutions providing debt financing to the venture on the basis of its cash generating capacity, and additional credit support arising from the contractual obligations of the service providers, as well as, in some cases, limited recourse to the project sponsors in the form of capped guarantees, temporary sinking funds, etc. The debt portion of a project finance structure may bring together different financing sources such as commercial banks, development banks, insurance companies, dedicated investors (e.g. infrastructure investment funds), and other institutional fixed income investors. Also, it can contemplate the succession, under certain conditions, of one type of lender by another (for instance, the planned take-out, after three years, of a bank syndicate by a group of insurance companies, provided pre-agreed upon performance indicators are met). The complexity of project finance structures typically demands that sponsor(s) select a financial advisor, often a specialized dedicated team housed within the bank's specialty industry leading groups or within its investment banking arm.

From the standpoint of a bank, being the financial advisor offers, on the one hand, the possibility of significant additional fee income in addition to greater visibility in the eyes of both project sponsors and investors. On the other hand, it poses a potential conflict of interest between its advisory role in securing the best

interests of the client and a most likely lending role. As in the mergers and acquisitions advisory arena, this opens the field up to competition from major corporate consulting firms and specialized boutiques. Nonetheless, easy access to
major project sponsors, close monitoring of industry specific developments,
sound valuation and negotiation skills, depth of knowledge of financial markets,
and, crucially, the ability to lead the loan and/or securities syndicates necessary
to bring a project to fruition make wholesale banks formidable competitors in the
project finance advisory arena.

Global payments and custody services

The time value of money makes an efficient payments and collection process
crucial for the optimization of a firm's working capital, thus banks have sought
to embrace this challenge to provide corporate customers with increasingly
sophisticated global cash management services for the secure and efficient settlement and short-term bridge financing of commercial trades.

The explosive growth of the securities markets over the past two decades has
made global administration and custody services for institutional clients (such as
broker-dealers, asset managers, and corporate trusts) a very important source of
revenue for a select group of international banks.

The offering of securities servicing that these banks can provide to investors
globally has been further enhanced over recent decades by the fact that an
increasing number of publicly traded companies have chosen to become listed on
foreign stock markets also. This can be accomplished through the issuance of
global depositary receipts (GDRs), negotiable certificates issued by a depositary
bank which represent ownership of a given number of a company's shares which
can be listed and traded in a foreign stock exchange. Companies can choose
between issuing GDRs, used to access two or more foreign markets, or American
Deposit Receipts (ADRs), for trading exclusively in the U.S. market.

The size of the contribution that transaction services can make to the scope and
operating results of a wholesale banking franchise is illustrated in Box 2.2. As
shown in Box 2.2 below, Citicorp's *Global Transaction Services* Division (GTS),
comprising *Treasury and Trade Solutions* and *Securities and Fund Services*,
accounted for over one-third of the revenues and approximately 40 percent of the
net profit after tax of Citicorp's wholesale bank, its Institutional Clients Group
(ICG) in 2011.

International investment banking

The role of the investment bank

The primary role of an *investment bank* is to design and realize financing structures that satisfy the objectives and constraints of both the issuers and investors.
In this regard, it is quite distinct from the role of a pure commercial bank, which
earns interest to carry on its own balance sheet the credit risk of the borrower, or

Box 2.2 Global transaction services at Citicorp

Citigroup's history dates back to the founding of City Bank of New York in 1812. In 1968, First National City Corporation, a bank holding company later renamed Citicorp, became the parent of Citibank. In 1998 Citicorp merged with the Travelers Group Inc. to form Citigroup Inc.

At year-end 2013, Citigroup had two major divisions: Citicorp, comprising the businesses the company had made the decision to retain in the aftermath of the 2008 financial crisis; and Citi Holdings, housing the assets and activities Citigroup were still in the process of orderly disposing of.

For 2013, Citigroup had earned US$13.7 billion on average total assets of US$1.88 trillion and average common equity of US$238.7 billion, corresponding to a return on average equity of 7% for the year. Citigroup's net income of US$13.7 billion resulted from a US$15.5 billion gain at Citicorp and a US$1.9 billion loss at Citi Holdings.

At year-end 2013 Citicorp comprised two major client groups: *Regional Consumer* and *Institutional Clients Group*, and *Corporate Center* (which included Treasury). Citicorp's net income of US$15.5 billion for the year resulted from gains of US$7.1 billion from Regional Consumer and US$9.5 billion from the Institutional Clients Group, and a net loss of US$1.2 billion by the Corporate Center.

Regional Consumer, the bank's retail commercial banking arm, was organized along four regional divisions: North America, EMEA (Europe, Middle East, and Africa), Latin America, and Asia. The Institutional Clients Group (ICG, the bank's wholesale banking arm) was organized along two major business divisions, *Securities and Banking* and *Global Transaction Services*.

Securities and Banking comprised the activities of corporate and institutional lending, investment banking (corporate finance advisory, fixed income and equity capital markets), structured finance and real estate, and the Private Bank.

Global Transaction Services consisted of *Treasury and Trade Solutions* (TTS) and *Securities and Fund Services* (SFS). TTS provided trade finance and cash management services for corporations, financial institutions and public sector entities worldwide. SFS provided a whole range of securities services (such as custody, clearing, agency services) to investors, asset managers, broker-dealers, multinational corporations and governments.

The table breaks ICG revenues between Securities and Banking and GTS. As can be observed, GTS accounted for approximately one-third of the bank's wholesale banking (ICG) revenues, while being also very well diversified globally.

Citicorp's Institutional Clients Group, Revenues 2013 (US$ million)

Region	Securities and Banking	Global Transaction Services (GTS)	Total
North America	9,045	2,502	11,547
EMEA	6,462	3,533	9,995
Latin America	2,840	1,822	4,662
Asia	4,671	2,703	7,374
Total	23,018	10,560	33,578

As can be observed in the table, GTS accounted for approximately one-third of total wholesale banking (ICG) revenues, while also globally diversified (75% international).

For the fiscal year 2013, GTS's net income amounted to US$2.9 billion, corresponding to over 30% of ICG's net income of US$9.6 billion and almost 20% of Citicorp's profit of US$15.5 billion. GTS's 2013 performance once again underscored its importance as a source of significant and stable earnings for Citigroup, a fact specifically acknowledged in its 2010 annual report by then CEO, Vikram Pandit, in his letter to shareholders as quoted below:

> *Citi's GTS franchise brings in highly stable revenues with relatively low capital usage, making it one of the most attractive businesses in the industry.*
>
> Source: http://www.citigroup.com/citi/investor/quarterly/
> 2011/ar10c_en.pdf, Page 6 of 2010 Annual Report

(Source: Authors, based on Citigroup Inc., 2013 Annual Report on Form 10-K filing with the SEC)

of a pure securities broker, which earns a commission to buy and/or sell securities on behalf of its primary client, the investor.

While having *issuers and investors* as their primary clients, investment banks can trade also for their own account with other market participants (or *counterparts*). The proper balancing of these inherent conflicts of interest (*issuer* versus *investor* versus *counterpart*) requires from investment banks the establishment of firewalls among the activities of *structuring and underwriting* of securities to be issued by an institutional client, *sales and trading* of securities on behalf of investors, and *proprietary trading* on their own account.

This is not new, as evidenced by the quote below, from the U.S. Securities and Exchange Commission (SEC) documenting its creation in 1934 (author's italics):

Based on the findings in these hearings, Congress – during the peak year of the Depression – passed the Securities Act of 1933. *This law*, together with the Securities Exchange Act of 1934, which created the SEC, was *designed to restore investor confidence in our capital markets by providing investors and the markets with more reliable information and clear rules of honest dealing.* The main purposes of these laws can be reduced to two common-sense notions: Companies publicly offering securities for investment dollars must tell the public the truth about their businesses, the securities they are selling, and the risks involved in investing. *People who sell and trade securities –* brokers, dealers, and exchanges – must treat investors fairly and honestly, *putting investors' interests first.*

(www.sec.gov)

The key elements of the U.S. Securities Act and Securities Exchange Act are present also in the securities legislation of most countries. There was, however, one aspect of capital markets legislation that was unique to the United States: the prohibition from engagement in securities underwriting, sales, and trading by depositary banks, introduced in 1933 under the Glass-Steagall Act. This prohibition was lifted fully in 1999, through the enactment of the Gramm-Leach-Bliley Act, yet, securities underwriting remained the exclusive domain of broker-dealers in the world's largest market economy in the ensuing years. This may help explain why the leading U.S. investment banks were able to evolve from private partnerships to major publicly traded companies, with market valuations by late 2006 comparable to those of the world's largest financial institutions.

The main revenue generating activities of an investment bank encompass:

- *securities underwriting*;
- *secondary market-making* in these securities for investors;
- structuring of, and market-making for *risk management instruments* (*derivatives*);
- *proprietary trading* in securities, commodities, foreign exchange, and derivatives;
- *credit* (typically short-term and secured) to issuers, investors, and trading counterparts;
- *mergers and acquisitions advisory* services.

Securities underwriting

As suggested above, the primary role of an investment bank is to act as the financial intermediary between issuers and investors. The type of security issued can range from the purest form of equity (common stock) to the simplest forms of debt (such as straight bonds, notes, and commercial paper).

The tension between debt (offering higher leverage without dilution of ownership) and equity (attracting the purest form of risk capital – superseded by all other financial claims – but with dilution of ownership) has led to the creation of a range of both *quasi-equity* instruments (such as convertible bonds, preferred stocks, and various forms of subordinated debt) and *asset backed securitizations*, the pooling of certain assets (such as commercial or residential mortgages, auto-loans or credit card receivables) against which securities are issued.

Finally, a securities issue can be a *public offering* – with no restrictions on sale to the public at large; or a *private placement* – restricted for purchase only by well-defined types of sophisticated investors. A private placement tends to be less costly for the issuer (because of less demanding registration requirements and legal responsibilities), but it also enjoys less secondary market liquidity than does a public offering. Cross-border transactions often combine both an unrestricted listing in the stock exchange of the company's country of origin and a restricted offering to qualified investors abroad.

From the standpoint of the investment bank, a securities offering encompasses four stages, *origination*, *structuring*, *underwriting* and *distribution*.

During the origination stage the investment bank seeks to demonstrate to the prospective issuer its superior execution capabilities in order to win the mandate to lead manage the transaction. The key areas of competence considered by the issuer are the bank's structuring, distribution, and secondary market trading (including continued sell side research support) capabilities. The structuring stage, conducted in intense cooperation with a dedicated team from the issuer, comprises: the design of the issue (type of security and price range, and issuer contractual covenants and obligations); the responsibility for and supervision of the due diligence process (conducted with the assistance of independent law and accounting firms hired for the particular offering); the necessary filings with the appropriate regulatory authorities; and, last but not least, assembling the securities underwriting syndicate.

The underwriting stage precedes final distribution to the market. Unlike loan syndicates, which normally provide a firm commitment from the underwriters to the borrower to place the entire amount of the facility, securities offerings are almost always on a *best efforts* basis: the lead underwriters commit *only* to engage their best efforts to sell the securities in the volume and price range indicated through a well-designed process of book building to take place during the distribution stage. A *road show* (one to two weeks during which the issuer meets face to face with investors selected by the lead underwriters) is often undertaken immediately prior to the launch of the offering to stimulate orders from investors. The underwriters provide a firm commitment to the issuer only after the examination of the book of orders built by their distribution (or sales) desks. Concrete evidence of the market's acceptance of the issue provides the basis for the final agreement between issuer and underwriters on both the amount and price of securities being placed. Full commitment is then finally given, and the underwriters' securities traders rush to their desks to fully distribute the issue.

Critical to the success of the offering is the investment bank's ability to place the securities with *final investors* (as opposed to *flippers*, who could be quickly selling them back in the secondary market, leading to immediate downward pressure on the market price of the security). This requires specialized sales forces organized for distribution according to the specificities of the issue (e.g. equity,

Table 2.3 Global debt and equity issues, 2013

Rank	Book Runner	Proceeds Amount (US$ Million)	Mkt. Share	Number of Issues
1	JP Morgan	481,187.22	7.8	1991
2	Deutsche Bank	412,015.78	6.7	1814
3	Citi	388,646.71	6.3	1656
4	Barclays	379,313.51	6.1	1440
5	Goldman Sachs & Co	371,645.06	6.0	1339
6	Bank of America Merrill Lynch	357,607.94	5.8	1760
7	Morgan Stanley	341,396.04	5.5	1579
8	Credit Suisse	253,336.04	4.1	1212
9	HSBC Holdings PLC	233,702.87	3.8	1234
10	BNP Paribas SA	201,801.15	3.3	787
11	RBS	152,372.48	2.5	702
12	Wells Fargo & Co	148,815.34	2.4	847
13	RBC Capital Markets	148,073.78	2.4	882
14	UBS	137,004.57	2.2	825
15	Nomura	113,020.94	1.8	648
16	Société Générale	104,599.21	1.7	385
17	Crédit Agricole CIB	98,043.75	1.6	408
18	UniCredit	86,217.14	1.4	342
19	Mizuho Financial Group	72,602.87	1.2	622
20	TD Securities Inc	66,650.19	1.1	434
21	Natixis	54,523.61	0.9	257
22	Daiwa Securities Group Inc	49,025.57	0.8	380
23	Sumitomo Mitsui Finl Grp Inc	40,119.90	0.6	309
24	Santander	37,056.83	0.6	195
25	CIBC World Markets Inc	36,524.98	0.6	220
	Subtotal with Book Runner	6,192,452.48	100.0	17373
	Subtotal without Book Runner	-	0.0	0
	Industry Total	6,192,452.48	100.0	17373

Source: Thomson Reuters Date: 2014-05-24 05:20:32 EDT

debt, hybrids), of the issuer (e.g. developed versus emerging), and of the type of investor (e.g. retail versus institutional with their respective sub-segments).

Table 2.3 presents the ranking of the top book runners of global debt, and equity issues for 2013. As can be observed, structuring, underwriting, and distribution fees from over 17,000 securities offerings totaling approximately US$6.2 trillion were up for grabs by investment banks and investment banking arms of universal banks.

Global fixed income

Fixed income securities play a fundamental role in complementing – and competing with – banks in the provision of credit to families, businesses, and governments.

As shown in Table 2.4, 15,148 fixed income offerings totaling US$5.6 trillion were distributed in the market in 2013.

Table 2.4 Global fixed income issues, 2013

Rank	Book Runner	Proceeds Amount (US$ Mil)	Mkt. Share	Number of Issues
1	JP Morgan	427,417.23	7.6	1632
2	Deutsche Bank	384,348.62	6.8	1558
3	Barclays	352,340.16	6.3	1239
4	Citi	344,498.97	6.1	1360
5	Bank of America Merrill Lynch	308,626.08	5.5	1417
6	Morgan Stanley	289,852.59	5.2	1277
7	Goldman Sachs & Co	286,693.53	5.1	968
8	HSBC Holdings PLC	242,708.80	4.3	1289
9	Credit Suisse	216,277.50	3.8	899
10	BNP Paribas SA	203,472.35	3.6	814
11	RBS	154,435.37	2.7	711
12	RBC Capital Markets	138,380.50	2.5	758
13	Wells Fargo & Co	135,925.32	2.4	701
14	Nomura	104,712.70	1.9	580
15	Société Générale	100,354.06	1.8	361
16	Crédit Agricole CIB	96,023.13	1.7	405
17	UBS	88,960.78	1.6	547
18	UniCredit	82,286.08	1.5	322
19	TD Securities Inc	70,604.52	1.3	474
20	Mizuho Financial Group	68,624.34	1.2	603
21	Natixis	54,355.09	1.0	254
22	Daiwa Securities Group Inc	43,369.88	0.8	356
23	Standard Chartered PLC	38,011.61	0.7	392
24	Commerzbank AG	36,276.91	0.6	160
25	CIBC World Markets Inc	34,685.56	0.6	191
	Subtotal with Book Runner	5,626,154.35	100.0	15148
	Subtotal without Book Runner	-	0.0	0
	Industry Total	5,626,154.35	100.0	15148

Source: Thomson Reuters Date: 2014-05-24 04:49:12 EDT

As can be observed, universal banks topped the ranking of lead underwriters of fixed income issues globally, similarly to what we observed for loan syndication (Table 2.2). However, the three non-universal investment banks listed (Morgan Stanley, Goldman Sachs and Nomura Securities) showed significantly higher rankings for fixed income (Table 2.4) than for loan syndications (Table 2.2): Morgan Stanley, 6th in fixed income versus 16th in loan syndications; Goldman Sachs, 7th in fixed income versus 12th in loan syndications; and Nomura, 14th in fixed income, not among the top 25 in loan syndications.

This is explained by the fact that fixed income securities, while a credit product, are a more tradable and liquid instrument than bank loans, and so much less demanding of potential medium-term carry in the underwriters' balance sheets.

The importance of the structure of a bank's balance sheet for its ability to compete for leadership of fixed income securities issues is further illustrated by

Table 2.5 All bonds in Euro, 2013

Rank	Book Runner	Proceeds Amount (EURO million)	Mkt. Share	Number of Issues
1	BNP Paribas SA	83,271.81	8.1	351
2	Deutsche Bank	73,547.99	7.1	356
3	HSBC Holdings PLC	67,508.65	6.5	299
4	Barclays	64,611.42	6.2	255
5	Société Générale	62,855.05	6.1	283
6	UniCredit	59,545.81	5.8	300
7	Crédit Agricole CIB	55,861.48	5.4	258
8	JP Morgan	52,932.60	5.1	208
9	Goldman Sachs & Co	43,339.27	4.2	165
10	Natixis	36,489.15	3.5	218
11	RBS	34,941.73	3.4	182
12	Citi	34,091.43	3.3	156
13	Credit Suisse	28,667.45	2.8	131
14	Morgan Stanley	26,200.21	2.5	119
15	Commerzbank AG	22,614.42	2.2	139
16	Bank of America Merrill Lynch	21,922.64	2.1	120
17	Banca IMI (Intesa Sanpaolo)	19,790.67	1.9	84
18	Landesbank Baden-Wurttemberg	18,333.71	1.8	135
19	Santander	17,747.97	1.7	99
20	BBVA	17,246.96	1.7	117
21	UBS	14,768.28	1.4	84
22	DZ Bank	14,699.51	1.4	119
23	ING	13,177.45	1.3	93
24	BMPS	11,135.93	1.1	1
25	Nomura	10,878.90	1.1	53
	Subtotal with Book Runner	1,033,996.73	100.0	1818
	Subtotal without Book Runner	-	0.0	0
	Industry Total	1,033,996.73	100.0	1818

Source: Thomson Reuters Date: 2014-05-24 04:52:58 EDT

an examination of the market for offerings in euros. Table 2.5 shows the ranking of the top 25 book runners of bonds in euros, totaling €1 trillion in 2013.

As can be observed, universal banks once again topped the book runners' ranking. However, when compared to Table 2.4, more Eurozone-based banks appeared among the top 25 (12 versus 7). Also, for all Eurozone banks listed in Table 2.5 (with the exception of Deutsche Bank, #2 in both Table 2.4 and Table 2.5), their ranking rose from Table 2.4: BNP Paribas rose from #10 to #1; Société Générale rose from #15 to #5; Unicredit rose from #18 to #6; Crédit Agricole rose from #16 to #7; Natixis rose from #21 to #10; Commerzbank rose from #24 to #15; and Intesa San Paolo, Landesbank Baden, Santander, BBVA, and ING previously outside of the top 25 rose to #17, #18, #19, #20, #23.

The reason for this goes beyond the possible closeness of these underwriters to issuers in their home countries. It is related also, as we will discuss in Chapter 6, with underwriters' greater appetite for credit risk in the currency of their primary and more stable funding sources.

Global equities

From the second century BC in Rome, where shares in private sector legal entities organized to engage in construction and other public services were traded in the Roman Forum and could be owned by non-citizens, through the milestones of the foundations of lively exchanges in shares of joint-stock companies in business and financial hubs around the world – such as Antwerp (La Bourse) in 1531, London in 1698, and New York in 1792 – stock exchanges have always been international in nature (Smith, 2003).

Table 2.6 shows the 2013 book runner ranking for global equity and equity related securities issues. Consistent with equity being the permanent capital base,

Table 2.6 Global equity and equity related issues

Rank	Book Runner	Proceeds Amount (US$ Million)	Mkt. Share	Number of Issues
1	Goldman Sachs & Co	91,246.09	11.4	411
2	JP Morgan	66,441.34	8.3	455
3	Morgan Stanley	61,172.31	7.6	427
4	Bank of America Merrill Lynch	56,962.32	7.1	414
5	Citi	51,058.13	6.4	372
6	UBS	49,543.84	6.2	310
7	Deutsche Bank	43,955.99	5.5	348
8	Credit Suisse	40,359.67	5.0	341
9	Barclays	36,979.71	4.6	272
10	Nomura	15,440.26	1.9	121
11	Wells Fargo & Co	14,383.19	1.8	187
12	RBC Capital Markets	11,549.60	1.4	160
13	Jefferies LLC	9,010.54	1.1	126
14	HSBC Holdings PLC	8,162.95	1.0	73
15	Daiwa Securities Group Inc	7,850.87	1.0	69
16	Macquarie Group	6,578.67	0.8	64
17	Sumitomo Mitsui Finl Grp Inc	6,421.97	0.8	63
18	BNP Paribas SA	6,353.32	0.8	55
19	Mizuho Financial Group	5,645.98	0.7	53
20	China International Capital Co	5,344.21	0.7	21
21	Haitong Securities Co Ltd	5,317.03	0.7	28
22	Société Générale	4,994.06	0.6	33
23	CITIC Group Corp	4,414.96	0.5	42
24	UniCredit	4,079.26	0.5	21
25	Credit Agricole CIB	4,006.26	0.5	23
	Subtotal with Book Runner	803,479.19	100.0	4464
	Subtotal without Book Runner	-	0.0	0
	Industry Total	803,479.19	100.0	4464

Source: Thomson Reuters Date: 2014-05-23 23:30:08 EDT

on top of which debt can be raised to pool the necessary resources to finance investment and growth, total equity and equity-related offerings amounted to US$803 billion, accounting for approximately 14 percent of total fixed income issues (US$5.6 trillion, Table 2.4).

As can be observed, while most universal banks listed in Table 2.4 are ranked highly in Table 2.6 also, the two leading U.S. investment banks – Goldman Sachs and Morgan Stanley – occupied two of the three top positions, ranking significantly higher than for debt underwritings. This should not be entirely surprising given: (a) the non-credit risk related and full book building nature of equity underwritings, which eliminate the balance sheet carry advantages of universal banks over investment banks for this type of activity; and (b) their long-standing position as leading U.S. and global broker-dealers, a segment for many years closed to U.S. depositary banks by the Glass-Steagall Act, as discussed previously.

Derivatives

A derivative is a financial contract whose value varies in response to changes in the price of an underlying asset that can also be traded in the market place. Derivatives are used to manage risk by transferring it from a party that wishes to reduce its exposure to another party that wishes to take on that exposure. Over the past 20 years, trading in derivatives has become a critical piece of the architecture of the global financial markets.

A *derivative* exposure can be a *hedge* – a sacrifice of potentially higher future returns to reduce risk; or a *speculative trade* – an uncovered calculated risk taken in the expectation of a financial gain. Classic examples of derivatives are *swaps* (commitments between two *counterparts* to exchange future streams of cash-flows, e.g. floating for fixed interest rate), and *futures*, transferable contracts promising delivery of a defined quantity of an asset at a specified price on a pre-determined date.

Banks design and trade in derivatives not only to help their clients manage risk, but also for their own account. When serving a client, the bank has the mission of providing the best match for the *hedge* or the *speculative* position desired by that client. When trading for its own account, the bank is itself the *counterpart* for the trade.

Similarly to what happens with securities trading, proprietary trading in derivatives poses internal conflicts of interest, therefore requiring from banks the establishment of internal firewalls (Apostolik et al. 2009: 155–67, *op.cit.*). Proprietary trading (of securities and derivatives) also implies higher risk of loss for the bank than market-making for clients in these instruments. For this reason, as will be discussed in Chapter 6, bank regulators have, in the aftermath of the 2008 global financial crisis, come to impose significantly higher capital charges for securities and derivatives trading, as well as restrictions on the scope and magnitude of proprietary trading permissible to banks.

Organized securities exchanges – almost without exception born as domestic cooperative type entities owned and run by the institutions trading in the particular exchange – have evolved, particularly over the past decade, to become major independent publicly traded corporations. Expanding trading volumes and increased internationalization of capital flows have further combined to push organized exchanges away from domestic single purpose trading venues (e.g. a stock exchange or a commodity futures exchange) and to multi-product trading venues with broad international scope.

The derivatives market can be divided into two: exchange traded derivatives and over-the-counter derivatives. Standardized derivatives contracts, such as options and futures contracts, are traded in organized exchanges, or central counterparties. Each party assumes the credit risk of the central counterparty (not each other's). In order to ensure that all trades are honored as contracted, the central counterparty, in turn, imposes real time margin requirements (cash collateral) on the parties to any trade. Less standardized (bespoke or tailor-made) derivatives are traded over the counter by market-makers on these instruments. These market-makers (also called swap dealers) are typically investment banks and investment banking arms of universal banks serving institutional clients such as asset managers, commercial banks, insurance companies, corporations, and government entities.

As of year-end 2012, total over-the-counter (OTC) derivatives notional amount outstanding was US\$633 trillion, of which US\$490 trillion was in interest rate derivatives, US\$67 trillion in foreign exchange derivatives, US\$25 trillion in credit default swaps, and US\$6.3 trillion in equity-linked and commodity derivatives (BIS 2013).

The total gross market value of OTC derivatives outstanding – defined as the total cost of replacing each outstanding contract at current market prices – was US\$24.7 trillion. Total gross OTC derivatives credit exposure, which deducts from gross market value the legally enforceable bilateral netting among counterparties, was US\$3.6 trillion.

As we will discuss in Chapter 6, in recent years a wide range of regulatory measures have been implemented in order to mitigate the complexity and lack of transparency associated with OTC derivatives trading. Swap regulation under the Basel III Capital Requirements Directive, the European Market Infrastructure Regulation (EMIR), and Title VII of the Dodd-Frank Act in the United States all push toward centralized clearing of trades through the imposition of substantially higher capital and collateral requirements for OTC bilateral trades.

Regulatory consistency among different jurisdictions is being pursued by legislators globally in order that prudential regulation of financial institutions and markets can result in both sustained stability and efficiency in the global financial system. To the extent that they level the playing field for financial agents around the world, these measures will most likely reinforce a trend, not without political tension, toward cross-border consolidation of organized exchanges.

Organized securities exchanges – almost without exception born as cooperatives owned and run by the institutions trading in the particular exchange – have evolved to become major independent publicly traded corporations, particularly over the past decade. Increasing trading volumes and internationalization of capital flows have further combined to push organized exchanges away from being single purpose trading venues (e.g. cash equities *or* commodities futures) and primarily domestic institutions, to multi-purpose trading (e.g. cash equities, *and* derivatives), services provided (e.g. trading, clearing, and custody), and geographies.

On the other hand, cross-border consolidation among organized exchanges is not without geo-political tensions and resistance from local financial institutions to the idea of migration of trading volume to foreign jurisdictions. The unsuccessful attempt by the London Stock Exchange (LSE) to seize control of the Toronto Stock Exchange (TMX) in 2011 exemplifies this phenomenon. In the end, however, a group formed by some of Canada's largest banks joined forces to outbid the LSE offer and take control of TMX (Jordan and Jeffs, 2011).

Looking ahead, however, competitive pressure for low-cost, real-time, reliable execution of centrally cleared trading of securities contracts should continue to push the management and boards of directors of organized exchanges around the world to seek control of expanded multi-purpose trading platforms and broader international reach.

Mergers and acquisitions advisory services

Mergers and acquisitions (M&As) are among the most important strategic decisions companies make. It is little wonder that investment banks, as experts in business valuation and financial structuring, should seek to position themselves as dominant providers of M&A advice.

As providers of credit to businesses, banks must be able to assess the financial impact of strategic decisions and investment decisions, such as an acquisition or a merger. As regional and/or industry specialists, they can identify – and effectively attract to the negotiating table – the ideal strategic counterpart for a divestiture, a merger, or an acquisition. Finally, as financial securities experts, banks can provide an investors' perspective on the merits of a particular strategic course of action and, possibly, assist with the financing of the undertaking.

Compensation for a bank's M&A advisory services combines a *retainer fee* (typically capped and often deductible from the success fee) and a *success fee*, payable upon completion of the transaction.

Table 2.7 shows that, in 2013, the world's top 25 M&As were involved in 8,932 closings for a total transaction amount of US$1.9 trillion. Also, and similarly to what we observed for equity offerings, the two leading U.S. investment banks, Goldman Sachs and Morgan Stanley, again topped the list.

Several of the world's leading international universal banks, particularly those highly ranked as book runners of equity underwritings (e.g. JPMorgan, Bank of America Merrill Lynch, Barclays, UBS, Deutsche Bank, Citibank, and Credit Suisse) were also among the top M&A advisors.

However, unlike the league table for securities underwritings, this list features several non-bank financial advisors (Lazard, Rothschild, Taubman, Centerview, Evercore, Moelis, LionTree, and PricewaterhouseCoopers).

These firms with their leading professional talent, often sourced from international investment banks (or the wholesale investment banking arms of universal banks), have clearly benefitted from the nature of their client

Table 2.7 Global M&A advisory

Rank	Financial Advisor	Ranking Value inc. Net Debt of Target ($Mil)	Mkt. Share	Number of Deals
1	Goldman Sachs & Co	617,383.70	26.0	401
2	JP Morgan	538,407.29	22.6	308
3	Morgan Stanley	519,199.55	21.8	334
4	Bank of America Merrill Lynch	516,352.04	21.7	237
5	Barclays	365,284.42	15.4	211
6	UBS	315,485.63	13.3	203
7	Deutsche Bank	245,497.52	10.3	204
8	Citi	233,578.52	9.8	229
9	Credit Suisse	210,450.78	8.8	250
10	Lazard	199,804.79	8.4	279
11	Guggenheim Securities LLC	143,644.39	6.0	16
12	Paul J Taubman	130,298.32	5.5	1
13	Rothschild	120,333.46	5.1	270
14	Centerview Partners LLC	105,216.86	4.4	35
15	Evercore Partners	88,537.56	3.7	123
16	Moelis & Co	84,271.23	3.5	110
17	BNP Paribas SA	80,569.36	3.4	123
18	RBC Capital Markets	79,683.75	3.4	146
19	Wells Fargo & Co	62,855.06	2.6	54
20	Jefferies LLC	55,108.73	2.3	117
21	HSBC Holdings PLC	53,773.31	2.3	78
22	Nomura	47,643.68	2.0	142
23	Macquarie Group	45,504.50	1.9	123
24	LionTree Advisors LLC	45,022.62	1.9	8
25	PricewaterhouseCoopers	39,975.41	1.7	451
	Subtotal with Financial Advisor	1,895,605.00	79.7	8931
	Subtotal without Financial Advisor	482,999.62	20.3	29149
	Industry Total	2,378,604.62	100.0	38080

Source: Thomson Reuters Date: 2014-05-28 12:00:20 EDT

relationships – offering purely strategic advice, without credit or market risk undertakings – while also effectively reinforcing their absolute independence from any potential conflict of interest as they embrace a new advisory mandate.

It seems unlikely, however, that non-bank financial advisors could outrank their leading bank competitors in M&A advisory given the advantages enjoyed by the latter by dint of their intense coverage of potential customers globally and their ability to claim privileged understanding of likely market responses to specific corporate initiatives, as well as their to ability to arrange, when required, the most appropriate funding.

It should be noted that several of these non-bank financial advisory boutiques specialize in at least one other major area, often asset management and/or private equity. While demanding a somewhat similar set of skills, M&A advice and principal investing embody an inherent conflict of interest, not very different from those faced by banks in M&A advice and either securities underwriting or proprietary trading. As a result, and similarly to how investment banks manage these potential conflicts, internal firewalls between M&A advisory and other units must be established – and known by clients to exist – such that the credibility and independence of the firm to provide the best service may be preserved.

Box 2.3 Global investment banking at Deutsche Bank

At year-end 2013, Deutsche Bank (Deutsche), headquartered in Frankfurt and Germany's largest bank, had total assets of €2.2 trillion.

Deutsche was organized along five divisions: *Corporate Banking and Securities* (CB&S), *Global Transaction Banking* (GTB), *Deutsche Asset & Wealth Management* (DeAWM), *Private & Business Clients* (PBC), and the *Non-Core Operations Unit* (NCOU).

CB&S consisted of two business divisions, *Corporate Finance* and *Markets*. Corporate Finance comprised the client coverage and the specialized product teams dedicated to the structuring of financing solutions for and providing M&A advice to institutional clients globally. Markets was responsible for sales and trading of fixed income, equity, equity-linked, foreign exchange and commodity instruments, in addition to structuring and implementation of financial risk management solutions for institutional clients.

The table below illustrates the importance for Deutsche of its global investment banking activities. As can be observed, CB&S accounted for approximately 43% of total net revenues and 47% of the profit before tax of the businesses the bank had committed to maintain.

Deutsche Bank, 2013 (€ million)

Division	Net Revenues	%	Income before	Tax %
CB&S	13,623	42.6	3,062	47.0
GTB	4,069	12.7	1,107	17.0
DeAVM	4,735	14.8	782	12.1
PBC	9,550	29.9	1,555	23.9
Sub-total	31,977	100.0	6,506	100.0
NCOU	867	-	(3,306)	
Consolidation Adj.	(929)	-	(1,744)	
Total	31,915		1,456	

Source: Deutsche Bank 2013 Annual Report on Form 20-F filing with the SEC, Financial Report, page 26

(Source: Authors, from Deutsche Bank's Annual Report 2013 on Form 20-F filing with the SEC)

Summary

In this chapter we have examined how the explosive growth of securities markets, the intensity of the shift from paper to digital contracting, settlement, and dissemination of information, and the deregulation of financial services on both sides of the Atlantic have combined over recent decades to push most leading commercial banks toward investment banking and internationalization.

We have observed that these banks, acknowledging the synergies between corporate commercial and investment banking have, eventually if not initially, chosen to combine these two product platforms under a single organizational structure – the wholesale bank.

We then explored in some detail the specific product offerings of both platforms.

In the realm of *international corporate commercial banking*, we examined:

- the basic elements of international trade finance and the mechanisms through which banks around the world cooperate with each other to mitigate information asymmetries and facilitate international commercial transactions among companies of all sizes;
- the origin, evolution, and workings of the international syndicated loan market, a critical source of financing for both major private sector and government institutions globally;
- the basic elements of international project finance, a traditional funding structure for large single-purpose capital intensive private sector endeavors, which has become increasingly relevant for the multiple source financing of infrastructure projects;
- the nature and workings of global cash management and securities services, offered by most international banks;
- the case of Citicorp's Global Transaction Services division, as an example of a highly successful approach to trade finance, cash management, and securities transaction services globally.

In the realm of *international investment banking*, we have examined:

- the primary role of the investment bank as agent and intermediary of financing structures designed to satisfy objectives and constraints of issuers and investors;
- the full range of investment banks' revenue generating activities and the nature of the internal conflicts of interest resulting from these activities;
- the basic elements and stages of the securities underwriting process and the nature of the competition for the book runner position for fixed income and equity issues globally;
- derivatives trading and the roles of investment banks as both market makers for customers and traders for their own account;

- the recent global trend towards consolidation of exchanges across financial instruments and geographies;
- the competitive aspects of cross-border M&A advisory services;
- the case of Deutsche Bank, as an example of a fundamental commitment to investment banking globally by an, originally, major domestic commercial bank.

3 International personal banking

Introduction

In Chapter 2, we examined how financial liberalization, technological change, and the explosive growth of securities markets combined to trigger a reinvention of the business of corporate banking globally. In this chapter, we explore how these same forces, combined with the recent tightening of legislation to prevent tax evasion globally, to influence the strategic choices made by financial institutions in their pursuit of international personal banking activities.

Under the heading The Concept of Personal Banking, we explore first the common aspects and key distinctive features of providing financial services to high net worth individuals (or private banking) and to the public at large (consumer banking).

Then, under the subheadings International Private Banking and International Consumer Banking, we examine separately the challenges for internationalization in each of these segments of personal banking services. We conclude each examination with real world examples of the business strategy and achievements of two major international personal banking services franchises, UBS (in international private banking) and American Express (in international consumer finance).

The concept of personal banking

Until the early 1980s, banks tended to divide the coverage of their individual customer base into two major groups: the consumer bank, serving the public-at-large; and the private bank, offering the more personalized attention of specialized banking executives to high net worth individuals and families.

Regardless of income level, net worth, or any other cultural and/or geographic consideration, an individual's need for financial services will always combine demands for payment services (such as checking accounts and debit cards), loan products (such as overdraft accounts, personal, auto, mortgage and home equity loans, credit card facilities), and investment or wealth management products (such as savings accounts, brokerage services, asset management, and insurance). The challenge for the bank is to establish and effectively manage personal banking offerings that most efficiently capture the profit potential from serving constituencies with different characteristics and priorities.

In response to this challenge, banks around the world have sought to refine their personal banking client segmentation strategies. In consumer banking, sub-segmentation tends to be guided by the customer's income level, as a proxy for his/her likely demand for credit and ability to borrow. In private banking, sub-segmentation is primarily determined by the customer's net worth, as a proxy for his/her likely demand for investment advisory and execution services.

The explosive growth of the securities markets globally from the late 1980s onward (see also Chapter 2) has made the ability to assist customers with overseas investments an absolute priority for a private bank. At the same time, large profit margins from consumer lending at home have led some banks to pursue aggressively the establishment of consumer finance franchises overseas.

Table 3.1 summarizes the fundamental distinguishing characteristics of these two main lines of personal banking services, private and consumer banking, laying the foundations for the discussion on the challenges for internationalization in each that follows.

International private banking

The shift to yield

Until the 1980s, high net worth individuals considered international private banks as primarily a provider of protection for their wealth from domestic turmoil and/or regulatory scrutiny. The fundamental change that has occurred in the nature of private banking over the past three decades has been the shift in priorities by high net worth individuals away from discrete protection of accumulated wealth toward yield.

This shift was, in large part, a consequence of the same forces that pushed corporate commercial lenders to engage in investment banking, as discussed in Chapter 2, namely the lowering of barriers to international capital flows, rapid technological change, and the explosive growth of securities markets. It was,

Table 3.1 Private banking versus consumer banking

Client banking group	Main source of revenue for bank	Segmentation strategy	Service apparatus	Internationalization challenge
Private	Wealth management; Fees	Geography; Net worth (stock of wealth)	Private Banker (or Investment Advisor) and support team plus access to above	Access to wealth management products globally
Consumer	Credit; Interest income	Geography; Income level (cash flow)	Branch network; Call centers; Automated services	To become a local bank overseas

Source: Author

however, reinforced by the sharp tightening and enforcement of legislation regarding tax avoidance and/or evasion in the aftermath of the global financial crisis of 2008.

As of year-end 2013, the largest penalty imposed on a bank for involvement in tax evasion was the US\$ 2.6 billion fine imposed on Credit Suisse Group AG by the U.S. Department of Justice, with formal admission of guilt for having helped Americans hide money from the Inland Revenue Service (IRS) (see Chapter 7), capping a trend begun in 2009 (Saltmarsh 2011).

The shift by high net worth clients away from protection of wealth to yield, combined with increased competition for client asset management share-of-wallet by banks and non-bank financial institutions, has pushed private banks (and private banking divisions of commercial and investment banks) to broaden and perfect their product platforms and distribution capabilities.

Product offering

The product offering of major international private banks typically encompasses the combination of very personalized delivery of the bank's set of core commercial banking convenience, lending, and investment products for individuals with a broad range of investment services, with international reach and tailored to the client's appetite for risk.

The range of products provided to private banking clients includes: payment convenience services; personalized credit facilities (including tax efficient financings for luxury items, such as boats, private jets); investment products (including third-party managed investment funds); brokerage services and investment advice; financial protection solutions (such as life, property, health, pension planning and directors and officers liability insurance); custody services (including safekeeping); trust services and inheritance planning.

Payment convenience services include benefits such as a free checking account and personalized monitoring of account balance and credit card dues for internally handled payment from clients' funds with the bank, ensuring that overdraft and interest charges are either avoided or reversed. This free of charge convenience is provided in the expectation that this personalized gesture by the bank will be more than compensated for by the fees associated with the provision of wealth management advisory and investment services.

Private banks often invite higher net worth individual clients to special relationship building events, such as investor conferences, art shows, and sponsored sports tournaments. This is similar to what is done by corporate and investment bankers for large institutional customers in wholesale banking.

As indicated above, a private bank's offering of investment services must include funds discretionarily managed by independent asset managers that cover the full spectrum of investment options of possible interest to its private banking customers.

The independent asset manager pays a fee to the private bank in order to have a place in the bank's investment products platform. This fee is, typically, a fraction of the full fees – entry fee plus annual management fee – charged by the asset manager to the bank's private banking customer.

The process of selecting third party funds to be included and maintained in the private bank's investment products platform requires careful assessment on the part of the private bank of the funds' performance (risk/return indicators) and of their manager's operating integrity.

The private bank must make clear to a customer that once an allocation is made to a third party investment fund, the responsibility for its financial performance resides fully with the manager of the fund. The customer, however, continues to look to the private bank for assistance on the monitoring of the performance of that allocation and for advice regarding its maintenance. As history has repeatedly shown, failure on the part of the private bank to conduct the necessary due diligence and monitor third party providers of services can cost the bank dearly in reimbursements to these customers, even when not legally bound to do so, as underlined by the €1.38 billion Santander offered to repay to private banking clients who lost money in the Madoff scandal (Penty and Burton 2009).

It is critical, therefore, that the private bank must not only understand their client's appetite for risk, but must communicate very clearly with the client, documenting appropriately investment decisions made, in order to prevent situations that could be characterized as either misrepresentation or failure to convey material information to clients.

Client coverage

Banks organize their coverage of wealth management clients according to region of origin and stock of wealth, with US$1 million in net worth being defined generally as the minimum threshold for private banking services (Maude 2006).

Other criteria, more directly related to potential revenue to be generated – such as the amount of investable assets – help the financial institution to sub-segment its private banking clientele into additional wealth brackets (e.g. high, ultra-high or mega-high net worth). The number of customers allocated to each relationship manager (or private banker) is a function of this further internal sub-segmentation, with more senior and investment savvy private bankers tending to be allocated to higher wealth bracket customers.

The internationalization of investment possibilities available to high net worth individuals, many of them characterized by significant short-term volatility and liquidity, forces private bankers to seek to be not only more knowledgeable about, but also much more in tune with, movements in global capital markets. They typically participate in early morning market meetings conducted by wealth management investment strategists, have the support of sell-side research reports produced by the bank on countries, industries, and individual issuers (often the same materials that are available to the bank's investment bankers), and maintain direct contact with the trading desks executing their customers' orders.

Generally, a private banker counts on the administrative support of one or more associates, who are also known to and can be directly accessed by the customer, for the handling of many of the time-consuming routine aspects of the banking relationship.

The competitive environment

During most of the twentieth century, Swiss banks' dominance of and leadership in private banking was based on Switzerland's political neutrality and its banks' commitment to secrecy, as well as their image of reliability and financial soundness. Increasingly, however, this dominance has been challenged by major leading universal banking franchises and international investment banks.

The pursuit of fully-fledged wholesale (corporate commercial plus investment banking businesses) banking strategies by most leading universal banking franchises (see Chapter 2) has, nevertheless, strengthened the ability of these institutions to present themselves to high net worth individuals as particularly well positioned to provide wealth management services. As a result, Swiss dominance in private banking has been challenged by both major international investment banks and leading universal banking franchises around the world.

This trend is illustrated in Table 3.2, showing the Scorpio Partnership Benchmark for the top 25 private banks globally in 2013. For the purpose of this ranking, assets under management refer to the total value of clients' funds invested either through or under the advice of the financial institution.

As can be observed, 17 of the world's 25 largest private banks[1] appear also among the top 25 global book runners of debt and equity issues shown in Table 2.3 of Chapter 2. Regarding the presence of Swiss banks among the top ranked private banks in the world, we should note that, in spite of the competitive pressures discussed above, at year-end 2012 they remained relatively dominant.

Bank of America's acquisition of Merrill Lynch in the context of the U.S. subprime crisis (see Chapter 4) boosted it to second in the ranking, very close to the bank ranked first, UBS. Nevertheless, the two largest Swiss banks, UBS and Credit Suisse, not only topped the table, but they showed higher rankings for wealth management (1st and 4th, respectively, in Table 3.2) than for book running of debt and equity transactions (14th and 8th, respectively, in Table 2.3). In addition, three other Swiss private banks (Pictet, Julius Baer, and Lombard Odier) ranked among the top 25 globally.

Nonetheless, competition in private banking is fierce, involving not only the world's major international banks, but also most leading private sector banks from around the world (including Banco Itaú, from Brazil, and Nordea from Sweden), and non-bank providers of wealth management services, such as Charles Schwab and Fidelity, from the United States.

In the case of Banco Itaú (Brazil), its acquisitions of the Latin American franchise of Bank Boston in 2004 (following Bank of America's acquisition of Fleet-Boston) and of Unibanco (then Brazil's third largest private sector bank) in 2008, gave the bank a solid number one position among all private banks operating in Brazil, and set the stage for the brewing of more ambitious international reach.

Table 3.2 Top 25 private banks worldwide by assets under management (31 Dec. 2013)

Global Ranking	Institution	AUM (USD billions)
1	UBS	1,966.9
2	Bank of America Merrill Lynch	1,866.6
3	Morgan Stanley	1,454.0
4	Credit Suisse	888.2
5	Royal Bank of Canada	673.2
6	BNP Paribas	395.1
7	Deutsche Bank	384.1
8	HSBC	382.0
9	JPMorgan	361.0
10	Pictet	338.1
11	Goldman Sachs	330.0
12	Julius Bär	282.5
13	Barclays	233.2
14	ABN Amro	231.7
15	Northern Trust	221.8
16	Wells Fargo	218.0
17	Lombard Odier	198.0
18	Santander	196.5
19	Bank of NY Mellon	185.0
20	Crédit Agricole	182.0
21	BMO Financial Group	171.7
22	CIC	141.8
23	Société Générale	116.3
24	Bank Safra Sarasin	115.6
25	Citi Private Bank	112.3

Source: Scorpio Partnership Global Private Banking Benchmark 2014 (Note: All results are rounded).

Organized along five major lines of business (retail commercial banking, consumer finance, wholesale banking, wealth management, and insurance) and ranking among the world's top 10 banks in market capitalization, Banco Itaú has, since 2010, made no secret of its international ambitions in private banking. In its Annual Report on Form 20 SEC filing, it notes that its client base in Latin America numbered 17,951 at the end of 2010, and "...private banking activity for Latin American clients had assets under management equivalent to R$118,295 million (US$70 billion equivalent), including R$92,824 million in Brazil, R$15,299 million in Luxembourg, and R$9,743 million in the United States."

Nordea Bank, formed in 2001 by the merger of all banking and financial services operations of Nordbanken (Sweden), Merita Bank (Finland), Unibank (Denmark), and Christiania Bank (Norway), was ranked among Europe's top 10 banks in market capitalization at year-end 2010.

Organized around three major business lines (retail banking, wholesale banking, and wealth management), Nordea was elected Best Private Bank in the Nordic Region by the 2010 and 2011 Euromoney surveys on private banking. By mid 2011, with €58 billion in assets under management, Gunn Waersted (Head of Wealth Management) was already emphasizing in formal presentations to investors that Nordea would increasingly engage in the pursuit of a significant presence in private banking and wealth management services outside its region of dominance (Waersted 2011: 8).

The threat to the dominance of Swiss and other traditional leading providers of global private banking services has been further heightened by the fact that higher net worth individuals have tended not only to establish more than one wealth management relationship for reasons not only of risk diversification or of key perceived competences of a particular provider, but also as a stimulus to competition (thus spurring better service at lower costs) among providers. Demand for quality wealth management has also led to the establishment of family offices, typically run by former private bankers who, as agents for and advisors to a small group of high net worth individuals, interact on their behalf with bank and non-bank providers of custody services (including safekeeping); trust services and inheritance planning.

More rigorous enforcement of regulations requires banks to ascertain the legitimacy of clients' funds maintained with them, including severe penalties for involvement in situations that can be ascertained as tax evasion schemes. An example of these penalties is the US$780 million fine imposed by the U.S. Department of Justice on UBS in February 2009 ("Called to Account", *The Economist*, 2009). The penalties resulted in higher costs of compliance and lower potential volumes for private banks. The competitive pressures described above have provided major incentives for much closer cooperation between wealth management and wholesale banking divisions. On the expense side, banks have sought to explore economies of scale and synergies of support function, such as marketing, compliance, and sell-side market research. On the revenue side, inter-divisional financial incentives for greater cooperation between private bankers and investment bankers to cross-sell respective capabilities have been put in place.

For the leading Swiss private banks in particular, these competitive pressures have pushed them toward placing much greater emphasis on investment performance as well as seeking to establish stronger physical presence – often in conjunction with their investment banking platforms – in selected overseas markets, as illustrated by the examination of UBS strategy at the end of this section.

UBS: a global approach to private banking

Brief history

In the early 1990s, Swiss Bank Corporation (SBC) and Union Bank of Switzerland, both commercial banks operating out of Switzerland, had a similar medium-term business proposition: to become world leaders in wealth management and investment banking, while remaining important commercial and retail banks in their home land (UBS AG Form 20-F, 2011: 13).

While Union Bank of Switzerland, then the largest Swiss bank, chose to pursue this strategy through organic growth, SBC opted for a cross-border acquisition path which included the purchases of O'Connor (a leading U.S. derivatives firm) in 1992, Brinson Partners (a U.S.-based institutional asset manager) in 1994, and the U.K. investment bank SGWarburg in 1995. In 1998, Union Bank of Switzerland and SBC merged to form UBS AG (UBS), and in 2000, with the objective of establishing a strong position in brokerage and wealth management services in the United States, UBS acquired PaineWebber.

Organization and 2011 performance

At year-end 2011, UBS was organized into five main divisions: Wealth Management & Swiss Bank, Wealth Management Americas, Global Asset Management, Investment Bank, and Corporate Center.

Wealth Management & Swiss Bank comprised two business units: Wealth Management, providing private banking services to clients around the world except for the United States; and Retail and Corporate banking, offering commercial banking services to individual and business clients in Switzerland. Wealth Management Americas provided private banking services to high net worth customers in the United States and Canada, in addition to being responsible for international business booked in the United States.

Global Asset Management offered UBS's discretionary asset management products to institutional and personal banking globally across all asset classes, traditional (e.g. equities, fixed income, currency) and alternative (real estate, hedge fund, infrastructure fund).

The Investment Bank offered capital markets, financial advisory and risk management services and products to corporate and institutional clients, including financial institutions and government and sovereign bodies.

Finally, Corporate Center provided "support and control functions for the Group in such areas as risk control, finance, legal and compliance, funding, capital and balance sheet management, management of non-trading risk, information technology, real estate, procurement, corporate development, and service centers" (UBS AG Form 20-F, 2010: 7).

Wealth management at UBS

Table 3.3 presents the breakdown of the contribution of each business unit to UBS's total pre-tax operating profit in 2011. While the figures have been extracted from the UBS AG Form 20-F 2011 Annual Report, they have been regrouped in this table, combining Wealth Management with Wealth Management Americas as opposed to with Retail and Corporate (or Swiss Bank) as per the UBS Group organizational structure.

As can be observed, UBS's wealth management (or private banking) business accounted for over 40 percent (30.7 percent for Wealth Management, 11.6 percent for wealth Management Americas) of the bank's profit before Corporate Core Center non-allocable expenditures and taxes in 2013.

Changing market conditions and regulatory tightening, particularly in regard to capital charges for credit and market risk (described in detail in

Table 3.3 Breakdown of UBS's 2013 operating profits before tax (CHF billion)

Business unit	Profit before tax	Share of profit (2011)
Retail and Corporate	1,512	19.2
Wealth Management	2,425	30.7
Wealth Management Americas	917	11.6
Global Asset Management	585	7.4
Investment Bank Sub-total	2,455 7,894	31.1 100.0
Core Center (incl. Legacy)	(3,751)	-
Total	5,350	-

Source: Authors from *UBS AG Annual Report 2013 on Form 20-F.*

Chapter 6), have pushed UBS toward rebalancing its business offerings with an emphasis on client oriented business activities and away from securities trading activities. As stated in the letter to shareholders by Chairman Kaspar Villager and Chief Executive Officer (CEO) Sergio Ermotti that accompanied the bank's results for the fourth quarter of 2011, "[UBS seeks to] center its strategy on its pre-eminent global wealth management businesses... As part of this strategy, the Investment Bank will be simpler, more focused and less capital-intensive... Our strategy reflects the changing market and regulatory environment."

International consumer banking

Until very recently, international consumer banking, defined as the provision of commercial banking services to individuals located in foreign countries, had been the realm of a handful of leading Organisation for Economic Co-operation and Development (OECD) banks targeting upper income and high net worth individuals.

The centerpiece of retail banking was the branch, where a customer would go to make a deposit, request a loan, or execute a commercial transaction. Until relatively recently the branch was also the place where credit decisions would be made or, at least, influenced by the recommendation of a bank officer with personal knowledge of the individual applying for the loan.

Over the past 30 years, however, the rapid evolution of telecommunications and data transmission technology plus continued refinement of credit scoring mathematical modeling (Mays 2004) have allowed financial institutions to not only engage in remote real-time transactional interaction with customers, but also to make quasi-instantaneous and depersonalized centralized consumer credit decisions.

It should not be surprising, therefore, that many banks, encouraged by the attractive margins typically associated with consumer lending, confident of the robustness of their business models, and perceiving the possibility of faster growth abroad, would become increasingly motivated to pursue consumer finance activities beyond their home base.

Going overseas in retail banking

The main obstacle for a bank considering entry into a new retail banking market is the existence of well-entrenched financial institutions already enjoying the advantages of significant distribution networks, well-known brands, and long histories of cultural integration with the customer base.

How, therefore, can a bank use its perceived strengths relative to the existing competition (product offering, risk management capabilities, pricing, distribution schemes, institutional image) to penetrate a foreign consumer banking market in order to achieve acceptable levels of sustained profitability within a reasonable time?

From the 1980s onward, entry by foreign banks into consumer banking markets around the world at an economically viable scale of operations has been facilitated by (i) the lowering in many countries – but still not all – of regulatory barriers, including permission to open branches and acquire domestic franchises; and (ii) technological change, driving the adoption by all banks of more commoditized and depersonalized financial services, therefore making customers gradually more alike in how they interact with the financial institution.

A bank may initiate its penetration of a particular foreign consumer banking market with the opening of a few branches. The consolidation of an important share in that market abroad typically requires at least the acquisition – with the capital and management commitments of such – of at least one major existing franchise, as was the case, for example, for Citibank in Mexico when it bought BANAMEX in 2001.

There are less ambitious focused approaches that have proven effective. Examples of these are niche type incursions abroad, such as India's ICICI Bank diaspora banking initiative (DiVanna 2004: 30), targeting Indian nationals in selected countries (such as the United Kingdom and Canada), and the ING (Netherlands) remote banking initiative ING-Direct, discussed in greater detail below.

Cross-border individual retail banking poses substantially different institutional challenges from private banking. Private banking customers perceive the foreign bank as a passport to the world. Therefore, only modestly sized operations in relation to the bank's headquarters are needed. In contrast, going abroad in retail consumer banking requires that the bank commit capital and personnel to make it a truly domestic bank overseas.

As a result, only a handful of banks, including Citibank, HSBC, and Banco Santander, have committed to a more global retail banking strategy. Most leading banks from the world's largest developed and emerging economies have chosen to pursue more narrowly focused geographic strategies.

A regionally focused strategy for international retail banking was the choice, for example, of BNP-Paribas, Unicredit, and Commerzbank toward selected countries in Europe; of Banco Itaú toward Latin America; and of Toronto Dominium toward the United States.

Let us now turn to the examination of concrete examples of these three basic alternative approaches to internationalization of retail personal banking activities: regional focus, with UniCredit Group (Italy); green field niche penetration, with ING Groep (Netherlands); and acquisition driven, with Banco Santander (Spain).

Alternative approaches to internationalization in retail

Regionally focused: the case of UniCredit Group

The UniCredit Group (UniCredit) resulted from the merger between Italian banks Credito Italiano SpA and UniCredito SpA in 1998. In 2005, UniCredit acquired the HVB Group (Germany) and in 2007 it absorbed the Capitalia Group (Italy), becoming Italy's largest bank.

The UniCredit-HVB merger brought about the formation of one of Europe's largest banks and also one of the region's most international consumer banking franchises.

Prior to acquiring the HVB Group (HVB) in 2005, UniCredit had already targeted Central and Eastern Europe for international expansion through acquisitions and bought local banks in Poland, Slovakia, Bulgaria, Croatia, Romania, the Czech Republic, and Turkey. HVB, while weakened by real estate losses over the three years prior to the transaction, was a particularly attractive franchise for UniCredit given its important presence in Germany and in Austria.

At year-end 2013, UniCredit had total assets of €845.8 billion, net worth of €46.8 billion, and had over 147,000 employees working in 17 countries. The bank had 8,954 retail branches: 4,171 in Italy, 851 in Germany, 290 in Austria, 1,003 in Poland, and 2,639 in other Central and Eastern Europe countries (Azerbaijan, Bosnia & Herzegovina, Bulgaria, Croatia, Czech Republic, Hungary, Romania, Russia, Serbia, Slovakia, Slovenia, Turkey, and Ukraine).

Revenues per region were 43 percent for Italy, 22 percent for Germany, 8 percent for Austria, 7 percent for Poland, and 22 percent for the group of other Central and Eastern Europe countries mentioned above.

UniCredit's commitment to a regionally focused international strategy was reflected in the excerpt below from Giuseppe Vita, Chairman of the Board, in his letter to shareholders accompanying the bank's 2013 annual report: "At UniCredit our objective is clear: to be a rock-solid commercial bank that drives the economy and unlocks Europe's growth potential..." (Unicredit Group 2013 Annual Report: 8).

Global niche approach: the case of ING Direct

ING Groep (Internationale Nederlanden Groep) was formed in 1991 by the merger of Nationale-Nederlanden and NMB Postbank Group, in the immediate aftermath of the lifting of regulatory restrictions on mergers between insurance companies and banks in the Netherlands (1990). Subsequently, between 1997 and 2000, ING acquired Barings Bank (U.K. investment bank) in 1995, Brussels Lambert (Benelux commercial bank) in 1998, and several U.S.-based insurance companies (Equitable of Iowa, ReliaStar, and Aetna Financial Services).

ING Direct, an in-house technological platform designed by ING to provide remote low-cost reliable commercial personal banking services to technologically savvy customers, was introduced initially in Canada in 1997. It expanded subsequently to Spain and Australia (1999), to France and the United States (2000), to Italy and Germany (2001), to the United Kingdom (2003), and to Austria (2004).

By year-end 2010, ING Direct offered commercial banking products (including payment services and mortgage loans) and other specialized financial services (such as e-brokerage, mutual funds and pensions) through the internet, call-centers, and direct mail to 24 million customers in these nine countries. Client funds entrusted to ING Direct worldwide amounted to €238 billion and loans amounted to €148 billion, over 25 percent of ING's total customer lending (€566 billion).

In 2008, in the context of the global financial crisis (see Chapter 4), ING was forced to make several commitments to the Dutch Government in order to obtain its support. Among these commitments was the promise to divest ING Direct USA. This condition was met in June 2011, with ING's sale of ING Direct USA to Capital One (originally a U.S. independent credit card issuer, which had been expanding through acquisitions into commercial personal banking since 2005) for US$9 billion.

At the time, ING Direct USA was the largest remote banking operation in the United States, with 7.7 million customers and €57 billion in entrusted funds. As part of the deal, ING agreed to a one-year transitional use in the United States by Capital One of its "ING Direct" trademark. As of December 31, 2013 ING Groep (ING) had total assets of €1,081 billion, net worth of €46 billion and had been reorganized along two major business divisions, NN Group and Banking.

NN Group comprised ING's insurance and investment management company, serving individuals and institutional clients in 18 countries. ING's Banking Division comprised Commercial Banking and Retail Banking. Commercial Banking, ING's wholesale banking arm, provided credit, payments, and investment banking services to institutional clients. Retail banking offered branch-based and direct banking services to individuals and small businesses. By year-end 2013, ING reported being well advanced in the process of combining traditional retail commercial banking and direct banking units into an integrated business model to be perceived by customers as easy and fair, and at a low cost (ING Groep NV Annual Report 2013).

Global acquisition oriented approach: Banco Santander

Banco Santander, the largest bank in Spain and one of the world's largest international banks, is primarily the result of a major domestic consolidation process during the 1990s, combined with a series of important cross-border acquisitions from the late 1990s onward.

Having acquired Banco Español de Credito (BANESTO) in 1994, Santander merged with Banco Central Hispanoamericano (BCH) in 1999, to become Spain's largest bank. Banco Santander's incursions into domestic commercial banking in Latin America began in the mid 1990s with the purchases of Banco de Venezuela (1996), Banco Rio (Argentina) (1998), and two mid-sized Brazilian banks, Banco Geral do Comércio and Banco Noroeste (1998).

Following the merger with BCH in 1999, Banco Santander pursued a more aggressive and non-exclusively Latin America focused expansion. In Latin America, it acquired Banca Serfin (Mexico), BANESPA (Brazil), and Banco Santiago (Chile) in 2000. In 2007, through its consortium bid with the Royal Bank of Scotland (United Kingdom) and Fortis (Belgium) for ABN Amro Bank (Netherlands), Banco Santander acquired Banco Real in Brazil.

In continental Europe, Santander acquired Banco Totta (Portugal) in 2000 and Santander Consumer in 2003, through the consolidation of previously established consumer finance subsidiaries in 11 continental European countries. In 2010, Santander acquired Allied Irish Bank's commercial bank in Poland as well as that country's third largest bank (Bank Zachodini WBK).

In the United Kingdom, Santander took over Abbey National in 2004, and proceeded in 2008 to absorb two other smaller mortgage lenders weakened by the financial crisis in 2008, Alliance & Leicester and Bradford & Bingley, thereby becoming the United Kingdom's third largest bank by deposits.

Finally, in the United States, Santander took a 19.8 percent equity stake in Sovereign Bancorp in 2005 and proceeded to acquire 100 percent ownership of this northeastern banking franchise in 2009.

At year-end 2013, Banco Santander had total assets of €1,116 billion and net worth of €84 billion. Net attributable profit to continuing operations was €4.4 billion for the year, distributed geographically as follows: 26 percent for Continental Europe (7 percent Spain, 6 percent Germany, 6 percent Poland, 7 percent other), 18 percent for the United Kingdom, 47 percent for Latin America (23 percent Brazil, 10 percent Mexico, 6 percent Chile, 5 percent Argentina, 3 percent other), and 10 percent for the United States (Banco Santander 2013: 45).

Banco Santander's strategic commitment to international retail banking had been explicitly renewed in the immediate aftermath of the 2008 global financial crisis. In his letter to shareholders in 2010, Chairman Emilio Botin noted that "(t)hese years of financial crisis have highlighted the fact that financial institutions with business more centered on retail banking have shown greater recurrence and less volatility in their results" (Banco Santander 2010: 8).

Consumer finance: internationalization challenges

Basic concepts in consumer lending

Consumer loans usually are either general purpose or asset specific. General purpose loans are credit facilities that are not tied to any specific consumption or investment objective, but simply contribute to an individual's overall cash flow needs. General purpose consumer loans are typically short-term (under one year) or revolving (with an open ended duration, but total repayment can be demanded by the lender at the end of every period), and tend to carry a floating rate of interest (e.g. current account overdrafts and credit card facilities); but they can also be of a medium-term nature (installment credit loans), often backed by some type of collateral, such as home equity loans, where the equity a customer has on a home is given as a guarantee to the bank.

Asset backed consumer loans are tied to a single pre-determined objective, normally an investment in the acquisition of a specific consumer durable (e.g. automobile financings) or a home (mortgage loans). The loan amount corresponds to a well-defined proportion of the total investment being made, the asset being acquired becomes a collateral guarantee of repayment, and the interest rate charged is normally fixed for the duration of the facility.

The total cost for a bank of making a loan equals funding cost plus operating cost (incurred in loan origination, credit process, monitoring and collection) plus loan losses plus, as applicable in certain jurisdictions, occasional transaction specific taxes.

The essence of consumer lending – loan origination, loan collection, and credit recovery (which often demands execution of guarantees and repossession of collateral by the bank) – requires physical proximity to the clients being financed. It also requires a minimum scale, so that lending costs can be diluted over a large number of similar transactions (Sinkey 1998: 457–81).

With regard to funding, while large credits to corporations and governments, whether in the form of bank loans or fixed income securities issues, can be efficiently distributed to third parties through the loan syndication and fixed income sales and distribution platforms of wholesale banks (see Chapter 2), small loans to individuals can be economically sold to third parties only if bundled to form a large and well-defined type of credit risk that can be efficiently securitized, more often than not, carrying an external credit rating (e.g. mortgages, auto loans, credit card receivables).

It is no wonder, therefore, that cross-border lending to individuals – many loans of relatively small amounts to a huge number of customers – is much more challenging economically from an operational standpoint than is cross-border lending to large institutions. As a result, international individual and small business lending endeavors tend to take the form of acquisitions of already existing retail lending networks in target countries, as illustrated by Unicredit's cross-border regional and Santander's multi-continental approaches.

The attractive margins of consumer financing activities (e.g. credit cards, auto loans, mortgage lending) by using hold-to-maturity credit exposure and by creating portfolios for securitization and distribution to third parties, have caused banks to acquire both commercial banking franchises and consumer finance and mortgage lenders at home and abroad.

Important examples of this trend were the acquisitions of Household Finance (United States) and Losango (Brazil) by HSBC (United Kingdom) in 2003, Abbey National (United Kingdom) by Banco Santander (Spain) in 2004, HVB (Germany) by UniCredit (Italy) in 2005, and Golden West (California) by Wachovia Bank (Eastern United States) in 2006. As examined in greater detail in Chapter 4, the 2008 financial crisis reinforced this tendency, as major banks around the world have, often with government assistance, absorbed the operations of other universal banks as well as of specialized institutions such as mortgage banks, consumer finance companies, and investment banks.

The financial crisis of 2008 forced banks to revisit their international strategies and to sacrifice internationalization in order to concentrate capital and management on initiatives that they perceived as more certain to produce stronger immediate results.

Such was the case for ING Groep in its sale of ING Direct USA to Capital One (see above). Other recent examples have been the announcements of the sales by HSBC (United Kingdom) of its U.S. credit card and retail operations to Capital One Financial Corporation (United States) on August 10, 2011, and by Bank of America of its credit card business in Canada to TD Bank Group (Canada) on August 15, 2011. Both of these transactions represented reversals from major consumer finance acquisitions engaged in by HSBC and Bank of America just a few years before (HSBC's 2004 acquisition of Household Finance, and Bank of America's 2006 acquisition of MBNA).

Stuart Gulliver, CEO of HSBC commented on its divestment that "... this transaction will reduce Group risk-weighted assets by up to US$40bn, which, together with an estimated post-tax gain of US$2.4bn, will allow capital to be redeployed over time" (HSBC 2011). This emphasis on streamlining the balance sheet with an eye towards growth in priority segments is evident also in the words of Bank of America CEO, Brian Moynihan, regarding the MBNA divestiture: "We have been transforming the company... and building a fortress balance sheet behind that [and] an international consumer card business under another brand is not consistent with that strategy" (Bank of America 2011).

International credit cards

The credit card is a twentieth century American innovation. Its origins can be traced to the early-1900s, when sales personnel in U.S. department stores began to give cards to their wealthier clients as a means to facilitate their immediate recognition as charge account customers. Department stores' credit cards became technologically more efficient in 1928, with the introduction of charga-plates: individually customized metal plates, which, when inserted in a recorder machine would automatically imprint the customer's name and address and some coded credit information onto the sales slip. By the mid 1930s, retailers had begun to extend credit to non-regular customers through cooperative charge systems, such as the Retail Service Bureau of Seattle which, by 1936, had over 1,000 retail establishments signed up to honor their customers' charges in case he/she failed to make the payment on the monthly itemized bill received from the Bureau (Mandell 1990: 457–81).

While the credit was essentially an operational enhancement of retailers' already existing credit practice of charge accounts for well-known local clients, for the oil industry it became an important instrument to secure brand loyalty from customers travelling further and further away from their local gas station. In the early 1920s, oil companies began to issue courtesy cards to be given by service station managers to their most frequent and trusted customers, a practice hotel chains as well as airlines began to follow. Yet, neither retailers' charga-plates nor the oil industry's courtesy cards had incorporated the revolving credit feature that would come to characterize, and play such a fundamental role in, the profitability of the credit card industry in future years.

In 1948, a select group of leading department stores in New York City (including Bloomingdale's, Saks, and Gimbel Brothers) decided to join forces and form a cooperative card operation. For the customer, the system offered the benefits of personal convenience (with one rather than several heavy metal plates to carry around) and increased prestige. For the participant retailer, it allowed for potential economies of scale in distribution and control of charge cards, and access to a broader customer base, in addition to the added benefit of membership in a credit bureau. In 1949, the first non-store issued multiple establishments was born, the Diners' Club (Diners) a charge card for use in upper scale restaurants in New York City. Diners would not become profitable until 1954, when, in addition to the fees collected from the participating merchants, it began to also charge cardholders a US$5 annual membership fee (Mayer 1997: 1303).

Simultaneous with this effort to build customer loyalty, a new development was taking place in the U.S. retail industry: the introduction of the individual revolving credit facility. A milestone in this process was Gimbel Brothers' introduction in 1947 of its rotating plan in New York, establishing monthly payments of one sixth of the balance on the customer's charge account plus an interest charge of one percent of the unpaid balance. In 1951, Franklin National Bank of Long Island, New York, introduced the first multi-store bank charge card.

The seeds were now planted for the birth of the true universal charge card, as we know it today, a most convenient means of payment accepted by merchants of all types in most geographies, and an automated credit instrument provided by the issuer to the cardholder. Early on, universal cards were either travel and entertainment (T&E) cards, such as Diners' Club, American Express, Carte Blanche, or bank cards, such as Bank of America's BankAmericard, Chase Manhattan's Charge Plan (CMCP, later Uni-Card), Preston State Bank of Dallas's Presto Charge, and National City's Everything card. This distinction would gradually disappear as competitive pressures pushed both T&E and bank cards toward consolidation, as evidenced by Citibank's acquisition of Carte Blanche in 1975 and Diners' Club in 1980.

In 1966, Bank of America announced it would "go national" through the licensing of its BankAmericard operation to other banks around the country. In response, a group of 17 northern central and eastern U.S. banks decided to form the Interbank Card Association (ICA), a cooperative type interchange to permit reliable and efficient clearing of charge obligations between one bank's credit card holder and a merchant served by another bank.

In 1969, ICA purchased the rights to the Master Charge brand from another bank consortium, the Western States Bank Card Association (WBCA), bringing both associations under the same umbrella. The original WBCA founders had been four Californian banks, Wells Fargo, Crocker National, First Interstate, and Bank of California). ICA would proceed to acquire Uni-Card from Chase Manhattan Bank in 1972 and to engage in aggressive internationalization throughout the

1970s, absorbing Eurocard[2] and the Joint Credit Card Company (a credit card cooperative involving National Westminster Bank, Midland Bank, and Lloyds Bank, and issuer of Access, the second largest credit card operation in the United Kingdom, behind BankAmericard's affiliate Barclaycard, both in 1974.

By year-end 1970, Bank of America – under pressure from its franchisees to set up a separate cooperative to set firm fee guidelines, align interests and objectives, enforce individual commitments, and treat participants equally – had already spun-off its BankAmericard operation to form National Bank Americard, Inc. (NBI). Under this new arrangement, NBI was also better prepared to explore ways to expand internationally beyond the ongoing initial licensing of BankAmericard to issuer banks in foreign countries. In 1974, NBI decided to form Ibanco to administer BankAmericard abroad, bringing together issuer banks from 14 countries in Europe, the Americas, and Japan. In 1976, NBI changed the name of its credit card (BankAmericard) and other foreign bank cards (such as Barclaycard, Sumitomocard, and Carte Bleue) to Visa, a word easily recognizable and understood globally. In 1980, ICA would follow suit and change the name of its MasterCharge card to MasterCard.

The 30 years that followed have been characterized by both the extraordinary broadening of electronic means of payment – from multi-purpose bank (immediate) debit cards to specific purpose money loadable cards, such as metro cards – and the explosive growth of the credit card industry itself as a provider of consumer financing around the world. This process has not been without tensions along the consumption chain – merchants, credit card companies (or acquirers), card issuers and cardholders. It has also triggered intense competition among the acquirers, for the fees to be earned from merchants for efficient and reliable clearing and collection of charges incurred by cardholders in their stores, and among credit card issuers, primarily banks, for the service fees and interest income to be earned from consumers.

The challenge of harmonizing efficient interbank clearance and secure collection for merchants and convenient automated payment solutions and consumer credit to consumers, given the degree of specialization and scalable economies associated with each of these activities, have combined to reinforce the trend initiated in the late 1960s in the United States with the formation of the ICA, WBCA and NBI: on one side were the acquirers (including Visa and MasterCard), focused on merchants to whom payment of credit card receivables was guaranteed in full and in a timely manner, and on the other were the credit card issuers (retail banks, mortgage banks, consumer finance companies, and large retailers) focused on consumers and providing both convenient automatic electronic payment and consumer credit.

Competition for consumers' share-of-wallet led banks to free themselves from exclusive relationships with a single acquirer. Banks around the world now issue debit and credit serviced by different acquirers, with both brand names, those of issuer and acquirer, appearing on the card. Furthermore, credit cards often now carry a third brand name, the so-called private label.

Private label credit cards are cards marketed to a particular retailer's customer base under pre-agreed revenue sharing conditions between the credit card issuer and the credit card distributor, or retailer (e.g. Citibank's AAdvantage MasterCard, marketed to American Airlines frequent fliers). This technique is commonly used by major credit card issuers to penetrate new emerging markets, in partnership with well-established retail chains (Sawaya 2007).

While often international – in the sense that they can be used for purchases abroad, charge cards are fundamentally domestic in settlement: they are distributed by issuers (domestic or foreign) to consumers resident of a country where the issuer has the necessary physical presence to properly assess cardholders' credit risk, collect payments due, and enforce the terms of the consumer revolving credit facility contract signed by each and every customer.

A global approach to credit cards: the case of American Express

The American Express Company (AMEX) entered the charge card business as a way to protect itself from the potential threat credit cards could pose to its traveler's check business. Traveler's checks, invented by Marcellus Fleming Barry, an AMEX employee in 1890 and patented in 1891, had become the leading payment solution for individuals travelling abroad: light to carry and in multiple denominations, with guaranteed acceptance by merchants signed-up by AMEX, and valid only upon a second signature at the time of purchase (Mandell 1990: 28).

The first AMEX charge card was launched in New York in 1958, in direct competition with Diners' Club. It commanded an annual fee of US$6, US$1 higher than Diners' Club, thus seen from the start as a premium product. AMEX's Gold Card was introduced in 1966, and the Platinum Card – with an annual fee of US$250 – in 1984, clearly establishing different customer segments for the company's charge card product line. It was only in 1987 that American Express finally decided to enter the consumer finance business by introducing its first credit card, Optima, allowing customers to carry a balance from month to month, on which interest income could also be earned.

In 2013, AMEX reported annual net income of US$5.4 billion on net revenues of US$33 billion from four major businesses: U.S. Cards, International Cards, Global Commercial Services, and Global Network & Merchant Services.

As of year-end 2013, U.S. Cards competition in the United States consisted of financial institutions large and small that issue general-purpose debit and revolving credit cards, in addition to Discover Financial Services, similarly to AMEX, both an acquirer and a credit card issuer. International Cards faced competition from multinational banks, domestic banks, other foreign banks, and other card issuing institutions operating in each country.

Global Commercial Services (GCS) provides expense management services to organizations worldwide through Global Commercial Card and Global Business Travel Services, allowing AMEX to lead in the global markets of commercial cards and travel management for businesses.

Global Network and Merchant Services (GNMS) operated a global general-purpose charge and credit card network for both AMEX's proprietary cards and cards issued under the Global Network Services (GNS) business. GNS develops

Table 3.4 AMEX net revenues and net income, 2010 (US$ billions)

Business	Net revenues	Net income
US Cards	16,995	3,193
International Cards	5,401	631
Global Network & Merchant	5,513	1,575
Global Commercial Services	4853	860
Corporate Center & Other	212	(900)
Total	32,974	5,359

Source: Authors, from *American Express Company Form 10-K Annual Report, 2013*, http://ir.americamexpress.com/Cache/1001184492.PDF?Y=&O=PDF&D=&FID=1001184492&T=&IID=102700

and maintains relationships with U.S. and foreign banks and other institutions to issue cards and attract merchants into the AMEX network. Gross revenues for AMEX per dollar spent by the consumer tend to be lower under a GNS-issued versus a proprietary card. Yet, because the GNS partner bank absorbs most of the operating costs and credit risk, the return on equity of the GNS business can be significantly higher for AMEX than that of the proprietary card business. Global Merchant Services (GMS) signs merchants into the AMEX network globally, offering point-of-sale servicing, settlement, fraud prevention, and marketing services.

The breakdown of net revenues (revenues net of interest expense) and net income among AMEX's four core business lines for 2013 is presented in Table 3.4. As can be observed, international operations (Global Network and Merchant Services, Global Commercial Services and International Cards) accounted for approximately half of AMEX's total net revenues and net income in 2013.

Summary

In this chapter we have explored how financial liberalization, technological change, and the explosive growth of the securities markets from the 1980s onward, influenced by stricter legislation against tax avoidance and evasion globally and greater enforcement, combined to influence the strategic decisions financial institutions have to make in the pursuit of market leadership and profitability in the business of international personal banking.

We divided our analysis into two distinct blocks: the provision of personal banking services to high net worth individuals (private banking) and to the public-at-large (consumer finance).

In the realm of international private banking we have examined:

- how the shift in priorities by high net worth individuals away from protection of acquired wealth toward yield has affected the product offering of private banking platforms, with much greater emphasis being given to investment advice, brokerage services, and third-party investment products;

- the resulting stronger demands on private bankers to be knowledgeable about the investment options of potential interest to their customers and at all times in tune with market movements globally;
- the fierce competitive environment in international private banking, involving not only the world's major international banks, but also most leading private sector banks globally determined to serve their domestic high net worth customers overseas, but also non-bank providers of wealth management services;
- a global trend for banks to seek to explore the potential synergies between private banking and investment banking to both reduce expenses (e.g. through integration and/or closer cooperation in marketing, compliance, sell-side research activities) and increase revenues (through interdivisional financial incentives for business origination); and
- the case of UBS, as illustration of the above and example of a most successful approach to global private banking.

In the realm of retail banking and consumer finance, we have examined:

- the challenge of internationalization in consumer banking, in particular the fact that an incoming bank into a new retail market is typically faced with the existence of well-established institutions already enjoying the advantages of significant distribution networks, well-known brands, and a history of interaction with and service to the local customer base;
- Three alternative approaches to international personal retail banking penetration:

  - Regional focus, with the example of UniCredit Group (Italy) towards Central and Eastern Europe; specific niche, illustrated by the ING Groep's (Netherlands) international ING-Direct initiatives, and major cross-border acquisitions, with the example of Banco Santander's (Spain) incursions into continental Europe, Latin America, the United Kingdom, and the United States.

- the internationalization challenges of consumer lending, in particular the critical importance of physical proximity to borrowers to both originate loans and collect;
- the process of internationalization of credit card companies, from domestic convenience charga-plate providers in the 1940s, to international travel and entertainment credit card issuers in the 1960s and, subsequently, to globally branded credit card acquirers (e.g. MasterCard, Visa, AMEX), earning fees from businesses that accept their cards around the world while allowing banks to assume the credit risk – and earn the interest associated with it – of their domestic customers;
- the case of American Express, an example of a highly successful approach to the credit card business globally.

Notes

1. These 17 banks are: UBS, Bank of America, Morgan Stanley, Credit Suisse, Royal Bank of Canada, BNP Paribas, Deutsche Bank, HSBC, JPMorgan, Goldman Sachs, Barclays, Wells Fargo, Santander, Crédit Agricole, BMO, Société Générale, and Citibank.
2. Eurocard was primarily a T&E card, the result of the merger between the Rikskort card of Sweden and the BHR card of the United Kingdom.

4 Bank failures and systemic crises

Introduction

The basic function of banking is to serve as provider of credit for a community or nation based on trust in its institutions. Bank failures are the most virulent manifestations of loss of trust and credit worthiness. The Latin derivation of bank is banca, the moneychanger's bench. Bankruptcy was the breaking or "rupta" of the bench once the contract between lender and borrower was no longer honored.

When King Edward III of England sought financing for the Hundred Years War, this included financing from his Italian bankers in Florence. However, in 1348 when he could no longer honor his obligations and repay his large loans to Florentine banking houses, he instigated the first international bank failures.

From 1551 to 1866, financial crises occurred approximately every ten years. American economist Hyman Minsky theorized that since the Renaissance, financial crises were often the effect of displacements, wars or revolutions, which provoked monetary instability, currency reduction through devaluation or excessive appreciation followed by depreciation which could trigger sovereign debt crises. "The incidence of banking crises proves to be remarkably similar in the high- and middle-to-low-income countries. Indeed, the tally of crises is particularly high for the world's financial centers: France, the United Kingdom, and the United States" (Reinhart and Rogoff, 2009: 141). From a societal perspective, bank crises and systemic failures bring in their wake erosion of trust in the financial system, its transactions, agents, and instruments. The repercussions of banking crises can invariably lead to sharp declines in tax revenues and higher deficits. The dangers include bank runs which can lead to the firesale of assets, and the consequences of capital flight, which instigates and exacerbates loss of confidence in the banking system as a whole.

Modern bank failures, systemic crises, and financial panics have occurred in all countries to varying degrees with major differences between domestic bank failures (such as in Canada in the 1970s and 1980s, which led to strict oversight of lending policies making Canada a model of prudent regulation), and large globally interconnected bank failures.

In this chapter we examine both specific individual bank failures and systemic crises (Barings, Crédit Lyonnais, Northern Rock, and German Landesbanken) and national or regional banking crises (U.S. Savings and Loan crisis (mid 1980s), Nordic banking crisis (1991–3), Japan's banking crises (1995–8), the U.S. financial crisis and global credit crunch of 2008, and the case of Iceland, where a near-sovereign default was incited by a collapse of the banking sector). Although Ireland, an EU member state and hence no longer able to exercise an independent monetary policy, was implicated directly in the EU sovereign debt crises, at the root of its financial distress was the failure of its banks rather than its debt to gross domestic product (GDP) ratio.

In Chapter 5, we examine sovereign debt crises and interlinkages with sovereign banking crises, from Latin America in the 1980s and 1990s, through Russia in 1998, to the European Union in 2010 to 2013.

Causes and precedents of financial panics

Asset bubbles

The economic historian Charles Kindleberger, described the 10 major financial "manias, panics and crashes" (Kindleberger and Aliber 2011: 11):

1. The Dutch Tulip Bulb Bubble, 1636.
2. The South Sea Bubble, 1720.
3. The Mississippi Bubble, 1720.
4. The late 1920s stock price bubble of 1927–9.
5. The surge in bank loans to Mexico and other developing countries in the 1970s.
6. The bubble in real estate and stocks in Japan 1985–9.
7. The 1985–9 bubble in real estate and stocks in Finland, Norway and Sweden.
8. The bubble in real estate and stocks in Thailand, Malaysia, Indonesia and several other Asian countries 1992–7 and the surge in foreign investment in Mexico 1990–9.
9. The bubble in over-the-counter stocks in the United States, 1995–2000.
10. The bubble in real estate in the United States, Britain, Spain, Ireland, and Iceland between 2002 and 2007 – and the debt of the Government of Greece.
                                                                        (Ibid).

Banking history proves that, ironically, bank failures and systemic financial crises are often more prevalent in times of economic growth, which involves greater capital mobility, liberalization, and deregulation without sufficient increased supervision (Kindleberger 1985; Bordo et al. 2001; Ferguson 2001; Reinhart and Rogoff 2009). According to Kindleberger, banking crises are often corollaries of real estate bubbles. Prior to most of these crises, inflated markets and promises of higher returns brought an increase in speculation, accelerating the bursting of the bubble with the loss of public and private assets, and land values. Economic historians including Rogoff, Reinhart, Bordo, and Jeanneney have attributed this to a direct correlation between banking crises and housing and real estate asset bubbles, from Japan (1992), to Sweden and Finland (1991), Argentina (2001),

United States (1929 and 2007), and Hungary, Iceland, Ireland, Spain, and the United Kingdom in 2008.

Asset bubbles include excessive lending to housing and construction sectors (Sweden, Japan Spain, and United States). Once the real estate bubble bursts, banks end up carrying a large number of non-performing loans.

Although smaller banks failed in the United States and other G-10 countries in the 1970s, within a decade, as technology and availability of information increased, financial crises began to accelerate: 1987, 1995, 1998, 2000, 2002, 2008, and 2011. As we discussed in Chapter 2, the explosive growth in securities markets from the late 1980s onward narrowed lending margins for corporate commercial banks, leading them to engage increasingly in investment banking activities. The expansion of secondary markets in an environment of financial liberalization allowed investment banks to act increasingly, not only as financial intermediaries between issuers and investors in the primary markets or as brokers in secondary markets, but also as proprietary traders in all types of securities for their own account.

After 1986, U.S., U.K., European, and Japanese banks began to expand their foreign subsidiaries, encouraged by fiscal incentives, interstate banking deregulation in the United States, and the opening of new markets in the former Soviet Union and Asia. By 1984, there was a shift in the type, size, and scope of trading transactions in the United States:

> The quantum increase in trading of financial instruments of all kinds, and the speed at which information on which trading decisions are based is supplied to institutions and individuals everywhere, has emasculated governments' powers to regulate their domestic money and capital markets from behind barricades that were established to protect them from events elsewhere. As a result, entire financial systems, and the regulations wrapped around them, that were built in the depression era of the 1930s (in the case of the United States) and in the postwar period (as in Japan) are swept by change.
>
> (Fallon et al. 1984)

Rogue traders and institutional collapse

Barings Bank (United Kingdom) and Crédit Lyonnais (France) (see Chapter 1) were among the most powerful and prestigious global banks, yet in 1995 they both imploded and within five years were completely absorbed and dissolved. Although these banks' initial triggers and final resolutions are at opposite ends of the spectrum, there are similar underlying shifts toward deregulation, expansion into foreign markets, competitive pressures and liberalization. Barings was destroyed by a new type of fraudulent activity, the rogue trader, which remained undetected for nearly three years.

Crédit Lyonnais, the largest state-owned bank in Europe, went into a liquidity crisis in 1995 when it was revealed that foreign subsidiaries had engaged in massive unsupervised fraudulent lending which highlighted the lack of home office oversight and due diligence. Resolution required state bailouts and Crédit Lyonnais' eventual dissolution and acquisition by Crédit Agricole.

Historical overview

Dutch tulip mania and real estate driven speculation

Amsterdam, part of the United Provinces by the 1620s, witnessed inflated property prices inciting real estate speculation among the wealthy burghers. The Amsterdam Exchange opened opposite the East India Company in 1631. "What was new in Amsterdam was the volume, the fluidity of the market and the publicity it received, and the speculative freedom of transactions" (Braudel, 1982). The vibrant Amsterdam exchange institutionalized futures trading in commodities with the "forward buying of herring before it has been caught and wheat and other goods before they had been grown or received" (de la Vega 1688). Although historians debate the extent of the damage and the number of speculators involved, the 1620s tulip mania based on the valuation of rare tulip bulbs introduced short selling, a futures market in tulips on the Amsterdam Exchange and the need for government intervention to quell market panic once the bubble burst in 1637.

British South Sea Bubble: futures markets and land speculation

In 1776, the English economist Adam Smith defined the stages of financial manias as "overtrading" followed by "negligence and profusion", then "revulsion and discredit" (Smith 1776). He was specifically referring to two seminal events of the early eighteenth century: the Mississippi Bubble in France and the South Sea Bubble in England. Although these speculative asset bubbles started out as a means of improving state finances, they quickly morphed into panics and bank runs. John Blunt, a wealthy British merchant, established the South Sea Trading Company in 1711 to help settle England's national debt by issuing shares in potential trading profits and selling the shares at reasonable valuation. However, as profits increased, by 1718 the South Sea Company had vastly expanded, with share prices increasing from a safe 100 pounds to 1000 in six months, based on rumors of immense dividends and future riches. Once the dividends decreased and the actual profits proved illusory, the bubble burst. In 1720, the House of Commons undertook an investigation leading to the Bubble Act of 1720 and "ruled that the directors of the South Sea Company, having been guilty of a breach of trust in lending money of the company on its own stock, should use their own wealth to make good investor losses" (Kindleberger and Aliber 2011: 140). This was the first instance of proprietary trading losses, officially disclosed and punished. The resolution was swift and unanimous as Parliament exonerated the Bank of England of any complicity and granted increased oversight powers over local banks and merchant houses. The powerful South Sea Trading Company was dissolved.

French Mississippi bubble: pyramid banking schemes

The situation in France was far more dramatic and had deeper and longer repercussions. At the death of King Louis XIV in 1715, France was without a central bank or regulatory oversight structure and suffered from a depleted Treasury and an inefficient and corrupt tax system. John Law, an inveterate Scottish gambler, but also a brilliant economist, proposed a plan to alleviate the public debt of 3,500 million livres tournois. Granted a charter to establish the first French state owned bank in 1718, Banque Royale, he began issuing stock in conjunction with the Louisiana Trading Company in the French-owned Mississippi lands. Law issued 200,000 shares at 500 livres tournois apiece, taking over monopolies of minting, tobacco sales, and taxes. However, within a year the shares became dangerously overvalued and were being sold and resold, and by the summer of 1720 there were "550,000 claimants for 2.2 billion in notes and 125,000 shares with a nominal value of 250 million, worth five times that amount at the market's peak. The claims were written down to one-twentieth of their stated value" (Kindleberger, 1993: 99). When early investors demanded to be reimbursed in cash, rumors started that the bank could not redeem the shares and panic set in. At the height of the speculative scheme shares worth 500 livres were being sold for 20,000 livres. The bank issued notes for 3 billion pounds, but had only 500 million in cash. In October 1720, the government closed the Bank, refused to honor the notes, and John Law, fearing for his life, escaped to Belgium.

Whereas England imposed strict oversight under the Bank of England without rejecting principles of capitalist ventures and financial innovation, for the next century France locked down all speculative activity: "French experience with John Law was such that there was hesitation in even pronouncing the word bank for 150 years thereafter" (Kindleberger 1985: 100) (see Chapter1).

Nineteenth and early twentieth century stock and commodity market swings and bank crashes

In the new world of transcontinental stock markets and commodities exchanges, nineteenth and pre-World War I bank crises were often caused by over speculation: railroad stocks (1846, 1857), gold (following the U.S. Gold Rush of 1849), and grain prices (1866, 1873). In 1857, over 1,000 U.S. banks failed as a result of the sudden drop in the price of railroad stocks, followed by a drop in commodities. The collapse of the Mires Bank in Paris and the Hamburg Bank impacted the Paris stock exchange. In 1866, a drop in U.S. cotton prices affected textile markets from India to Egypt, with contagion spreading from the London Stock Exchange to finance companies in Austria, Prussia, and Russia.

In 1873, the failure of Philadelphia banking firm Jay Cooke and Company incited large losses in commodities and railroad stocks provoking a recession in the United States and Canada. In 1890 to 1891, Argentinian real estate prices rose dramatically with excess issuance of bank notes, before dropping precipitously and causing a collapse of the currency. British and French investments in

Argentinian projects collapsed in value, causing the first near failure of Barings Bank in 1890. The Bank was rescued through a consortium led by the Bank of England, Bank of France, Imperial Bank of Russia, and the Rothschild's. In 1890, Barings could not be allowed to fail as it could have provoked a systemic crisis in the entire British banking sector (unlike the situation in 1995 when Barings was no longer considered to represent a global endemic risk). Over speculation in railroad bonds following the market crash of May 1893, provoked runs on banks in Chicago, Omaha, Detroit, San Diego, and Milwaukee.

By 1900, U.S. banks functioning without interstate or federal regulation used New York as their clearing house. New York's large banks, heavily invested in the Stock Exchange, did not have sufficient liquidity to meet sudden large redemptions. Trust companies, which functioned as a combination of commercial deposit and investment banks, were the most vulnerable. In October 1907, the New York Stock Exchange, reacting to currency and gold price fluctuations in Paris and London, coupled with weakening commodity prices in the United States, caused panic among trust companies. The New York Knickerbocker Trust could not meet its obligations, with US$60 million on deposit, but only US$10 million in cash. As in 1893, resolution depended on JP Morgan assuming the role of lender of last resort, bringing together the heads of all major New York banks to arrange a loan to Knickerbocker in order to quell the panic and stop the flight of gold from New York.[1]

Stock market crash and its impact on U.S. banks

Until the 1980s, the most significant event in American financial history was the Crash of 1929. From October 1929 until the newly elected President Roosevelt's first fireside speech on bank closures on March 4, 1933, over 10,000 banks failed. Unprotected depositors lost US$2 billion in savings in the absence of Federal deposit insurance. Unemployment rose to 23 percent in 1932, and stocks lost almost 80 percent of their value. The crisis instigated the creation of regulatory and structural firewalls imposed between the banking, securities, and insurance sectors under the Glass-Steagall Act of 1934, the creation of the Securities and Exchange Commission, the expanded oversight role of the Federal Reserve and the Office of the Comptroller of the Currency (OCC). These reforms remained intact, although in diluted form, until the final repeal of Glass-Steagall in 1999 with the passage of the Gramm-Bliley-Leach Act.

US bank failures and systemic crises in the 1980s: precursor to 2008

Penn Square

Between 1982 and 1989, U.S. bank failures and the collapse of the savings and loan industry imposed consolidation, mergers and a transition from small- and medium-banking establishments toward too-big to fail banks. Penn Square, a faltering community bank in Oklahoma City, launched an oil and gas department in 1976, based on Government-encouraged oil and gas exploration in the wake of the 1973 Crisis. In July 1982, Penn Square failed after years of granting loans based on non-existent or poor collateral, and based on the belief that "a bank did not have to lend its own deposits, because it could lend other banks' deposits. Penn Square could earn interest lending its own funds, but could generate far greater earnings with very little risk by arranging loans and collecting fees as a middlemen" (Singer 1985: 19). Penn Square, as a regional bank, was entitled to deal with large money center banks, including Continental Illinois National Bank and Trust Company of Chicago, the eighth largest U.S. bank holding company. In order to guarantee its loans, "at its zenith Penn Square could legally lend up to three million dollars at one time", then engage in "over lines" through other banks" (Singer 1985: 19–20). Continental in turn began to sell off these loans to larger institutions, including Chase Manhattan. Although banks' auditors and, by 1980, the Office of the Comptroller of the Currency issued warnings of "financial, operational or compliance weaknesses" (Singer 1985: 73), bankers only saw a growing balance sheet. Once the bank collapsed, it was revealed at hearings that loans were granted upon request with almost no due diligence or collateral required. When it was declared insolvent, Penn Square had US$37 million in capital and identifiable losses of US$20 million. Due to lack of disclosure and weak oversight, Chase Manhattan, although not held legally responsible, took months to unravel which loans were on its books and which had been sold to correspondent banks.

Resolution: Penn Square was taken over by the Federal Deposit Insurance Corporation (FDIC). Within a few months, over 25 banks in Texas, Tennessee, Kentucky, and across Oklahoma failed or were listed as problem banks. By 1984, "the FDIC's list of problem banks had risen to 617, a post-Depression record" (Singer 1985: 153). The bank was liquidated, its president was indicted in Chicago, but never convicted in Oklahoma, and acquitted on all charges as not having intended to defraud.

US savings and loan: the first U.S. mortgage debacle

Banking historian Martin Mayer commented on the demise of the U.S. savings and loans (S&Ls) in the late 1980s: "the saddest story in the long history of the relationship of American government and American banking is the collapse of the savings and loan industry in the 1980s and early 1990s" (Mayer 1997: 361). The failure of Home State Savings Bank in 1985 set in motion a chain reaction of over 700 savings and loans failures. Between 1984 and 1991, 1,400 savings and loans and 1,300 banks failed in the United States (Bordo et al. 2001).

These S&L institutions were not banks, which took deposits, but essentially community pools of money in which members bought negotiable shares (Mayer 1997). Associated with the housing reforms of the early 1930s, part of the Federal Home Loan Bank system, and directly associated with mortgages and the housing market, they had nearly gone bankrupt many times. In the 1970s, these institutions were allowed to engage in property development, make commercial loans, buy junk bonds, and invest in non-financial business. Starting in 1982, changes in regulation and individual state rules for savings and loans allowed arbitrage between state and federally chartered mortgages (especially in California, which had the highest rate of new mortgages), giving institutions charged with protecting the savings of their clients, the right to use insured deposits for non-regulated ventures, including junk bonds. (The Nolan Act allowed savings and loan "operators in effect to own stock in and lend money to whatever business ventures they might like to attempt" (Mayer 1997).)

Resolution: By 1987, as hundreds of savings and loans began to fail, the U.S. Government was forced to intervene. Congress passed the Financial Institutions Reform, Recovery and Enforcement Act of 1989 (FIRREA), which would become a model for the good bank–bad bank concept applied in the Nordic and subsequent banking crises. The Financial Institutions Reform Recovery and Enforcement Act contained the following key provisions:

1. The creation of the Office of Thrift Supervision (OTS) within Treasury as the regulator of all thrifts.
2. Imposition of stricter minimum capital and accounting requirements for thrifts.
3. The establishment of the tax payer funded Resolution Trust Corporation to conduct the necessary reorganization of the Savings and Loans industry, and organize federal mutual savings associations.

The purpose was to resolve failed thrifts and manage deposition of assets. The original Act called for US$50 billion: "to close, sell or merge institutions and dispose of assets" and "minimize taxpayer costs and avoid serious dislocation in markets."

European domestic bank failures with international repercussions

Credit-Anstalt

Post-World War I and the collapse of the Austro-Hungarian Empire, the first major failure was the May 1931 collapse of the lead Austrian bank, Credit-Anstalt, created by the Rothschild's in 1855 to finance trans-European railroad ventures (see Chapter 1). The Austrian Central Bank and Credit Anstalt had been pillars of stability and sound investments. However, under pressure from the German monetary crisis and war reparation payments coupled with German hyperinflation in the early 1920s (see Chapter 1), the bank accumulated bad loans due to tremendous depreciation in real estate and land values and the takeover of smaller failed institutions.

In May 1931, unable to pay back a large international loan, it was revealed that its reserves were reduced to 165 million shillings with losses of 140 million shillings. The Austrian Government was forced to guarantee bank liabilities, and

Rothschild's offered a bridge loan, but the news of the bailout created panic across Germany and Austria. Under Austrian law, once a bank lost half its capital, it had to be declared insolvent and closed. The subsequent shock to the German and newly formed Eastern European banking sector accelerated political and economic turmoil. Although the Bank for International Settlements (see Chapter 1) was founded in 1930 to help coordinate central bank policies, it did not have the mandate to support intervention in the Credit Anstalt collapse.

Herstatt and Franklin National-Technical FOREX failures

Between the end of the Great Depression and the 1970s, there were few bank failures in Europe, as, after World War II, economies slowly recovered under nationalization, government run industrial and economic policies, and strict regulation. In the United States there were few bank failures as banks functioned under the strictures of Glass-Steagall. There were two Foreign Exchange (FOREX) related transactional failures in 1974: Bankhaus Herstatt, in Germany, and Franklin National Bank in the United States. In October 1974, Herstatt failed after daily closure of the settlement system in Germany did not take into account outstanding positions in New York, defaulting on more than $600 million in claims. When the Bundesbank stopped clearing all accounts, Hertstatt's counterparties were immediately affected due to "the asynchronous settlement of funds", which gave its name to the Herstatt risk. Although this issue may be anachronistic in the era of instantaneous electronic transactions, the danger was severe at the time. The failure of Franklin National was triggered by the refusal of other banks to take the counterpart of Franklin's forward FOREX contracts, or to lend it federal funds.

Herstatt instigated the G-10 central banks' decision to set up the Basel Committee on home and host country regulations for foreign banks, leading to the 1983 decision to give home and host country joint responsibility for oversight of foreign banks (see Chapter 6 on bank supervision).

The failure of Banco Ambrosiano through misappropriation of funds and corruption will be examined in Chapter 7. The transactions and losses incurred as a result of rogue trader activity will be examined in Chapter 7 also. However, we will examine the case of Barings Bank in this chapter, as the actions of the trader Nick Leeson were the direct cause of Barings' failure and dissolution.

How one trader destroyed a global bank

In the United Kingdom, following Big Bang in 1986 (see Chapter 1), British merchant and investment banks, including Barings, adopted U.S.-style liberalization, privatization, and deregulation. In order to maintain competitiveness British banks entered into securities and trading, often with insufficient due diligence and lack of experienced staff.

In July 1992, Nick Leeson, an aggressive young trader, was sent to Singapore to execute trades on SIMEX on behalf of numerous accounts, including Barings

Security Japan, Barings Futures Singapore, and Barings Securities HK. Without additional management supervision he was placed in charge of back office operations. As he began to take on higher risks, losses accumulated to GB£23 million in 1993, and GB£208 million in 1994. Coming from the back office, Leeson (like Jerome Kerviel at SocGen in 2008 (see Chapter 7) created fictitious accounts to cover the trades. His superiors in London had little knowledge of derivatives traded on exchanges and continued to believe that Barings was a lead player on SIMEX, despite the fact that the trades were fictitious. As the losses accumulated in late 1994, Leeson needed the Nikkei to remain stable or to rise, but the Japanese economy began to veer off course. As Leeson was unable to explain his strategy nor its success, there had been a series of internal memos since 1993 expressing concern. Yet, as profits seemed to soar, management ignored these warnings, and by December 1994 the false account held 65,000 options worth GB£1.8 billion. When an earthquake struck Kobe on the morning of January 17, 1995, the Nikkei sank by 175 points and Leeson lost GB£105 million in one session. Leeson continued to increase his position, requesting more funding until he finally and single-handedly lost a total of close to GB£830 million of the bank's money.

Investigations and reports submitted after the crisis revealed that between 1991 and 1995, Barings strove "to merge old style banking with a freewheeling security business" (Darnton 1995). Asian operations grew rapidly, but without additional monitoring. Furthermore, London management did not understand the instruments nor the methodology and was, therefore, unable and unwilling to exercise any oversight. In January 1995, within hours of being informed of the magnitude of the problem, the Bank of England decided that contagion in the City was unlikely as the issue was solvency not liquidity. The response occurred in a global crisis environment barely a year after the Spanish bailout of Banesto, which had to be folded into Santander, the ongoing losses at Crédit Lyonnais, and with the peso crisis in full force and Mexico threatening to default. Leeson, fleeing Singapore in February 1995, was captured, tried, and jailed.[2] Barings was sold for the symbolic amount of GB£1 to the global Dutch bank ING, which absorbed its GB£660million loss.

The lessons learned were to include not allowing the same trader to have access to back office operations at the same time as taking trading positions. By 2008, however, the Barings model reappeared in Société Générale, and in 2011 in UBS, where both instances involved back office manipulation of accounts and the creation of false accounts.

Crédit Lyonnais: the largest state-owned bank failure and dissolution

Crédit Lyonnais was both too big to fail and too big to save. Chartered in 1863 as the first French joint stock deposit bank (see Chapter 1), it extended credit to regional industry in the economic expansion of the 1860s to 1880s. The largest French bank in the world by 1910, it had branches in over 100 countries.

In 1992, as the largest and best capitalized French bank, rivaled in Europe only by Deutsche Bank, Crédit Lyonnais was considered a model of universal banking. However, in constant pursuit of additional assets and territorial market share, it began to carry problem loans on its balance sheet, many to dubious international clients.

Between 1988 and 1993, the bank lost nearly FF10billion on a disastrous U.S. film studio deal, FF2 billion on the failed U.K. Canary Wharf real estate deal, FF500 million to Marseilles tycoon Bernard Tapie, who was subsequently indicted for financial fraud, and FF4 billion to poor investments in Russia. Economist George Kaufman, writing on state-run international banks, noted that "they are a superb vehicle for governments to use to pass on political favors to their supporters, direct credit to favored sectors and raise revenues by creating monopolies" (Kaufman and Kroszner 1997).

Extending credit according to French industrial policy, the bank held stakes in all major industrial groups. In 1981, it acquired a Rotterdam bank with a checkered past, renamed Crédit Lyonnais Bank Nederland, which aggressively provided loans totaling almost FF2.5 billion to ventures in California with little or no due diligence. This lending included a leveraged buyout of the U.S. film studio MGM. When Italian financier Paretti defaulted on these loans in 1991, under U.S. laws regulating foreign ownership of U.S. companies, the U.S. Securities and Exchange Commission (SEC) intervened and brought suit against Crédit Lyonnais, which in turn had to sue Paretti. Investigations revealed that Paris had given approval to these deals without any due diligence or oversight of its subsidiary. "The state failed to distinguish between the roles of regulator and owner", noted *The Economist* (July 5, 1997).

In 1994, the French press began to investigate what was dubbed "the Banking Scandal of the Century" (*Le Point*, March 26, 1994) revealing that losses, initially estimated at FF500 million, had ballooned to nearer FF6.9 billion. In January 1995, the losses had mounted to FF50 billion, forcing the State to announce a second bailout.

As the last fully-owned French Government bank in 1995 (SocGen had been privatized in 1987, BNP in 1993), the bailout had political implications which affected economic decisions. Between 1988 and 1993 Crédit Lyonnais doubled its assets, and even with the losses in 1994 it held FF350 billion in assets, remaining the largest non-Japanese world bank. In 1995, Crédit Lyonnais was not insolvent despite the massive losses incurred, but it could not control, unravel, or independently take charge of its balance sheet as the Government was the lender of last resort. After the currency crisis of 1992, in a sluggish economy, the French Government justified bailing out the bank, which had 2,000 domestic branches and employed globally approximately 32,000 persons, noting that the "costs and disruption of closing Crédit Lyonnais would have been far greater than the restructuring plan and that no-one was in any case willing to buy the bank without a state guarantee of liabilities" (Kamm, 1996).

The scandal, resolution, and final privatization revealed a crony management culture, lacking in transparency, disclosure or accountability. The bank was accused of "aggressive lending and investment policy ... without there being sufficiently strict monitoring of exposure" (EU Commission Decision, 1995).

There was concern that endemic risk would spread to become a crisis of confidence in the system.

Following three government bailouts and lesser cash injections to the amount of nearly FF145 billion, Société Générale and BNP issued an official complaint that the government provision of aid to Crédit Lyonnais was in violation of Article 92 and Article 93 of the Maastricht Treaty on market distortion. This was the first instance of the EU Commission being called upon to intervene. The 1998 agreement between the EU Commission, the French Government and Crédit Lyonnais provided for a final bailout of nearly FF100 billion (US$20 billion) and a commitment to privatize the bank by the October 1999. The resolution also required the sale and disposal of bad loans through the creation of a separate bad bank entity, the Consortium de Réalisation (CDR), modeled on the 1991 Nordic SECURUM model.

However, unlike the independent Securum, CDR was established originally as a subsidiary of Crédit Lyonnais, despite the EU Commission specifically calling for the separation of CDR and the bank. CDR was dissolved within a year and in 1998 partial privatization began.

In order to avoid German and other foreign banks and insurers gaining a majority shareholding, the French government prolonged privatization until 2003 when it encouraged a rapid merger with Crédit Agricole. Within a decade, Crédit Lyonnais' international corporate and investment brand was fully absorbed into Crédit Agricole and France's oldest deposit bank disappeared.

German Landesbanken

Although the German economy continues to be the strongest in the European Union, the banking sector remains vulnerable, with major divergences between the two remaining German megabanks Deutsche Bank and Commerzbank, who account for approximately 35 percent of domestic market share and the fragmented Landesbanken sector. In 2009, 65 percent of the German banking sector remained within public banks, with over 400 savings banks (Sparkassen) and nearly 2,000 cooperative banks. Postbank (acquired by Deutsche Bank in 2010) had the largest number of branches. During the EU crisis, German bank bailouts represented only 25 percent of GDP (compared to almost 300 percent of GDP in Ireland).

First established as regional savings banks in 1818, Landesbanken functioned alongside savings and thrifts and cooperative saving banks to help finance small- and medium-sized enterprises up to World War II. Reconstituted in 1949, Landesbanken became full-service regional banks to help finance the reconstruction of infrastructure in the export driven recovery of the 1970s. By the 1980s, however, under deregulation, liberalization, and increased international competition, they began to consolidate in order to remain competitive: Württembergische Sparkasse BadenWurttemberg evolved by absorbing smaller Landesbanken in the period 1998 to 2005.

In 1995, following its decision on state subsidies to Crédit Lyonnais, the EU Commission turned its attention to other state subsidized banking sectors.

It decided that by 2002 Landesbanken ownership had to adhere to market principles, transforming them into joint stock corporations. Under the Brussels Concordance in 2005, Germany was obliged by the EU Commission on Competitiveness to withdraw state guarantees for banks.

No longer required to serve as credit institutions for local Mittelstand (SMEs), Landesbanken began to diversify and consolidate, but under pressure to compete and maintain profitability they jumped into structured investment vehicles (SIVs) and collateralized debt obligations (CDOs) without having experienced staff, and unfamiliar with the necessary business and risk management models. By August 2007, the Landesbanken were among the first financial institutions to post losses. These losses reached almost €1.6 billion in the case of WestLB, and within three years it was shut down; SachsenLB and LB Rheinland-Pfalz collapsed in 2008 and were absorbed into Landesbank BadenWürttemberg. Bayern LB owned jointly by Bavaria and community savings banks required a €10 billion euro bailout, revealing, in the process, fraudulent lending practices and the concealment of losses.

Landesbanken was forced to abandon plans to compete in international investment banking and reduced their financial holdings. The EU Commission imposed on the remaining nine Landesbanken (reconsolidated into four) the implementation of significant cost savings, staff reductions, the repayment of all bailout funds, and the elimination of all state guarantees by 2013. The savings bank sector under further consolidation was also sharply reduced, from over 400 banks to 85 banks (Engels 2010).

UK Northern Rock: precursor and warning

Northern Rock was created in 1965 through the merger of two nineteenth century mutual building societies, which provided mortgages and construction loans to their communities in Northern England. In 1994, expanding through the acquisition of building societies, it changed status to become a bank. Maintaining its offices in Newcastle upon Tyne, it grew into one of the top five UK mortgage lenders, and it listed on the FTSE 100 Index in 2000. Between 2004 and 2006, bank profits increased from GB£228.9 million in 2002, to GB£309.5million in 2004, and GB£443.0 million in 2006 (Northern Rock Plc 2006). In 2007, the group increased its loan portfolio of securitized notes by GB£6.1bn. Its annual report stated that the bank had a diversified portfolio of high quality liquid assets, confirmed by the Independent Auditors' Report. With 76 branches and mortgage centers, postal and internet operations, Northern Rock sought to become one of the three leading mortgage lenders in the United Kingdom.

However, the market became volatile through 2007, and in August 2007, BNP decided to suspend three investment funds with exposure to the U.S. subprime mortgage market. The Bank of England was given notice that Northern Rock was in difficulty and provided short-term emergency loans. When the BBC revealed that Northern Rock had to seek short-term emergency loans, it set off a panic and a subsequent public relations disaster symptomatic of all rumor generated bank runs.

On September 14, 2007, a photograph appeared in the global media and on the front page of the *Financial Times* showing older, middle-class pensioners queuing up to withdraw funds, despite statements that the bank appeared solvent. Within days the bank lost 32 percent of its market share, with all 76 branches across the United Kingdom affected.

The Bank of England announced that it would intervene, in an effort to calm depositors and the market. On September 17, 2007 Chancellor of the Exchequer, Alistair Darling announced the guarantee of all deposits. By early 2008, Northern Rock became the object of various bids until the Treasury recommended its nationalization in order to protect savers. Subsequent investigations revealed weak oversight, a lack of due diligence, and poor management. By August 2008, in an increasingly volatile global market, Northern Rock needed GB£3 billion in stability funding, despite restructuring efforts. Split into two groups in 2010 and in 2011, Virgin Money bought Northern Rock, renamed Virgin Money Plc, and Northern Rock's personal loans were sold to One Savings Bank, backed by U.S. private equity firm JC Flowers. The UK Asset Resolution Authority, created in October 2010, became responsible for winding down the mortgage book and managing the loan book losses. Merged with Bradford and Bingley in August 2013, the bank had to repay an additional GB£9 billion pounds to taxpayers.

Country and regional banking crises

Nordic banking crises and resolution model

Nordic banks, originally merchant and trading houses, expanded into retail and commercial banks from 1830 to 1870. While Swedish banks focused on domestic timber, fishing, and trade, Finnish banks turned from domestic to international markets, with trade focused on Russia.

After the fall of the Soviet Union, Finland lost its key trading partner, provoking a deep recession. Skopbank collapsed in September 1991, followed by the nationalization of three other banks "that together accounted for 31% of system deposits" (Reinhart and Rogoff 2009: Table A5-7). Norway, although outside of the European Union and European Free Trade Area (EFTA) was not left unscathed. Price slumps in commodities, the shipping, petroleum, and fishing sectors had a significant impact. The banking sector almost collapsed and the State had to intervene in 22 domestic banks including Christiana.

As a member of the European Union, Denmark was directly impacted by German reunification. As the Danish (and Swedish krona) pegged to the common European currency unit (ECU) were underpinned by the Deutsche mark, banks suffered heavy losses, and the banking sector had to be consolidated and restructured (Caprio et al. 2003).

However, the most severe problems occurred in Sweden in the aftermath of the 1985 deregulatory measures when "quantitative restrictions on the volume of bank lending were abolished" (Drees and Pazarbasioglu 1998). Where previously government industrial policy dictated credit allocation, commercial and savings banks began to expand lending in the sectors of housing and real estate, and the economy saw a surge in stock market participation. The Swedish economy, with historically high savings rate and low inflation, began to experience reduced rates of savings and rising inflation following Government-imposed tax reforms in 1990. In a volatile environment these plans backfired as the market plunged and asset prices collapsed. The European Union currency crises of 1992 attacked the krona, as the Riksbank insisted on maintaining the currency peg to the ECU until November 1992.

In December 1992, the Swedish Parliament passed legislation to establish the Bank Support Authority, an independent agency working in close coordination with the Riksbank, the Ministry of Finance, and the National Debt Office. Two major banks, Nordbanken and Gotabanken, were declared insolvent. The goal was to save the banks, without sparing their owners.

Banks were divided into three categories: those that could regain solvency; those that fell below capital adequacy ratios, but could recover; and those that were beyond saving. Two bank asset management corporations were set up (AMC), Securum and Retriva, to assume and address bad debt in the form of non-performing loans through the sale of assets. Although owned by the Swedish state, the company had to maintain full independence, with political backing from all parties. The portfolio covered approximately 1,000 insolvent companies. According to the official SECURUM AB Report, by mid 1994 "of the 790 Swedish limited share companies in Securum's client list register, 70 percent were declared bankrupt and liquidated" (Bergström et al. 2003). The others were restructured or sold. The final cost to taxpayers was significantly lower than initial expectations. The Swedish State retained a 20 percent stake in Nordbanken and, in order to consolidate the sector, Nordbanken acquired Gotabanken in 1993.

The International Monetary Fund (IMF) did not have to intervene as the Swedish Treasury assumed the task of stabilizing the banking sector and the economy without compromising its sovereign credit worthiness. Nordbanken, previously state-owned, was privatized and merged with Finnish Merita in 1997 to form Nordea. The Swedish system was not corrupted by derivatives, with barely a hedge fund and little securitization. With only six banks, the Swedish banking system was manageable, homogeneous, and transparent.

This model was successful for a number of reasons: "(1)... political unity behind the resolution policy, (2) a government blanket guarantee of the financial obligations of the banking system, (3) swift policy action where acting early was more important than acting in exactly the right manner, (4) an adequate legal and institutional framework for the resolution procedures including open-ended public funding, (5) full disclosure of information by the parties involved, (6) a differentiated resolution policy minimizing moral hazard by forcing private sector participants to absorb losses before government financial intervention, and (7) the proper design of macroeconomic policies to simultaneously end the crisis in both the real economy and the financial sector" (Jonung 2009: 1).

In Finland, banks began consolidating in the 1980s, creating Union Bank of Finland, which in 1995 merged with Kansallis-Osaka-Pankki to become Merita.

Unlike other country resolutions, the Nordic banks created cross-border organic mergers starting in 1997 with Nordbanken-Merita to form Nordic Baltic Holdings. Within three years the crisis was resolved. Nordic Baltic Holdings merged with Denmark's Unibank (focused on equity and investment activities) and Norway's Christiana Bank to create the cross-regional NordeaAB. The merger combined Nordbanken-Merita's expertise in internet banking with Danish investment and Norway's trade expertise. NORDEA, the largest bank in Sweden, Finland, and Denmark after 2004 opened branches in the new EU member countries Estonia, Latvia, Lithuania, and Poland.

Although the sector suffered losses in 2008–10, Swedish banks, Swedbank and Nordea maintained their lead positions in the European Union until the incursion of Russia's Sberbank in 2012.

Japan: the Japanese banking-industrial sector nexus – its strengths and weaknesses

From the 1950s through the 1990s, six major banks in Tokyo held one half of the nation's bank deposits. Starting in the mid 1970s, there was a sharp increase in consumer credit and mortgages after the long post-World War II period of austerity. After the global crash of 1987, asset prices fell sharply, and by 1992, the Nikkei had fallen 60 percent from its 1989 peak.

Despite internal weaknesses, Japanese banks remained the most highly capitalized in the world, and the largest by total assets (see Chapter 1). However, cultural norms under the keiretsu system of industrial bank holdings, aided by government policies, did not allow banks to fail and ignored internal reform, efficiency, and transparency. Under government dictated competition policy, if a bank was deemed vulnerable other banks were required to bail it out at government controlled interest rates. In a system of cross shareholdings when a firm was in trouble, the lead bank was obligated to establish a rescue package. Even when banks held large numbers of non- or under-performing loans, Japanese industrial firms were reluctant to downsize, and banks were unwilling to reduce or stop loans, even to clearly bankrupt companies (Enright et al. 2005). In 1990, after decades of expansion, monetary policy tightened, and by 1991 the real estate bubble had burst.

Daiwa

In 1994 to 1995, Daiwa, Japan's tenth largest bank with approximately US$85 billion of its US$176 bn assets invested in the United States collapsed. On July 13, 1995, Toshihide Iguchi, a bond trader in New York, admitted forging 30,000 trading slips over a period of 11 years of dealing in government bonds for the bank's New York branch, accumulating losses of US$1.1 billion. Like Nick Leeson at Barings, knowledgeable about back office and compliance procedures, he covered his losses by selling off bonds in custodial accounts and falsifying records. The Japanese Ministry of Finance delayed notifying U.S. authorities for almost one month, underscoring the lack of cooperation and deep cultural and institutional incompatibilities.

In November 1995, U.S. regulators ordered Daiwa to close its U.S. operations. Daiwa Bank Ltd never recovered and a year later was merged into Sumitomo Bank. One year later, Yasuo Hamanaka, a copper trader at Sumitomo Corporation, a subsidiary of the Sumitomo Bank, pleaded guilty to fraud in trading losses of US$1.8 billion. These trading scandals exposing fundamental oversight and risk management failures, were followed by the first post-World War II regional bank failure, that of Hyago Bank.

The failure of 13 financial institutions in Japan in 1995 can be traced to two decades of collusive regulation, an incestuous relationship between regulators and institutions, structural defects, a lack of transparency, and the impact of the real estate bubble. Non-performing loans reached 13 percent of gross outstanding loans. Despite reform attempts in 1996, the impact of the 1997 Asian currency crisis placed further pressure on Japanese banks, which held US$495.5 billion in sovereign debt from Thailand, Indonesia, Malaysia, and South Korea.[3]

In March 1998, under the Financial Function Stabilization Act, the government injected ¥1.8 trillion into 21 banks. A year later, under the Prompt Recapitalization Act, the government injected a further ¥6.7 trillion into 15 banks. From 1999 to 2003, the entire sector underwent consolidation and reform through a series of large domestic mergers: IBJ merged with Dai-Ichi, Kangyo and Fuji into Mizuho Financial Group; Mitsubishi UFJ Financial Group merged to become the second largest global bank. By 2008, Japan had three huge international mega-banks: Sumitomo Mitsui, Mizuho Financial Group, and Mitsubishi UFJ. Benefitting from sector-wide restructuring prior to the financial crisis of 2008, Japan emerged relatively unscathed from the global financial and debt crisis.

U.S. subprime meltdown and U.S. government response

By the end of 2000, the U.S. economy had grown for 39 straight quarters, and large banks appeared to be diversified, profitable, and well capitalized. However, "from 1978 to 2007, the amount of debt held by the financial sector soared from $3 trillion to $36 trillion, more than doubling as a share of gross domestic product" (Financial Crisis Inquiry Report 2011: xvii). By 2005, the 10 largest U.S. commercial banks held 55 percent of the sector's assets, more than double the level held in 1990.

By 2004, the threat of an economic slowdown resulting from the terrorist attacks of September 11, 2001 had been averted. Basel II, a new international regulatory regime incorporating the lessons from the 1997 Asian and 1998 Russian financial crises, had been approved by the G-20 finance ministers for gradual implementation through 2007. By mid 2006, bank executives, credit rating agencies, and regulators were confident that the risk management techniques employed by leading banks globally could prevent a major crisis. Yet between March and September 2008, Bear Stearns and Lehman Brothers, two venerable U.S. investment banks, collapsed. In September 2008, the U.S. Department of the Treasury was forced to provide outright financial backing in an attempt to avert the risk of collapse of the entire U.S. financial system, in exchange for *de facto* ownership control of the two government sponsored mortgage lenders Fannie Mae and Freddy Mac, and AIG, the world's largest insurance company. By early October of that year, the U.S. Congress approved the creation of the Troubled Asset Relief Program), a US$700 billion Treasury commitment for the recapitalization of private sector banks: what had gone wrong?

The build-up to the U.S. financial crisis

The financial crisis of 2007 to 2009 was sparked by a severe deterioration in the health of the U.S. mortgage market that began in late 2006, after a six-year period of unprecedented growth in the housing market. Extremely low interest rates between late 2001 and late 2004 (Federal Funds Rate below 2 percent per annum, and 1 percent between July 2003 and July 2004), combined with double digit annual increases in real estate prices (11.5 percent per annum between 2000 and 2005) increased the risk appetite of both mortgage lenders and borrowers. Highly irresponsible credit granting, particularly in the form of aggressive subprime lending, and unchecked abuses by the financial industry of securitization techniques and derivatives, with the blessing of credit rating agencies, generated a real estate credit bubble of gigantic proportions. At year-end 2006, investors around the world held US$8.6 trillion in U.S. mortgage backed securities.

At its root, the financial crisis of 2008 was not very different to earlier financial crises. A period of excessive optimism on the part of lenders and borrowers was followed by an abrupt reversal in expectations, causing severe balance sheet problems for banks, and the risk of systemic contagion, with potentially dramatic economic consequences, triggering a government-sponsored bailout. What made this crisis unique – and particularly dangerous – was the fact that it was nurtured over a relatively long period of time (2001-2006) in the world's largest economy, home to the world's most creative financial market, and the world's most widely-used currency.

Subprime mortgages had been created originally for home buyers considered riskier than normal. Their repayment terms were quite different from conventional mortgages, including steep hidden fees and adjustable interest rates, lower during an initial teaser period and to be reset at much higher levels after two to three years. Increasing appetite for risk appetite on the part of mortgage lenders and investors led to a progressive lowering of credit standards. Zero down payment adjustable rate mortgages to high risk borrowers, in many cases without proof of their incomes, became relatively common practice. Subprime mortgage lending expanded six-fold in five years, from US$100 billion in 2000 to US$600 billion in 2005.

Industry excess in the use of securitization was a fundamental cause of the real estate credit bubble. Co-agents in this process were mortgage securities originators, initially large private-sector mortgage lenders such as Countrywide and Washington Mutual, the government-sponsored enterprises, Fannie Mae and Freddie Mac, investment banks, and credit rating agencies.

Fannie Mae, or the Federal National Mortgage Association, was founded in 1938 as a government-owned agency to acquire housing loans from banks and thrifts, increasing the availability of home loans. In 1968, with the aim of removing Fannie Mae from the Government's balance sheet, Congress approved its reorganization as a publicly traded corporation. Fannie Mae had been, *de facto*, privatized; but it was perceived by the market as a *hybrid*, a private sector company that could count on special government support, or a *government-sponsored enterprise* (GSE).

In 1970, Congress chartered a second government sponsored enterprise GSE, Freddie Mac (Federal Home Loan Mortgage Corporation), allowing Fannie Mae and Freddie Mac to acquire non-Federal Housing Administration (FHA) backed mortgages. It authorized the GSEs to *securitize* their loans portfolio, bundling housing loans and issuing securities to be sold in the market place, backed by the pool of loans assembled, the so-called mortgage backed securities (MBSs).

Fannie Mae and Freddie Mac enjoyed a virtual monopoly on securitizing fixed rate loans within their authorized loan limits. But in the 1980s with the help of Wall Street, mortgage lenders began to securitize loans that the GSEs were unwilling to buy, including adjustable-rate mortgages (ARMs). As loans were pooled into a structured finance security, they could be sold in tranches, lower yield – lower default risk for risk averse investors, higher yield – higher default risk for more aggressive investors. The complexity of these structures led investment banks to bring in the services of credit rating agencies to examine the likelihood of default of securities traded in the market place.

From the mid to late 1990s to the mid 2000s, private sector mortgage lenders with the help of Wall Street and the participation of credit rating agencies were successfully packaging and selling their own mortgage backed securities in significant amounts. They would become dominant: between 2003 and 2005, as the GSEs' share of the total mortgage securities market declined from 57 percent to 37 percent.

The ratings provided by credit rating agencies were essential, not only to guide pricing and facilitate investment banks' placement of securities with investors at large, in the United States and abroad, but also to determine the amount of capital banks, domestic and foreign, were required to allocate to carry positions. The explosive growth of mortgage-backed investment products accounted for the extraordinary increase in revenues by credit rating agencies structured finance departments between 2000 and 2007. In 2002, in the wake of the dot.com bubble, Federal Reserve Chairman Greenspan described mortgage markets as "a powerful stabilizing force", focusing two years later on the advantages of "large extraction of cash from home equity".

However, mortgage credit risks, rated based on the recent period of strong credit performance, did not incorporate the deterioration in underwriting standards by lenders or the likelihood of future destabilization or decline in home prices.

The final layer of the subprime credit bubble was the improper use of derivatives (see Chapter 2). Derivatives are financial instruments, which, like securitization, should be expected to facilitate credit flows and contribute to a more efficient allocation of resources throughout the economy. Unfortunately, misguided use of two particular types of derivatives, collateralized debt obligations (CDOs) and credit default swaps (CDSs), added additional layers of risk to the U.S. real estate credit bubble in formation.

Lower-rated tranches of mortgage-backed security (MBS) structures were harder to sell to investors, not only because they embodied a higher risk of default, but because they included higher capital charges for banks. A creative solution was the development of the mortgage backed securities collateralized debt obligation (MBS CDO). Investment bankers would take the lower investment grade tranches of an MBS structure and repackage them into a new security, the MBS CDO. Securities firms proposed – and rating agencies agreed – that because the MBS CDO was a pool of many, for example, BBB-rated mortgage backed securities of different origins, risk reduction from diversification ensued and a higher credit rating for the new CDO than for the underlying securities became possible. Approximately 80 percent of the tranches of CDOs created from triple-B to A rated tranches of outstanding MBSs were rated triple-A. Between 2003 and 2007, CDOs issued by Wall Street with lower tranches of MBSs as collateral amounted to US$700 billion.

Credit default swaps (CDSs) are financial contracts through which a certain credit risk is transferred from one party to another in exchange for a premium. It is a form of insurance and a derivative, in that the value of the contract varies with changes in the default risk of the underlying credit exposure covered by the contract.

In 1998, AIG Financial Products, a unit of American International Group (AIG), began selling credit default swaps on a variety of financial assets. Benefitting from the guarantee of its triple-A rated parent, AIG Financial Products was able to earn attractive premiums in exchange for underwriting third parties' credit risk. Banks on both sides of the Atlantic were willing to pay a premium to reduce the amount of regulatory capital required against certain assets. As CDSs were not formally treated by insurance regulators as insurance contracts, reserves against potential losses on these positions were not demanded. AIG's CDS business grew from US$20 billion in 2002, to over US$500 billion in 2007, of which over 15 percent had been written against MBS CDOs.

Early signs of trouble and FED response

As real estate prices began to decline in the second half of 2006, the first signs of trouble emerged. Subprime foreclosures rose from 3 percent in early 2006, to 5 percent at year-end, an upward trend that would continue, reaching 15 percent in 2009.

As default rates increased, subprime lenders began to have difficulty selling on these loans to Wall Street and, through Wall Street, to investors at-large. Much of their funding came from repo agreements which required them to buy back from Wall Street loan portfolios that defaulted quickly.

By late 2006, a few smaller subprime lenders had already declared bankruptcy. On April 2, 2007, New Century, one of the country's largest subprime lenders, filed for Chapter 11 bankruptcy protection. By mid 2007, the deterioration of the housing sector began to impact severely the hedge fund industry. About a dozen funds that were heavily invested in the bottom tranches of MBSs and MBS CDOs, including two managed by Bear Stearns, collapsed.

The Federal Reserve interpreted that these difficulties with mortgage portfolios were not of a systemic nature and could be managed by the financial sector. Concerned with inflation risk, the Federal Reserve decided in its August 7, 2007 meeting to maintain the Fed funds rate at 5.25 percent.

On August 9, 2007, BNP Paribas, France's largest bank, suspended customer withdrawals, alleging that U.S. housing market conditions prevented proper valuation of these funds' mortgage investments. In September 2007, Northern Rock failed. An immediate loss of confidence permeated European financial markets, as evidenced by the rise from 0.4 percent to 2.4 percent in the TED spread between three-month LIBOR (the rate at which banks borrowed from each other) and U.S. Treasury rates. In the beginning of the fourth quarter, several major financial institutions, including Citicorp, Merrill Lynch, Lehman Brothers, and HSBC, reported large subprime losses. Shortly after, Countrywide Financial, the country's largest subprime lender, was acquired by Bank of America. By year-end, the rate of subprime foreclosures had reached 9 percent, and US$100 billion on U.S. mortgage holdings had been written down by the financial industry globally.

The Federal Reserve began a process of monetary easing (bringing the Fed funds rate from 5.25 percent in August 2007 to 4.25 percent and then 3.5 percent in January 2008). In December 2007, it introduced two emergency lending programs, one for domestic depository banks, the Term Auction Facility (TAF), and a second for foreign central banks. TAF was initially a US$20 billion pool of funds for short term financing, made available to domestic depository institutions to bid for, with a broad range of assets, including mortgage backed securities serving as collateral. In addition, a major foreign exchange swap program, seeking to mitigate the negative effects of a shortage of U.S. dollars to foreign banking sectors, made US$24 billion available to selected central banks.

Bear Stearns

The fifth-largest U.S. investment bank, Bear Stearns, was judged among the best run and best capitalized in the securities industry in 2007 (Boyd, 2007). Established in 1923, the firm was known as aggressive and innovative. It had three businesses: Capital markets, Global Clearing Services, and Wealth Management. Its profit center was its fixed income business, but from 2004 to 2007, it also became the most important underwriter of U.S. mortgage-backed securities. This included "a substantial presence in the subprime mortgage market, providing lines of credit to many subprime mortgage originators including New Century Financial, which collapsed in 2007" (Bergstresser, Rose and Lane 2009: 3). By the end of 2006, "mortgage related securities were the largest part of Bear's balance sheet, representing about 31% of the securities it owned" (ibid: 2).

In order to access the market for securitization transactions, a number of big banks, including Bear Stearns, Morgan Stanley, Deutsche Bank, and Barclays acquired mortgage originators. However, as an investment bank, Bear Stearns, like Lehman, did not have access to the Federal Reserve discount window and depended entirely on the market for "its liquidity and funding" (ibid: 3).

Triggers

According to the findings of the Financial Crisis Inquiry Report 2011, Bear Stearns' collapse was caused by: "exposure to risky mortgage assets, its reliance on short term funding and its high leverage". These practices were provoked and fostered by "weak corporate governance and risk management ... (and) an executive and employee compensation system based largely on return on equity" (ibid: 291), which encouraged rapid high risk, high yield transactions and culture. Although credit rating agencies began to express concerns, these banks were still considered resilient and capable of meeting all their obligations. By February 2008 the losses accelerated at an alarming pace.

Between March 10 and March 18, 2008, despite emergency measures led by the Federal Reserve, Bear Stearns "burned through nearly all of its $18 billion in cash reserves" (Ryback n.d.: 11). On March 11, the Federal Reserve announced a new emergency lending program, the Term Securities Lending Facility (TSLF), allowing non-depositary financial institutions to benefit from liquidity support through up to four-week swaps of mortgage related assets for government bonds. Nevertheless, on March 13, two weeks prior to TSLF becoming operational, Bear Stearns collapsed under the weight of its highly leveraged MBSs and MBS CDOs exposure carried by short-term funding. Over the next few weeks, negotiations with JPMorgan Chase and government officials led to the acquisition of Bear Stearns by JPMorgan Chase for US$1 billion in stock, with the Federal Reserve's exposure to its distressed assets limited to US$29 billion.

These two actions by the Federal Reserve, the establishment of the TSLF program and its liquidity support in the acquisition of Bear Stearns by JPMorgan Chase, provided a short-lived respite to financial markets.

Threat of turmoil: treasury steps in

By late Spring 2008, as market conditions deteriorated, government authorities began to understand that the U.S. financial system was facing an unprecedented crisis that could not simply be resolved by the central bank, as lender of last resort against collateral to solvent banks, and the FDIC on a case-by-case take-over of individual insolvent institutions. Once the solvency of Fannie Mae and Freddy Mac came into question, the financial soundness of the U.S. and the global financial systems was at risk. On July 14, the Bush administration asked Congress for permission for Treasury to inject capital into Fannie Mae and Freddy Mac. In a separate announcement, the Federal Reserve indicated that it would be making short-term loans against acceptable collateral available to GSEs as it had done for banks.

Although privately owned, Fannie Mae and Freddie Mac were still seen by the market as enjoying special U.S. government support. In early summer 2008, the GSEs were once again acquiring and/or guaranteeing over 70 percent of all mortgages originated. On Sunday, September 7, the government seized control of Fannie Mae and Freddie Mac. This decision was triggered by fear of the consequences for the U.S. housing industry if the GSEs were allowed to fail and the disastrous global implications of such an event, given that many financial institutions around the world, including central banks, held trillions of dollars in exposure to these GSEs. A Treasury backed emergency credit line in the amount of US$100 billion was made available to each of the two companies in exchange for convertible preferred stock, earning accrued interest and giving the government *de facto* control of destiny and ownership of the GSEs.

Lehman, failure, market turmoil and the
U.S. government response

On Monday, September 15, markets around the world were faced with two major announcements: Lehman Brothers, one of the most important U.S. investment banks with over US$600 billion in financial liabilities and a high degree of interconnectedness to major depositary financial institutions domestically and internationally, had filed for bankruptcy; and another major Wall Street bank, Merrill Lynch, had been acquired by Bank of America.

Seeking to mitigate the negative consequences of a global credit crunch resulting from a likely collapse of the interbank market, the Federal Reserve announced two measures: a substantial expansion of the scope collateral financial institutions operating in the U.S. – depositary or non-depositary, domestic or foreign – could pledge in exchange for short-term funding; and the formation of a US$70 billion pool (through commitments of US$7 billion tranches by ten of the world's largest financial firms) to be made available to any of these companies in the aftermath of Lehman's failure.

Within a week of the Lehman Brothers' filing for bankruptcy, Goldman Sachs and Morgan Stanley, the last two large surviving independent Wall Street securities houses, decided to convert to bank holding companies, coming under closer scrutiny, but also under the umbrella liquidity protection of the Federal Reserve as lender of last resort to banks against acceptable collateral.

On Tuesday, September 16, government authorities announced that AIG, crippled by margin calls from counterparts on its huge MBS CDS exposure, had been taken into *conservatorship*. Similarly to Fannie Mae and Freddie Mac, an emergency US$85 billion credit line was made available to the company in exchange for convertible preferred accruing interest and giving the U.S. government a *de facto* 80 percent equity interest in the company. The rationale for the government bail-out of this private sector insurer was the risk of collapse for the entire financial system, given the high levels of exposure of many major international financial firms to AIG through AIG Financial Products' CDSs, mortgage-related or not.

On September 16, Reserve Primary Fund, a private money market fund, announced that its shares had broken the buck, meaning that their value had fallen below US$1 as a result of the fund's exposure to Lehman Brothers' commercial paper. This sent a wave of uncertainty throughout the money market industry, causing withdrawals in excess of US$100 billion in less than 48 hours. Treasury, again, was forced to respond, by putting in place the Exchange Stabilization Fund, a US$50 billion insurance program allowing participating funds to pay a modest asset-based premium in exchange for a government backstop guaranteeing investors full redemption at least US$1/share of any balance outstanding on September 19. In addition to this Treasury initiative, the Federal Reserve made available a new credit facility for banks to purchase commercial paper from money market funds, enhancing the liquidity of these funds.

On September 25, Washington Mutual (WaMu), the country's largest saving and loan, and seventh-largest commercial banking franchise, was seized by regulators and promptly acquired by JPMorgan Chase for US$2 billion in stock.

Within days of WaMu's absorption by JPMorgan Chase, Wachovia Bank, the country's fourth-largest commercial banking franchise was also close to collapse. The cause for its impending insolvency was the deterioration in the mortgage portfolio of Golden West, another major private label mortgage lender that it acquired for US$80 billion in stock in 2006. An initial government supported deal with Citibank for US$2 billion was supplanted by a no strings attached US$ 15 billion acquisition of Wachovia by Wells Fargo Bank.

On September 29, the U.S. House of Representatives turned down a proposal by Treasury Secretary Henry Paulson and Federal Reserve Chairman Bernanke – an initial version of the Troubled Assets Relief Program (TARP) – to empower the U.S. Treasury to acquire up to US$700 billion in illiquid mortgage backed securities from financial firms. A massive securities sell-off ensued, causing the S&P to fall 9 percent, its largest drop in over 20 years. A second version of TARP, dividing it in two US$350 billion tranches with disbursements under Congressional supervision, was approved on October 3, giving Treasury the ammunition to push for recapitalization of the entire banking system. The new legislation also raised the FDIC protection to individual depositors from US$100,000 to US$250,000.

On October 3, the recently converted bank holding companies Morgan Stanley and Goldman Sachs obtained voluntary private sector capital infusions, Morgan Stanley from Mitsubishi UFJ (US$9 billion), Goldman Sachs from Berkshire Hathaway (US$5 billion), both in the form of convertible preferred stock. Yet, TARP funds remained unused, as financial institutions resisted selling their troubled assets at the high level of discount necessary. On October 14, the Treasury announced that it would use US$250 billion in TARP funds to inject capital into private sector financial institutions, with US$125 billion to go immediately into the nine largest banks and US$125 billion to be allocated to other financial firms throughout the country.

In late November 2008, the government agreed to buy another US$20 billion of Citicorp's convertible preferred stock and to guarantee US$250 billion of the bank's riskier assets. Conversion of the bank's preferred stock (including the US$ 25 billion from the first round of TARP) gave the government a one-third ownership stake in the company. The first round of divestment would take place in September 2010, when the U.S. Treasury was able to sell to the market approximately one-sixth of its holding, corresponding to a 5 percent equity stake in Citicorp, for US$5.9 billion through a secondary offering led by Morgan Stanley.

In early 2009, Bank of America faltered under the weight of its mortgage backed securities exposure, which included portfolios absorbed as a result of the acquisitions of Countrywide and Merrill Lynch. The government agreed to buy another US$20 billion in Bank of America's preferred stock and to guarantee US$100 billion of risky assets. Bank of America was able to retire its TARP obligations without having to accept dilution of common equity ownership.

The Dodd-Frank Act, approved by Congress in July 2010, lowered the US$ 700 billion ceiling for TARP to US$475 billion. Approximately US$250 billion had been allocated to banks, US$70 billion to AIG, US$60 billion to the automakers Chrysler and GM, and US$30 billion to non-bank financial institutions. Some US$65 billion remained available for possible disbursement in federal programs designed to stimulate mortgage loan modifications, small business financing and consumer lending.

Considering the dramatic consequences that followed the failure of Lehman on September 15, 2008, questions continue to be asked as to whether the bank should have been rescued by the government in the way that AIG and Bear Stearns were.

While this debate may never be settled, three important factors should be mentioned (Swagel 2013):

1. The Federal Reserve did not believe Lehman possessed the necessary legal authority to back the financial assistance needed to prevent a subsequent bankruptcy filing; and unlike the Bear Stearns' rescue where liquidity was provided to support a transaction in which the investment bank had been taken over by a bank holding company, this never materialized for Lehman.
2. The Treasury did not technically have access to TARP funds to either attempt to rescue Lehman directly or guarantee its operations for the private foreign acquirer still considering a transaction (Barclays Bank, United Kingdom).
3. The Federal Reserve and Treasury saw the Lehman situation not as a lack of liquidity, but of clear insolvency, and distinct from liquidity support for the JPMorgan acquisition of Bear Stearns or the AIG rescue (an ownership takeover by the government, backed by sound operating assets of one of the world's largest insurers).

The TARP amount of US$475 billion does not include capital infusions by Treasury in the GSEs, Fannie Mae and Freddie Mac (approximately US$250 billion). Also, it does not take into account transaction specific credit facilities put together by the Federal Reserve for liquidity support of JPMorgan Chase, upon its acquisition of Bear Stearns in March 2008, and to AIG Financial Products. These facilities totaled approximately US$70 billion.

In financial terms, the U.S. subprime meltdown crisis required the Treasury to put over US$700 billion in capital at risk (some 5 percent of GDP) to save the financial system. It forced the Federal Reserve, as short-term lender of last resort (against collateral), to substantially expand its credit exposure to the financial sector, more than doubling its balance sheet between mid 2007 and mid 2009, from US$903 billion on August 8, 2007 to US$2,041 billion on July 29, 2009. It provoked a severe economic recession, with serious fiscal and monetary implications.

As of 2013, government funds allocated to rescue the financial system have been fully recovered. The 2009 American Recovery and Investment Act (US$787 billion in tax cuts and new government spending), as well as the continued extraordinary monetary easing by the Federal Reserve through 2013, helped mitigate the longest period of high rates of unemployment in the U.S. economy since the Great Depression.

In line with the Basel III accord, which sets the minimum standards for bank regulation for national jurisdictions (see Chapter 6), much tighter minimum capital, minimum liquidity, maximum leverage, and significantly more demanding guidelines for the reporting of risk exposures and internal governance procedures have been imposed on banks globally (particularly those identified as systemically important financial institutions (SIFIs). In addition, similarly to provisions established under Title II of the Dodd-Frank Act in the United States, legislation empowering bank regulators to preemptively intervene in troubled financial institutions to ensure orderly liquidation at no cost to taxpayers are in the process of being implemented by national jurisdictions around the world (see Chapter 6).

Private sector implications

The subprime meltdown crisis had important consequences for the structure of the U.S. banking industry. According to the FDIC, as of year-end 2011 there were 6,290 commercial banks and 1,044 savings institutions in operation in the U.S., down from 8,315 commercial banks and 1,589 savings institutions in 2000. The number of failed institutions – an average of five per annum between 2000 and 2004, zero in 2005 and 2006, and three in 2007 – reached 25 in 2008, 140 in 2009, 157 in 2010, and 92 in 2011. Also, at year-end 2011, 772 banks remained as problem financial institutions, compared to 94 in 2000.[4]

The crisis not only decimated the largest mortgage lenders but also fundamentally altered the structure of the U.S. investment banking sector: Bear Stearns and Merrill Lynch were acquired by JPMorgan Chase and Bank of America; Lehman Brothers, was placed in liquidation, subsequently having its Western and Asian corporate finance divisions purchased by Barclays (United Kingdom) and Nomura Securities (Japan); and Goldman Sachs and Morgan Stanley remain as primarily investment banking franchises, but voluntarily converted into bank holding companies.

Iceland and Ireland: at the intersection of banking and sovereign debt financial crises

Iceland

Iceland, a tiny island nation of almost 326,000 inhabitants with a parliamentary system and strong environmental policies joined the European Free Trade Area (EFTA) in 1994, but remained outside of the European Union and Eurozone.

The economy, dependent on geothermal energy sources and fishing, was largely state-owned, with electricity, telecommunications, and the banking sectors all under state control. As with its wealthier Nordic neighbors, competitiveness, deregulation, and liberalization in the 1980s and 1990s, encouraged rapid privatization and entry into global markets. Iceland's largest bank, Landsbanki, assumed the functions of the central bank: "In 1986, the Act on Commercial Banks and Savings Banks granted banks the right to set deposit and lending rates. The financial markets began to deepen with the share of loans rising relative to GDP" as money market and FOREX transactions increased (Porter and Ketels, 2009). In 1987, with the decline in the profitability of the fishing sector, Iceland (like Ireland later) provided tax incentives to encourage foreign investment, and "[c]apital flows were fully liberalized starting with long term flows in 1994 and then short term flows in 1995" (ibid). In this deregulated environment, the three main banks dramatically increased their balance sheets, but the economy overheated with currency volatility and double digit inflation. By 2004, "private sector banks started to compete aggressively with the state-owned Housing Finance Fund by introducing lower mortgage rates" (ibid, p.5). In 2006, the currency came under pressure as current account deficit and foreign debt accounted for about 120 percent of gross domestic product (GDP). By 2007, the financial sector had become the largest sector of the economy. The three large banking groups, Glitnir – created from a consolidation of small, previously state-run banks, Kaupthing Bank, the largest group specialized in SMEs, and formerly state-owned Landsbanki, made acquisitions in the United Kingdom and the Netherlands. In 2007, "the banking sector had significantly increased its level of foreign debt from 6% in 1995 to 138% of GDP in 2004" (Porter and Ketels, 2009: 8). Total assets of the three banks rose to more than $168bn. Although the economy appeared to be booming, inward FDI remained low and domestic savings rates were falling.

In September 2008, foreign investment suddenly dried up and investors demanded withdrawal of krona denominated funds and securities from the overheated Icelandic Stock Exchange and banks. The currency depreciated, and within a few weeks Icelandic banks defaulted. At the time of the default, the gross external liabilities of the banking giants extended to 900 percent of Iceland's GDP (Spruk 2010).

In October 2008, the three banks were declared insolvent and nationalized, their boards and senior management fired and replaced. The leadership of Kaupthing and the Chief Executive Officer (CEO) of Glitnir were indicted on criminal charges of stock manipulation, misuse of bank funds, and corruption. After three years of litigation seeking to protect taxpayers from foreign liabilities incurred by UK and Dutch depositors, Glitnir repaid its creditors in full, including 500 British councils and charities. In March 2013, Iceland repaid its IMF loan of US$443 million. Under new management, the banks returned to profitability, focusing on domestic lending and investment in geothermal energy, green technology, and local industries. Outside of the EU and Eurozone, Iceland was able to set out its own regulatory decisions, devalue its currency, and meet the IMF criteria.

Ireland

The Irish economic crisis of 2008–2013 was triggered by a banking crisis, specifically the collapse of the country's largest bank, Anglo Irish, resulting from a confluence of asset bubbles, internal governance failures, and poor regulatory oversight. The crisis in Ireland required the resolution of both the domestic banking crisis and the sovereign debt crisis, with bailouts provided under the aegis of the troika of the European Union, IMF and European Central Bank. According to the Commission of Investigation Report, April 2011, the banking crisis was not instigated by complex products, such as subprime mortgage instruments or derivatives, but by a "plain vanilla property bubble compounded by exceptional concentration of lending for purposes related to property and notably commercial property" (Regling and Watson, 2010). Since the 1970s, six banks had dominated the Irish banking sector, focused on local lending and property loans: Bank of Ireland, Allied Irish Bank, Anglo Irish Bank, Irish Nationwide Building Society, Irish Life and Permanent, and Educational Building Society. Ireland, historically afflicted by famine, dispossession, poverty, and civil strife, placed heavy emphasis on land ownership which accounted for the largest percentage of loans. An impoverished rural economy, Ireland joined the European Community (EC) in 1973 to benefit from agricultural subsidies and to break its economic dependency on the United Kingdom. The Irish economy benefitted from a young, skilled, English speaking labor force, and high levels of foreign direct investment flowed in, especially from the United States. An attractive tax regime with low rates of corporate tax added to the attractiveness of Ireland as an investment location. By 1989, Ireland had become a global back office service provider for New York banks and financial institutions. Between 1994 and 2008, dubbed the Celtic Tiger, Ireland saw massive foreign capital inflows as high tech, pharmaceutical firms, and banks established operations there. The economy grew by 6 percent annually between 1997 and 2007. Meeting all the membership criteria, Ireland joined the Eurozone on its launch in 1999. Irish banks looked for wholesale short-term borrowing in the Eurozone, while increasing lending to the construction sector. In 1999, the Financial Services Authority was established to oversee general stability, but without primary responsibility for evaluating problems. An initiative to introduce a corporate governance code for credit institutions and insurance by the Central Bank in 2005 was diluted in 2007, as banks became largely self-regulating.

In this highly competitive environment, Anglo Irish aggressively pursued loans in domestic and EU markets as profits soared, and the construction sector accounted for 20 percent of GNP by 2006. Bank of Ireland and Allied Irish, wanting to emulate Anglo's success, increased their loan books.

Anglo Irish: instigator and culprit

Established in Dublin in 1964, when the three main banking groups (Bank of Ireland, Allied Irish, and Ulster Bank) were separated by geographic and political allegiances, Anglo Irish specialized in bridging loans on mortgages until 1982.

Sean Fitzpatrick,[5] CEO since 1979, focused on mid-size business mortgages. However, by the late 1980s he began to push for more aggressive expansion, merging with City of Dublin Bank, and acquiring Irish Bank of Commerce in 1988, as he sought to expand the U.K. loan book. Within a decade, Anglo Irish had a presence in Austria with acquisition of Royal Trust Bank and Crédit Lyonnais Austria in 1998. He set up a private banking division, allowing the bank to take on equity stakes in property development projects. There began to be greater collusion between government regulators, banking officials, and Anglo Irish clients. A weak board of directors was overwhelmed by Sean Fitzpatrick's directives calling for less regulation in 2003. By 2005, the credit committee was often bypassed in loan-making decisions, and loans were granted without due diligence or assessment of the collateral. When property prices peaked in 2006, demand fell. With the start of the global credit crunch in mid 2007, lending to households and non-financial companies reached 200 percent of GDP. In March 2008, in the wake of the collapse of Bear Stearns, a Merrill Lynch report in London mentioned Anglo's high risk portfolio. After the collapse of Lehman and the fear of contagion throughout the EU banking sector, the Irish coalition Government along with all other Eurozone countries gave blanket guarantee to all depositors and bond holders of the six main domestic banks including Anglo Irish. Anglo Irish officially declared a shortfall of €7 billion. At the trial of Sean Fitzpatrick, it was revealed that the number had been plucked from thin air, and the total of non-performing loans and bets on property was closer to €30 billion. Subsequent criminal investigations revealed that, in 2007, one of Anglo Irish's largest shareholders, Sean Quinn, owned a stake in the bank through derivative transactions. Once his stake began to fall in mid 2007, in order to avoid liquidating his position all at once, the bank lent him funds to meet his margin calls until the entire scheme collapsed in 2009. Sean Fitzpatrick and board members amassed massive loans from the bank to the amount of €155 million, which were hidden from the official audit and regulators. Once all accumulated losses were revealed, the amount rose to €62 billion (Ahearne 2011), half of this derived from Anglo Irish Bank. The bank was nationalized in December 2008. Despite €4 billion in fresh capital in December 2009, Anglo's share price fell 98 percent when it was delisted and nationalized.

The resolution of Anglo Irish involved moving the majority of non-performing loans into the public National Asset Management Agency (NAMA). All banks were nationalized and the Irish taxpayers were forced to assume a crushing debt burden. Ireland required IMF/EU loans in November 2010, as residential prices fell 47 percent. The EU Commission allowed recapitalization in 2010, with the real losses estimated at €17.7 billion in March 2011.

The bailout of Irish banks cost the government €29 billion, close to 20 percent of Irish GDP. With unemployment at 14 percent, pension funds decimated, the entire system collapsed under the weight of debts totaling €70 billion. In July 2011, Anglo Irish ceased to exist. It was merged with Irish Nationwide Building Society, renamed the Irish Bank Resolution Corporation and is to be wound down in 10 years.

Summary

Bank failures and the endemic repercussions in domestic and regional economies illustrate the warning issued in the BIS Report 2001: "The expansion of credit is an essential ingredient in the build-up of imbalances in the financial system and in any concomitant excessive accumulation or misallocation of real capital" (BIS 2001: 139).

Each of the cases examined in this chapter demonstrates how expansive credit allocation, a lack of sufficient and rigorous internal and external supervision, controls, and legal restrictions, government-banking, industrial or real estate sector collusion, and short term high yield oriented policies have contributed to institutional failures.

Notes

1. Morgan established a system issuing bonds, which the banks in the syndicate would turn over to the Clearing House, which would then pay for them by issuing certificates credited to the city's account at First National and National City banks, keeping the banks afloat until the Treasury stepped in and issued bonds and certificates to back the notes.
2. Released in 1999, he regained notoriety in 2008 as a paid expert on the Société Générale copycat scandal.
3. In comparison, Germany's exposure was US$29 billion, and U.S. exposure was US$21.5 billion. See Chapter 5 on the impact of sovereign debt exposure.
4. None of the major private sector independent mortgage lenders from the early 2000s remain. Countrywide and Washington Mutual were acquired by Bank of America and JPMorgan Chase, respectively. Golden West, the cause of Wachovia Bank's failure, was, with Wachovia, absorbed by Wells Fargo Bank. IndyMac, initially taken over by the FDIC and later sold, was stripped of a huge portion of its toxic balance sheet and sold to a private equity investor. And the GSEs, Fannie Mae and Freddy Mac, were returned in full to government ownership.
5. Following the crisis, Sean Fitzpatrick was indicted for fraud.

5   Sovereign debt crises and the ramifications for international banking

Introduction

History shows that sovereign debt crises can both cause systemic domestic banking crises[1] and result from large scale bank failures:[2] "A high incidence of global banking crises has historically been associated with a high incidence of sovereign defaults on external debt" (Reinhart and Rogoff 2009: 73). Domestic banking crises, while disruptive to national or regional economies, once contained,[3] can avoid the danger of markets pricing in a sovereign default. Banking crises can also produce "a 'sudden stop' of lending to countries at the periphery", that is, emerging economies (idem: 74).

Since 1815, "most sovereign defaults have occurred because a defaulting government's past policies left it ill prepared to face an unexpected turn of events (in other words, a shock). War, regime change, other forms of political instability and sharp deterioration in terms of trade are examples of shocks" (Standard and Poor's, 2011: 6).

From Bretton Woods and the creation of the International Monetary Fund (IMF) in 1944 (see Chapter 1), until the 1970s, the assumption was that sovereign states could renegotiate their loans, receive temporary external emergency support and, therefore, avoid default. Walter Wriston, the late Chief Executive Officer (CEO) of Citibank, "wrote that countries don't go broke, as any country, however badly off it may be will own more than it owes. Inevitably the joke in financial circles became: Countries don't go broke, just the banks that lend to them" (Rhodes 2011: 133).[4]

In 2005, following Argentina's 2001 unilateral default on foreign debt owed to both private sector and multilateral agencies, the Executive Board of the IMF conducted a review of sovereign debt restructurings in order to understand the determinants of and prospects for regaining access to markets following a crisis. In February 2012, Greece successfully launched the largest sovereign debt restructuring in history (€205 billion). However, as of 2013, ongoing litigation against Argentina calls into question the legal robustness of sovereign debt restructurings. In April 2013, an examination by the IMF Executive Board concluded that:

(i)   sovereign debt restructurings are often too little, too late, with delays caused by the difficulty in introducing early resolution and fear of contagion;
(ii) creditor participation in recent preemptive (that is, prior to default) debt restructurings, the current market-based approach, has not proven to be sufficiently robust to overcome collective action problems, as evidenced by the ongoing Argentine litigation;
(iii) the changing composition of official lending calls for a clearer framework for official sector involvement; and
(iv) since lending in arrears to the country emerging from a sovereign debt crisis remains the most promising way for it to regain market access post-default, consideration should be given to extending the lending in arrears policy to official arrears. (IMF, 2013).

Progress on these fronts should further reinforce the IMF's ability to act preemptively with effectiveness in sovereign debt restructuring situations. Also important for this goal would be the successful completion of the doubling of its equity capital to US$720 billion, announced by the Executive Board in 2010, but as of mid 2013 still pending formal Congressional approval in the United States, its largest quota holder.

The correlation between fiscal deterioration, currency crises, and cross-border sovereign defaults from the Middle Ages to the present day has been well established by Reinhart and Rogoff (2009). Throughout the nineteenth century, the promise of vast riches incited waves of investment in Latin America, resulting in booms and busts in fragile political systems and economies. In the following section, we consider a number of sovereign debt crises in a range of emerging economies from the 1980s to present. We examine the causes of each crisis and the course of action adopted in response.

The 1980s Latin American debt crises

The 1980s Latin American debt crisis was the first sovereign debt crisis to challenge the orderly resolution framework conceived under the 1944 Bretton Woods Conference, which heralded the establishment of the IMF. It also set the stage for Basel I, the first international accord on bank regulation reached in 1988, as detailed in Chapter 6.

Mexico 1982 and Basel I

Mexico's sovereign default in 1982 was followed by similar outcomes throughout the region. These multiple sovereign debt crises would only begin to be fully resolved in July 1989 when Mexico and its foreign creditors finally reached a restructuring agreement – the first Brady Plan – imposing a 35 percent reduction in the principal due to private foreign creditors.

Mexico faced a further sovereign debt crisis in late 1994 to early 1995, when a delicate process of political transition caused an abrupt interruption in foreign capital inflows. This currency crisis (in some ways similar to Turkey in 2001) was resolved without losses being imposed on foreign creditors of Mexican sovereign debt, through the establishment of a new IMF agreement for Mexico that superseded the terms and conditions of the agreement established in 1989. It did, however, cause a major restructuring of the Mexican banking industry (see Chapter 8).

The build-up to the crisis: 1974 to 1982

Characterized by modest levels of domestic savings, Latin American economies had historically depended on foreign capital inflows to support growth. However, what had, over the course of decades, been a quite thorough credit assessment process by banks involved in cross-border hard currency lending, particularly of non-trade-related facilities, suddenly became in the mid 1970s a seemingly inexhaustible outpouring of general purpose medium-term credit availability.

As a result of the Organization of the Petroleum Exporting Countries' (OPEC) first oil embargo in late 1973, the price of a barrel of oil more than tripled in 1974, from US$3 to US$10. This led to a major wave of surplus petrodollars being deposited with the London branches of money center banks.

Attracted by the significantly higher yields obtainable from Latin American borrowers than from their traditional Organisation for Economic Co-operation and Development (OECD) corporate borrowers – and encouraged also by an environment of relative political stability and economic growth prevailing in Latin America – these banks began to commit larger and larger shares of their balance sheets to the region.

For major oil importing countries such as Brazil and Chile, the easy access to financing at relatively low interest rates provided much needed respite from the immediate and substantial trade deficits resulting from the oil price hike. Additionally, it allowed for continued and increased borrowings by governments to cover ongoing expenditures. For oil exporting countries such as Mexico and Venezuela, the windfall from oil revenues combined with the easy money from the petrodollar recycling to generate both government and corporate private sector spending and borrowing sprees.

A second tripling of oil prices in 1979 (from US$12 to US$36 per barrel, as a result of the Iran–Iraq war), while further escalating the amount of surplus petrodollars available for recycling in the Eurodollar market, had different effects across the region. For oil importing countries, it triggered the beginning of a more serious process of belt tightening. For oil exporting countries, it led to a second – albeit short lived – spending bonanza.

Adding to the danger of the massive borrowings in foreign exchange was the nature of the medium-term debt being contracted, almost exclusively floating rate based (typically 6-month LIBOR). When the U.S. Federal Reserve – seeking to curb inflationary pressures arising from the second oil price spike – decided in 1979 to raise its federal funds target rate from 7 percent to 13 percent, the spill-over to the Eurodollar market was immediate. The U.S. federal funds rate – and, consequently, also the 6-month LIBOR – would continue to increase, peaking at almost 20 percent in 1982.

By year-end 1982, when oil prices finally began to decrease, Mexico's foreign debt had reached US$82 billion (almost 60 percent of gross domestic product (GDP)). For Latin American as a whole, foreign debt had reached over US$390 billion, over 50 percent of which (US$220 billion) was owed to commercial banks.

Mexican default and struggling through: 1982 to 1988

On September 1, 1982 the Mexican government announced the nationalization of its domestic banking system, crippled by loan losses arising from the economic recession and major asset-liability mismatches resulting from borrowing in U.S. dollars to lend in Mexican pesos.

Five days later, on September 6, as massive capital flight persisted in spite of the 70 percent peso devaluation over the course of that year, the Mexican government declared it was suspending principal repayments on its foreign debt. Too much debt at peak interest costs combined with the decline in the price of its major export commodity to push the largest Latin American economy into default. In similar predicaments, other countries in the region decided to follow Mexico's example, suspending principal repayments.

Nevertheless, at this stage, OECD governments, multilateral agencies, and banks acknowledged the crisis as purely a major liquidity, rather than solvency, problem. Between 1982 and 1984, US$23.5 billion in new money and US$41 billion in restructured debt (at higher fees and spreads) were arranged by private sector banks.

By mid 1985, it had become clear that much stronger economic growth was necessary for Latin American countries to meet their debt service obligations. Important domestic policy initiatives, such as monetary tightening and reduced government expenditures to curb inflationary pressures, and more realistic exchange rate policies, such as mini-devaluation type regimes to ensure international competitiveness, combined with increased support from multilateral agencies to allow for some temporary respite. Yet, it was too little too late. In February 1987, Brazil declared a moratorium on interest payments to commercial banks. Shortly thereafter, banks began to announce very substantial increases in reserves against losses on their Latin American exposure, including increases of up to 25 percent for Citibank and 54 percent for Bank of Boston.

The seeds had been sown for a period of voluntary market-based debt reduction mechanisms. Some of these initiatives, such as the debt-equity swaps largely utilized in Chile, Mexico, Brazil, and Argentina, not only allowed for the retirement of a few billion dollars in debt but, perhaps more importantly, began to provide secondary market prices for the different countries' sovereign debt, an important ingredient to the multiple party negotiations that were to follow.

Crisis resolution: the Brady plan

In early 1989, the incoming U.S. administration presented the core elements of its plan to deal with the decade-long sovereign debt crisis assailing Latin America: a voluntary exchange by banks of their existing Latin American exposures for new credit enhanced facilities with a significant discount on principal, this exchange taking place simultaneously with country-specific economic reforms agreed with – and subject to close supervision by – the IMF.

Named after Nicholas Brady, the U.S. Treasury Secretary, the first Latin American *Brady Plan* for Mexico was finally announced in early July 1989, after several months of intense negotiations involving not only the banks (represented by a bank advisory committee led by William Rhodes of Citibank) and the Mexican Government, but also U.S. Government officials and representatives of the multilateral agencies.

The Mexican Brady Plan offered creditors the following menu of choices:

(i)   a 30 year *discount bond* with a 35 percent reduction in principal and market interest rates, the principal collateralized by a zero coupon U.S. Treasury bond purchased by Mexico, in addition to an 18-month guarantee of interest payments; and/or

(ii) a 30 year *par bond* (no principal reduction) with the same collateral as the *discount bond*, with a fixed interest rate of 6.25 percent per annum (as compared to market rates of 10 percent); and/or

(iii) *new money* commitment at market rates of 25 percent of total exposure, half of which to be disbursed in the first year, the remainder over the following two years.

As it turned out, 90 percent of total commercial bank exposure was swapped for Brady bonds: 49 percent for discount bonds and 41 percent for par bonds. Mexico's foreign bank debt had been reduced by 35 percent and transformed from large individual bank loans and/or syndicated facilities into marketable securities.

By the mid 1990s, eleven Latin American countries had completed their sovereign debt restructurings under the Brady Plan, issuing over US$200 billion in bonds with US$70 billion in debt reduction being absorbed by international banks.

Asian currency crisis, 1997

The Asian crisis of the late 1990s followed the general pattern of previous sovereign debt crises: great optimism by lenders and borrowers, in this case by the mid 1990s, convinced of the "East Asian miracle that was seen as capable of delivering rapid economic growth over an extended period"; significant foreign capital inflows; rapid increases in asset prices, especially in the real estate sector; and a reversal of all the above as economic growth slows down and corporate and financial balance sheets begin to deteriorate (Collyns and Senhadji, 2002: 3).

The build-up to the crisis: 1991–7

Annual GDP growth in the ASEAN-5 (Indonesia, Malaysia, Philippines, Singapore, and Thailand) averaged approximately 8 percent in the 1990s through 1996.

Asian countries also accounted for close to half of total foreign capital inflows to developing countries in 1996. As a result of the wave of optimism that fueled increasing foreign capital inflows and bank lending, asset prices rose substantially between 1991 and 1997 across the East Asian economies. Stock markets generally peaked around 1997, at an average 165 percent higher than at the beginning of the decade, and property prices, while harder to ascertain with precision due to limited information, followed this path, but with great variation among different countries, with peaks in 1993 for Thailand, 1996 for Singapore, 1997 for Hong Kong and Malaysia, and less pronounced property price swings in Indonesia, Korea, and the Philippines (idem).

As export volumes from the Asian tigers began to weaken in 1996, as a result of increased competition from China, Vietnam, and other emerging economies) and trade surpluses began to deteriorate as a result of oil price increases, economic growth began to slow down and asset prices began to falter. Non-performing loans began to increase, particularly in those countries where banks' relative exposure to the commercial real estate market was greater.

Transparency and corporate governance failures in lending practices further exacerbated the potential for a credit rupture, as illustrated by the situation in Korea, where bank lending with explicit government blessing to chaebols, large industrial conglomerates perceived as fundamental to the country's economic growth and global competitiveness and, as such, too big to fail, was widespread.

Trigger

The Asian sovereign debt crisis of 1997–8 was triggered by a speculative attack on the Thai baht in June 1997 that quickly spread throughout the region. Market perception of widespread and severe balance of payments vulnerabilities made initial domestic interest rate hikes – the classic first line of defense against potentially large currency devaluations – ineffective. For banks, losses resulting from credit exposure to over-leveraged corporate balance sheets were further aggravated by serious currency mismatches on their own balance sheets.

As in pre-debt crisis Latin America, international banks had lent imprudently in East Asia. However, this time the international banks most exposed to cross-border credit risk in East Asia were not American. Japanese banks were by far the largest creditors, with US$114.8 billion outstanding at year-end 1997, followed by German banks (US$48.6 billion), French banks (US$42.8 billion), and British banks (US$32.2 billion) (Hughes and MacDonald, 2002: 387).

Resolution

The sovereign debt restructuring programs the IMF supported in the different countries all called for monetary tightening, to restore confidence in the currency and stabilize foreign capital flows, and fiscal tightening, to regain creditworthiness while taking into consideration the cost of cleaning up the financial system, for some countries estimated to reach 15 percent of GDP (Fisher, 1998).

In Thailand, for example, the government was forced to shut down 59 of 90 financial institutions, and nationalized four banks. Korea's was the domestic financial system most affected by the crisis, shrinking from 33 banks and over 2,000 non-bank financial companies in 1997, to 10 banks and 400 non-bank financial institutions in 2000.

Between August and December 1997, three of the ASEAN-5 countries signed stand-by credit support agreements with the IMF: Thailand, for US$3.9 billion, Indonesia for US$9.8 billion, and Korea for US$21 billion. The Philippines reached its stand-by credit support agreement in the amount of US$1.9 billion with the IMF in March 1998. Malaysia, which enjoyed stronger underlying fundamentals (including a better regulated and capitalized financial system), declined IMF support. It chose to fix its exchange rate at RM3.80 per US dollar (10 percent above the level at which it traded immediately prior to the announcement), and simultaneously imposed strict controls on capital accounts.

As shown above, not one sovereign debt default – or, for that matter, any haircut on sovereign debt owed to private sector lenders – resulted from the Asian crisis. However, the 1997 Asian crisis brought to the forefront matters of insufficient disclosure and poor internal corporate governance practices that had been, until then, neglected by bank regulators. These matters were to be specifically addressed by the 1998 Basel II Accord (see Chapter 6).

Russia: sovereign debt crisis and global interconnectivity, 1998

Post-World War II, banking relations between the West and the Soviet Union were politically motivated, as the United States and Western Europe sought to make investment inroads as a means of opening closed markets across the Soviet Union. The Soviet leadership veered away from strict isolationism in the 1950s to détente in the early 1970s. The Soviet Union maintained strict supervision over regional bank lending and investment. Foreign currency and trade transactions went through London, but as U.S. leaders saw economic liberalization as a means to penetrate the Soviet bloc, American banks were encouraged to lend to Central and Eastern European countries. Under this principle, Chase Manhattan bank (United States), led by David Rockefeller, and Crédit Lyonnais (France) were allowed to have representative offices in Moscow. These transactions were considered safe under the assumption that "Moscow would not allow any COMECON member to default or even reschedule for economic, political and image reasons" (quoted in Portes, 1977).

Following the collapse of the Soviet Union in 1991, inward FDI flows steadily increased between 1994 and 2007, from zero to approximately 4.5 percent of GDP. However, portfolio equity investment net inflows had a rockier trajectory, reaching a peak of 1 percent in 2002, followed by a sharp downturn in 2004 to 2005, before reaching almost 2 percent in 2007 (Werker et al. 2011).

As the government set about selling and privatizing state assets from 1991 to 1994, including oil, gas, mineral, and commodity holdings, these rapid conversions occurred in a volatile environment plagued by an inability to conduct due diligence, a lack of regulatory and legal safeguards, and vast corruption. In 1995, the entire Russian stock market "was valued at a little over $15bn – less than a third of the prevailing market capitalization of Walmart" (World Bank 2010). Between 1993 and 1997, the central bank was plagued by turnover and weak leadership.

In 1993, hyperinflation reached 874 percent, and was coupled with massive capital flight. By 1994, although the central bank had stabilized and attempted to impose reforms, confidence in banks was very limited. Russia lacked a commercial code, regulatory regime, bankruptcy recourse mechanisms, and deposit insurance mechanisms.

Following five years of chaotic and uneven central bank leadership and monetary policy, 1996 seemed to herald a turnaround in the country's situation, with the extension of World Bank loans and potential agreements for IMF loans. Inflation fell from 131 percent in 1995, to 22 percent in 1996, and 11 percent in 1997. There was a surge in inward FDI and Russia's credit rating improved. Nevertheless, tax collection was riddled with inefficiencies and corruption, massive capital flight continued, and a large proportion of domestic industry relied on barter for exchange (Chiodo and Owyang, 2002). Dependent on commodity and oil prices, the Russian economy was severely affected by the Asian crisis in 1997, and the subsequent worldwide drop in oil and commodity prices. The Central Bank "defends the ruble, losing nearly $6 billion" (idem: 10). By August 1998, as banks collapsed, Sberbank held 85 percent of all household deposits, after taking over the deposits of six large banks. 1998 saw "a decrease in real output of 4.9 percent" (ibid).

On August 13, 1998, annual yields on ruble denominated bonds rose to more than 200 percent. Stocks lost more than 75 percent of their value between January and August, 1998. On August 17, the Russian Government announced a devaluation of the ruble, with a widening of parity bands to the US$ from 5.2–7.3 to 6–9.5. The Kremlin declared a 90-day moratorium on payments by commercial banks to foreign debtors. On September 2, 1998, the ruble was allowed to float, and within three weeks, it had lost two-thirds of its value. Inflation, down to 27 percent in 1998, began to rise rapidly (Rabobank 2013). By November 20, 1998, the country could no longer honor its commitments.

The Russian economy began to improve in 1999, with growth of 6.4 percent, the result of a global increase in oil prices. In July 1999, the IMF provided a US$4.5 relief package. Inflation steadily decreased from a high of 85 percent to 21 percent by 2000.

Upon becoming President on December 31, 1999, Vladimir Putin initiated a series of strong reforms geared toward bringing back foreign investors. He promised to curb the power of the oligarchs who had stripped assets from state owned companies for personal enrichment, to establish rule of law, and to clarify and impose a strict tax regime, including a flat 13 percent income tax rate and a reduced tax on profits. Putin forced a change of management at Gazprom, Russia's largest and most powerful privatized gas and oil conglomerate. The major banks were renationalized and Sberbank went from near default on bad gas and oil lease loans in 1998 to being the largest bank in Russia, with 48 percent of domestic retail deposits and 33 percent of domestic loans. Most of the reforms were more cosmetic than substantive, however, as Russia continued to be fraught with endemic corruption and collusion between the government and industrial sectors.

Between 2000 and 2005, the economy stabilized, benefitting from rising oil and gas prices and EU dependency on Russia for energy supplies. Between 2002 and 2007, foreign banks were allowed to slowly enter the Russian market, led by Citibank, HSBC, Société Générale, Unicredit, Raiffeisen Bank, and Goldman Sachs.

The impact of the Russian sovereign debt crisis: the first U.S. hedge fund failure

Long Term Capital Management (LTCM), a hedge fund established by Nobel laureate economists, Robert Merton and Myron Sholes, and led by former-Salomon trader, John Meriwether, based its success on sophisticated mathematical models, formulated on the belief that risk could be quantified, that markets were inherently efficient, and that liquidity would always be available. LTCM worked under the premise that their mathematical models captured market irrationality and that extreme market shifts were infinitesimal, and "(f)rom 1995-1997, LTCM had an annual average return of 33.7% after fees" (Connor and Woo, 2003: 10).

Oblivious to the political reality and the irrationality of currency fluctuations in poorly governed fledgling democracies in Asia and Russia, LTCM specialized in high-risk arbitrage deals in U.S, Japanese, and European bonds. Leveraged to banks for US$120 million, and carrying US$1.25 trillion in financial derivatives and other exotic instruments, it was caught off guard by the Russian default, the "'perfect storm'– everything went wrong at once. Interest rates moved the wrong way, stocks and bond prices that were supposed to converge diverged, and liquidity dried up in some crucial markets" (Coy et al., 1998). Once Russia devalued the ruble in mid August 1998, defaulting on Treasury bills, LTCM lost US$553 million within four days, and by the end of August the amount reached US$1.9 billion in assets and 45 percent of their capital.

Resolution

Concerned that "[i]f the fund were forced into a sudden and disorderly liquidation, markets around the globe would be disrupted" regulatory authorities in the United States determined that the only solution to the LTCM crisis was a private sector solution (Eichengreen and Mathieson 1999). Under the auspices of the Federal Reserve, the New York Federal Reserve, under William McDonough, repeated the Barings (1890) and JPMorgan (1907) scenario, bringing together JP Morgan, Merrill, Morgan Stanley, Goldman, Salomon Smith Barney, Bankers Trust, Chase, Lehman, Credit Suisse, Deutsche, Barclays Capital, UBS, Société Générale, and Paribas to form a consortium creating a bailout package of US$3.6 billion.

LTCM's inability to integrate geopolitical factors into its risk assessment, disregard of the potential ramifications if the models failed, and hubris in trying to corral market volatility, should have served as a warning. By September 1998, LTCM had US$100 billion in assets, largely borrowed, and declining in value. It also had thousands of derivative contracts with more than US$1 trillion in exposure. If LTCM had been allowed to fail, the derivative contracts held by major banks would have defaulted. LTCM should have been a lesson in the danger of overleveraging and hedging on transactions dependent on externalities as well as mathematical models. However, LTCM was perceived as an individual case, not as part of a larger pattern or as a warning to future hedge funds.

Argentina 2002: a still unresolved sovereign default

In January 2002, President Duhalde announced a moratorium on all Argentina's sovereign debt, including monies due to the IMF, the World Bank, and the Paris Club. This sovereign default imposed losses in excess of 75 percent of principal on private foreign creditors. In July 2014, a U.S. court ruled that Argentina must repay those hedge fund debt holders who had rejected the previous debt restructuring, in effect bringing about a second default. As of end-August 2014, this remains unresolved. The lessons learned by all, sovereign governments, the IMF and other multilateral agencies, and private sector investors, helped shape the handling of Greece's sovereign debt crisis in 2010.

The build-up to the crisis

Argentina emerged from the 1980s Latin American debt crisis facing a problem common to most of its neighboring countries: the destabilizing effects of inflation. Its response to this challenge was to attempt a silver bullet, a constitutional commitment to a 1:1 fixed exchange rate between the Argentine peso and the US dollar. In line with the Convertibility Law, approved by the Argentine Congress in late 1991, the Argentine Treasury was obliged to guarantee, in full and at any time, the exchange of one Argentine peso for one US dollar.

Market perception of the Government's commitment to the fiscal discipline necessary to sustain the newly-imposed fixed exchange rate regime led to its almost immediate success: the inflation rate dropped from over 2,000 percent in 1991 to 13 percent in 1992, and 1 percent in 1998; and GDP growth exceeded 5 percent per annum throughout this period, 1995 excepted (as a result of the effects of the 1995 Tequila Crisis, felt throughout Latin America).

Important vulnerabilities had, however, begun to build with the deterioration in Argentina's balance of trade and public finances. On the external front, the fixed exchange rate caused the costs of imports and of foreign borrowings to drop, leading to expansion of both trade deficit and foreign indebtedness. On the fiscal side, the Argentine Government maintained the federal fiscal deficit between 1.5 percent and 2 percent of GDP, but failed to capture substantial fiscal excesses in the provinces, a politically contingent liability that materialized as the crisis erupted. By year-end 1998, federal public sector debt remained at 50 percent of GDP, but external vulnerabilities had mounted, with Argentina's foreign debt-to-exports ratio reaching 450 percent. Moreover, declining global competitiveness had made Argentina's exports highly dependent on its large MERCOSUR neighboring partner, Brazil.

Trigger and collapse

Two major interconnected external events finally triggered the collapse of the fixed exchange rate regime in Argentina: the 1998 Russian crisis, which caused capital flight from emerging economies globally, and the almost 100 percent devaluation of the Brazilian Real between January and March 1999, in large part due to the deterioration in Brazil's external accounts following the 1997 Asian and the 1998 Russian crises.

As exports deteriorated, uncertainty regarding the continuity of the fixed exchange rate regime – which required the Central Bank to maintain US dollar reserves equal to the nominal amount of Argentine pesos in circulation – built rapidly. Domestic interest rates shot up, GDP growth turned a negative 3.5 percent in 1999, the unemployment rate increased from 12 percent in 1998 to over 20 percent in 2000, the federal fiscal deficit jumped from 2 percent in 1998 to 4.1 percent in 1999, and 6.3 percent of GDP in 2001.

A series of emergency measures followed. In January 2001, the IMF approved a US$14 billion rescue package (against Argentina's commitment to certain severe fiscal adjustments), disbursing US$3.6 billion. In April, without consultation with the IMF, the Government introduced new export subsidies and import taxes, effectively tinkering with the fixed exchange rate regime. In June 2001, the Argentine Congress gave the Central Bank permission for selective currency backing under the 1991 Convertibility Law.

These measures failed to restore confidence in the sustainability of the economic regime in place. A spiraling political deterioration followed, with the resignation of President De La Rua in December 2001 and the admission by interim President Saa of a likely sovereign default. In January 2002, President Duhalde – the fifth President in just three weeks – announced a debt moratorium on all Argentine sovereign debt, including monies due to the IMF, the World Bank, and the Paris Club, and the end of the Argentine convertibility regime. By year-end 2002, public debt to GDP had reached 135 percent (up from 63 percent in 2001), in part due to a 12 percent drop in GDP in 2002.

Historically, most sovereign debt restructurings have been consensual, even when involving significant discounts on principal owed to foreign private creditors (as was the case under the Brady Plan for Latin American countries in the late 1980s. and for Greece in 2010). Argentina chose to unilaterally impose a large write down on the principal plus accrued interest due to private foreign creditors, while simultaneously suspending negotiations with the IMF and the Paris Club. Argentina's unilateral and non-negotiable offer to private bondholders was finally put forward on January 14, 2005: the conversion of US$81.8 billion of principal plus US$21.4 billion of past due interest at 30 cents on the dollar, or a loss of 70 percent on principal plus accrued interest. Holders of 24 percent of the total amount eligible to conversion chose not to tender their bonds under these conditions. A second round of eligibility (under even less favorable conditions) was presented in 2010, raising the amount of private sector sovereign debt restructured to 92.6 percent.

Benefitting from the commodity export boom that followed its debt moratorium in January 2002, Argentina was able to repay its debt of US$9.8 billion in full to the IMF in 2006. However, as of mid year 2014, holders of US$6 billion in defaulted bonds outstanding continued to pursue the Argentine government in U.S. courts. On June 16, 2014 the U.S. Supreme Court refused to hear Argentina's appeal to a lower court decision ordering Argentina to pay holdouts in full. The holdouts winning argument before the U.S. Supreme Court was that paying restructured bonds (due on June 30) without paying holdouts violated the principle of *pari passu* or equal treatment for all bondholders. Since payments of debt service on restructured bonds plus full payment to holdouts would amount to an unacceptable balance of payments to Argentina, the country was left facing a choice between defaulting on the restructured debt or reaching an out-of-court agreement with holdouts.

Lessons from the fallout

While fortunate in the timing of its 2001 unilateral default – benefitting from the foreign exchange relief provided by the early 2000s commodity boom – almost 15 years later, Argentina had still not succeeded in normalizing its relationship with foreign creditors. As a consequence, a series of questionable actions had to be taken by the Argentine Government to increasingly tap private domestic savings to manage the nation's public sector debt. These actions included the nationalization of private pension funds in 2008, since then becoming significantly larger buyers of public sector debt. Furthermore, it set Argentina on a path of manipulation of the inflation index, thereby reducing the nominal cost of the mostly inflation-indexed domestic public sector, and of imposing other restrictive measures on individual access to foreign exchange, such as limits on the amount of foreign exchange an individual can purchase for foreign travel.

All in all, important lessons for borrowers, creditors, and multilateral agencies emerged from Argentina's 2002 sovereign debt crisis. For borrowers, the Argentine case serves as a reminder of the importance of international sovereign credibility. Thirteen years after its unilateral default, Argentina has not yet been able to restore market confidence and engage sustainably foreign investors in support of its economic development. For private foreign creditors and multilateral agencies, the importance of timely and proactive cooperation under the umbrella guidance of and monitoring by the IMF became abundantly clear, as evident from the handling of Greece's sovereign debt crisis in 2010.

The European Union sovereign debt crisis of 2010–12

The Eurozone sovereign debt and banking crisis represented a unique case, directly related to the structure of the European economic and monetary union. For the first time in history sovereign countries with mature economies and stable democratic regimes suffered cross-border contagion directly correlated to their dependency on one central bank, the European Central Bank (ECB), one monetary policy, and for the 17 member countries of the European Monetary Union or Eurozone within the 28 member European Union, one currency, the euro.

After the horrors and devastation of World War II, the economic and infrastructure recovery of Europe was spearheaded in 1948 by the American-led Marshall Plan, intended to redress Soviet influence across the continent. In the aftermath of the Marshall Plan, European leaders, led by the French Finance Minister, Robert Schumann, established the European Coal and Steel Community in 1951. This project would lead to the Common Market established under the Treaty of Rome in 1957, which set the guidelines for the Economic European Community (EEC) between France, West Germany, Italy, the Netherlands, Belgium, and Luxembourg. In the following three decades, as the project evolved into a more complex institutional, commercial, economic, monetary, and social policy union, the core countries led by France and West Germany were joined by the United Kingdom, Denmark, Ireland, Greece, Spain, and Portugal. In February 1992, these twelve nations signed the Treaty on European Union (the Maastricht Treaty) which came into effect on November 1, 1993. In 1995, the European Union absorbed three European Free Trade Association (EFTA) members: Sweden, Austria, and Finland, bringing to 15 the total number of member states. The next round of enlargement occurred in 2004 under the Treaty of Accession, under which ten countries joined the EU: Czech Republic, Estonia, Cyprus, Latvia, Lithuania, Hungary, Malta, Poland, Slovenia, and the Slovak Republic. This was followed by the accession to the EU of Romania and Bulgaria in 2007, and Croatia in 2012, bringing to 28 the total number of EU member states.

The Maastricht Treaty (Article 105–9) codified the conditions under which an economic and monetary union would be established by 1999, with a single currency, one central bank, the ECB, and a common monetary policy. Countries would cede sovereignty of their central banks to the European System of Central Banks as members of the Board of the ECB. With this they relinquished their ability to independently devalue their currencies. Importantly, the Maastricht Treaty did not provide an exit clause. Having chosen to opt out of economic and monetary union, the United Kingdom, Denmark, and Sweden have retained the ability to assume these functions.

In order to become a member of economic and monetary union, countries have to meet specific convergence criteria: inflation rates must not exceed the average of the three best performing countries by more than 1.5 percent; the general budget deficit must not exceed 3 percent of GDP; the debt to GDP ratios must not exceed 60 percent of GDP. Once countries chose to meet the criteria it was assumed that with subsidies and internal fiscal discipline the weakest countries would retrofit their economies in line with the strongest: Germany and France. Ironically, as early as 2003 when the German-led Stability Pact sought to require that all member countries adhere to the criteria or risk penalties, both France and Germany already exceeded the minimum debt to GDP ratio of 60 percent.

The Lisbon Treaty of 2007 clarified the political structure of the EU, but continued the very complex balance between sovereignty and supranational authority over economic, financial, fiscal, and social policies. Therefore, despite these requirements and political and economic convergence, under the division of responsibilities in areas of exclusive and shared competencies, countries maintained sovereignty over their fiscal, and budgetary policies as well as the supervision, oversight, and regulation of their domestic banking sectors. European monetary integration and a European central bank preceded fiscal and regulatory harmonization. The ECB, as defined in the Maastricht Treaty and in its original charter, did not clearly specify its role as lender of last resort in a cross-border crisis. Furthermore, the initial attempts at cross-border regulation formulated in the Financial Services Action Plan (1994–2004) did not clarify the lender of last resort function.

European monetary union

First conceptualized in the European Payment Union of 1950, the idea of a unified currency remained theoretical until the Werner Committee Report of 1970, which established the blueprint for the irreversible convertibility of currencies and the irrevocable fixing of parity rates, but which retained the option of maintaining national currencies. Jacques Delors, the first President of the European Commission and former French Finance Minister, set out the Delors Plan establishing the concept of one central bank and one unified currency zone. The European Central Bank, modeled after the price stability principles of the Bundesbank and the Board structure of the Federal Reserve, was to set policy and to ensure monetary stability.

In March 1998, despite skepticism among American and British economists, the Nobel Prize winning economist Robert Mundell, declared that "Monetary Union will do much to integrate Europe's commodity, factor and capital markets. It will increase Europewide competition and revolutionize financial markets. It will spur rationalization, mergers and takeovers in the European banking industry and commercial firms. [...] EMU will change the way Europeans think about themselves and about a multiregional continental market that has become the largest in the world" (Mundell 1998: 10).

Economic and monetary union came into effect in 1999 with the successful introduction of the euro at a rate of 1 euro: US$1.18, described as "arguably the most momentous currency innovation since the establishment of the US dollar in 1792" ("Europe's Adventure Begins", *The Economist*, 1998). For a decade, Mundell's predictions came to pass as the euro maintained parity range with the dollar and the ECB gained global prestige and credibility. Nevertheless, there were deep structural weaknesses: lack of fiscal, banking, and regulatory harmonization, and lack of political union.

In 1999, when eleven countries joined the Eurozone, followed by the late entry of Greece in 2001, the ECB policy encouraged major EU banks to carry sovereign debt of all member economies. Until 2010, the classic assumption was that in mature economic regions, sovereign debt was a perfectly safe asset. The entry of the ten new member states in 2004 imposed a new economic burden and posed an economic challenge. Their accession increased the EU's population by 20 percent, but GDP by only 5 percent. Despite the increased costs of subsidies, the EU peripheral countries (Greece, Portugal, and Spain) continued to enjoy the benefits of recipient countries.

EU responses to the financial crisis of 2008

The demise of Lehman and the subsequent shock to the global financial system was initially perceived as an American phenomenon. However, by October 2008 it was made public that Spain, the United Kingdom, Ireland, and Germany, as well as non EU members Norway, Switzerland, and Iceland, had substantial exposure to U.S. subprime mortgage loans. The German public and media were shocked to learn that from 2005 onward, the former state subsidized German Landesbanken had sought high yield, high risk transactions, and began to suffer liquidity and solvency problems by mid 2007 (see Chapter 4). Within one week, the Belgian–Dutch Fortis and French–British Dexia collapsed. The United Kingdom called on all its major banks to accept capital injections and undertook the partial privatization of Royal Bank of Scotland, Lloyds, and Barclays. Only HSBC was able to recapitalize without government aid. From October to December 2008, EU governments acted in concert, rapidly deciding to guarantee all bank liabilities, to begin harmonizing and increasing current account deposit insurance, and requiring all major banks to accept injections of capital. Through early 2009, in coordination with the U.S. Federal Reserve, the ECB began expansionary emergency measures providing Medium Term Refinancing Operations (MROS) for Eurozone banks.

However, near-defaults in Iceland, Hungary, and Latvia, and the endemic weakness in all new member states with the exception of Poland, made it clear that the ECB and the IMF had to assume far more aggressive roles, often on an ad hoc basis, when a country within or outside of the Eurozone was in danger of financial collapse or default. Ukraine required an IMF loan (with further loans in 2011 and 2014), as did Hungary in October 2008 (and again in 2011). In the eight Central East European accession countries of 2004, almost 80 percent of their banking sectors had been acquired by or were majority held by Austrian, Italian, and Swedish banks. While the authorities feared that these institutions would divest, they did not, and in within less than two years, EU banks appeared to have recovered and were beginning to post substantial profits for the last quarter of 2009.

However, a highly volatile political environment across Europe made it very difficult to carry out deeper structural reforms. Riots, changes of governments, a rise of extremist movements at both ends of the political spectrum, and general distrust of government and markets incited the public's perception that large banks' ability to repay government bailouts and maintain bankers' salaries and bonuses occurred at the expense of taxpayers and stakeholders.

The Greek crisis: the catalyst

The cradle of Roman-Hellenic civilization, Greece was absorbed into the Ottoman Empire from 1453 until its independence in 1832. Through the nineteenth and up to the mid twentieth century, Greece, like Ireland, Spain, and Portugal remained a rural economy with immature markets and weak banking sectors, dependent on French and British investment. Suffering horrific deprivations under German occupation in World War II, Greece began to recover in the 1950s through conservative fiscal and monetary policies combined with the development of the shipping and tourism industries. However, the country remained poor, rural and deprived of industrial diversification through the 1970s. From the nineteenth century, tax evasion, bribery and corruption remained endemic (Roscini et al., 2011). Greece joined the European Community in 1981, despite well acknowledged structural and economic challenges, and began the process of harmonization and adherence to EU rules and regulations.

Throughout the 1990s, Greece benefitted steadily from EU subsidies. It broadened its tax base, reduced inflation, and maintained a stable exchange rate for the drachma – the weakest currency in the European Monetary System basket of currencies. However, the public sector was bloated, with extremely high social benefits and pension costs despite low productivity. The Greek financial sector was reasonably sound, but Greek banks carried an inordinate amount of government debt. In 1999, despite the fact that Greece was unable to meet the economic and monetary union criteria, political pressure prevailed and, by 2001, Greece was integrated into the Eurozone. As late as 2006, Greece provided official data to Eurostat indicating that the budget deficit met the convergence criteria of less than 3 percent. Through 2009, the deficit approached 15 percent of GDP, and the actual debt to GDP ratio was revealed to be 113 percent – at best. By late 2009, it had become clear that Greece would not be able to meet its sovereign debt obligations. Yet in March 2010, when Greece finally admitted that it could not meet its short-term obligations, the markets still judged that the crisis could be contained as Greece represented only 2.7 percent of the €13.1 trillion EU economy. In May of that year, despite commitments by the IMF and ECB, a new danger loomed, as it became clear that previously safe EU banks were heavily exposed to Greek sovereign debt. The fear of a Greek default was exacerbated by revelations of French banks' higher than assumed exposure to Greek government bonds.

The first rescue: European financial stability facilities

Between March and May 2010, the EU and the ECB sought to find an equitable solution, which would allow both banks and the private sector to avoid major losses while granting Greece some reprieve. The greatest fear was regional contagion. Greece's "repeated statistical misstatements" (Roscini et al., 2011), coupled with the government collapse, increased the sense of urgency as global markets lost confidence in the Eurozone. The mandate of the ECB permitted lending to banks only and not to sovereign nations, which required the intervention of the IMF. The United Kingdom refused to take part in any bailout package, and the German public was initially very reluctant to provide unconditional aid.

With the creation of the Troika (European Commission, ECB, and IMF) in May 2010, a blueprint for the European Financial Stability Facility was finally established. A compromise between private and public interests, it was incorporated in Luxembourg as a private organization, informally under EU oversight, and coordinating with the German Debt Management Office and the European Investment Bank, which allowed it to raise funds to provide loans to countries in financial difficulties. Among the Eurozone members on the governing board, Germany's participation was the largest. The European Financial Stability Facility was charged with functioning as a temporary, smaller version of the IMF, created solely for the purpose of country bailouts. Through the IMF and the EU, Greece received a separate bailout package of €110 billion, to be distributed in three tranches between May 2010 and 2013. The initial commitment to the European Financial Stability Facility was €440 billion, increased to €700 billion within a year. These funds coexisted with the EU Financial Stabilization Mechanism, and with an additional safety net provided by the IMF. Greece was granted a separate rescue package, but the European Financial Stability Facility could address the challenges facing other countries, in particular Portugal.[5]

However, this bailout imposed draconian austerity measures on the Greek economy, from a reduction in the size of the public sector, through wage and pension cuts, to stabilizing the public debt and establishing fiscal discipline. Despite the three years of recession that followed, which saw the economy shrink 25 percent, and unemployment remain stubbornly high at 27.6 percent in 2013 (with even higher rates of youth unemployment), Greece required two further bailout packages.

In May to June 2010, as the EU announced a coordinated almost US$1 trillion Emergency Fund to bolster the euro and guarantee a safety net for all Eurozone economies, extreme volatility in financial markets settled somewhat, creating a sense of relief and respite. However, Greece remained unstable, and Portugal, Spain, Italy, and Ireland were forced to adopt strict austerity measures under IMF and EU monitoring. Although not a Eurozone member, even the United Kingdom was forced to implement draconian austerity measures.

Ireland 2010: an exceptionally deep banking crisis

In the early 2000s, following a decade of export and FDI-led growth, the Irish economy embarked on a domestic credit expansion boom. Rapidly rising property values stimulated both investment in commercial and residential real estate, and borrowers' appetites for consumer loans. The integration of the Irish financial system into the Eurozone facilitated access to cheap wholesale funding. In the five years from 2003 to 2008, net foreign liabilities of the Irish banking system increased from 20 percent to 70 percent of GDP, with wholesale funding accounting for 55 percent of total assets. By mid 2008, bank assets had grown to approximately 500 percent of GDP.

Ireland's property price downturn had begun in 2007, but following the collapse of Lehman Brothers in September 2008, wholesale funding to Irish banks dried up, bringing the Irish banking system to the brink of insolvency.

The immediate reaction of the Irish Government was to seek prompt recourse to the Eurosystem. In early 2009, this was followed by the transfer of distressed property and commercial real estate assets from bank balance sheets to the government-backed National Asset Management Agency (NAMA), the large-scale government support for two failed banks (Anglo Irish and Irish Nationwide), and major equity investments in other banks, with a total fiscal cost estimated at 40 percent of GDP.

A steep economic recession ensued, with the unemployment rate jumping from 9.5 to 13.6 percent in 2010, and real GDP dropping approximately 8 percent between 2007 and 2010. As a consequence, tax revenues fell sharply, driving the fiscal deficit – before the fiscal cost of bank support – to 10 percent of GDP from fiscal balance in 2007.

By late 2010, the credibility of Irish sovereign creditworthiness had been severely compromised. Government guarantees were no longer sufficient to restore confidence in the country's banking system. External official support was urgently needed.

This official support was formally achieved in December 2010, when the IMF approved a three-year Extended Fund Facility (EFF) arrangement for Ireland in the amount of €22.5 billion as part of an €85 billion financing package that involved the European Financial Stabilization Mechanism (EFSM) and the European Financial Stability Facility (EFSF), in addition to bilateral loans provided by the United Kingdom, Sweden, and Denmark. In conjunction with the granting of this facility to Ireland, the European Central Bank committed to continued liquidity support to Irish banks.

From sovereign debt to regional banking crisis: 2011–12

The stress tests of 2010 (and 2011), administered by the European Banking Authority on 93 banks, indicated that only a handful were undercapitalized or in potential risk of failure. As Deutsche Bank, Barclays, and BNP, unwilling recipients of capital injections in 2008, were able to repay these monies, and other banks appeared ready to follow suit, these results appeared to lend credence to talk of a steady recovery. However, continuing political volatility in Greece, Italy, and Spain was in fact symptomatic of a far more fragile landscape, one fraught with public distrust of banks and markets. The sense of relief was short-lived, as the extent of bank exposure to other peripheral countries became evident: "Europe must come clean on the extent of its losses" (*Financial Times*, 7 June 2010).

An August 2010 report by the OECD revealed that equity in French and German banks barely covered total exposure to Greek, Spanish, and Italian assets

(Blundell-Wignell and Slovik, 2010). By fall 2011, Société Générale's exposure totaled €4.2 billion, that of Crédit Agricole €3.4 billion, and BNP €5b billion. The collapse of the Irish banks revealed EU bank exposure to Ireland of €509 billion, with Germany carrying the highest exposure at €138 billion. In December 2010, is was finally revealed that French banks held the highest exposure to Greece in the amount of €53.5 billion (Jenkins et al. 2010).

As Martin Wolf noted, "Banks are on a Eurozone knife edge" (Wolf, 2012) as a "combination of vulnerable sovereigns with exposed banks" led to political implosions and fomented extremist factions at both ends of the spectrum with anti-EU, anti-euro, anti-market and anti-bank platforms. Weakness in financial regulation before 2008 and lack of oversight in public finances across the EU through 2009 allowed banks to increase exposure to sovereign debt without any warning signs.

Collapse of Dexia: danger of cross-border contagion

The sudden collapse of the French–Belgian bank, Dexia, on October 4, 2011 further impressed on markets that the crisis was not resolved and that serious emergency measures were necessary in order to avoid cross-border contagion. It discredited the latest round of stress tests administered in July 2011 under the European Banking Authority, established in London in 2010. Among the seven of the 93 banks examined deemed unsound, Dexia received the highest rating.

Like Fortis, Dexia was created in the first wave of cross-border consolidation in 1996, when Crédit Local de France merged with CREGEN of Belgium. In 2011, it had massive reciprocal obligations following huge losses due to failed municipal lending. Belgium, France, and Luxembourg were forced to rescue Dexia as it became public that the bank had global risk exposure of US$700 billion, of which US$34 billion was to Greece. The French arm of Dexia was merged into the state-run Caisse des Depots, the Belgian arm acquired by the Belgian State. The second collapse of Dexia implicated by association its largest trading partners: Morgan Stanley, Goldman Sachs, and Commerzbank.

Greece experienced ongoing turmoil, unable to meet its obligations that would allow it to receive the second tranche of its bailout. EU banks could no longer avoid disclosing that they were overleveraged and undercapitalized. National scrutiny, market and political pressures were compounded by the new requirements of Basel III, despite the extension in Basel III implementation from 2013 to 2015–19, requiring banks to meet higher capital adequacy requirements and higher Tier I capital requirements. Santander, UBS, Société Générale and U.K. banks still claimed they could self-recapitalize, but in reality this was as dubious as their ability to self-regulate.

ECB to the rescue

On December 22, 2011, Mario Draghi, the new head of the ECB, announced the Long Term Refinancing Operation (LTRO), in which 523 banks would be eligible to borrow a total of US$640 billion or €489 billion. Instead of the ECB moving money through the IMF or directly buying bonds, the ECB assumed the role of lender of last resort in an emergency program to provide three-year loans to EU banks. This judicious decision allowed the ECB to remain within its mandate, to extend the scope of its activities without imposing an undue political burden on national central banks. The ECB decision was complemented in December 2011, by the German-led Fiscal and Budgetary Compact, which would impose far stricter supervision and oversight over national budgets.

On March 2, 2012, a second phase of LTRO took place, affecting an additional 800 banks, of which 400 recipients were German financial institutions, including the finance arms of major car companies. France borrowed €150 billion, Italy €260 billion, and Spain €250 billion, intended to bolster the failing savings banks. In 2013, the European Stability Mechanism replaced the European Financial Stability Facility.

Spain's Bankia and the second stage of the ECB rescue

An unexpected crisis in Spain caused another panic in June 2012, when the Spanish savings bank, Bankia, created through consolidation of seven failed saving banks (cajas), failed. The Spanish economy almost collapsed under the debt-fueled housing and construction bubble, which remained unchecked through 2010. Ironically, at less than 90 percent, Spain's debt to GDP ratio was much better than in other peripheral countries, and its retail and corporate banking sector was solid, led by Santander and BBVA.

The collapse of property values and the construction industry brought about the failure of mortgage banks (see Ireland, Chapter 4). The newly-elected center-right Spanish government was forced to turn to the EU for an unprecedented €160 billion rescue package. The impact of the crisis drove unemployment rates to 26.2 percent, compared with 17.4 percent in Portugal (*Financial Times*, October 24, 2013), and a deep recession ensued, lasting from 2011 to 2014. Spain began to see a fragile recovery in 2014, as foreign private equity groups began to buy up cheap toxic assets and foreign investment resumed.

Beginning of resolution and recovery

On July 26, 2012, Mario Draghi pledged that "[w]ithin our mandate, the ECB is ready to do whatever it takes to preserve the euro. And believe me it will be enough" (*Financial Times*, July 26, 2012). With this statement, markets surged in London, Madrid, and Paris, followed by New York. Despite some hesitation from the more hardline bankers at the Bundesbank, in September 2012, the German Constitutional Court voted to agree to Germany's participation as chief donor to the European Stability Mechanism, with a limit of €190 billion for any bailout. These actions began slowly to shift Europe out of the crisis and toward a slow and painful recovery.

The Banking Union (see chapters 6 and 9) and EU-wide regulatory reforms were implemented in 2014. Nevertheless the remaining challenges are threefold:

- an EU-wide resolution mechanism for failing banks and preventive measures;
- expansive supervisory and monitoring powers granted to the ECB;
- an EU-wide standardized deposit insurance scheme put in place.

Despite signs of renewed confidence in early 2014 in Europe, and specifically in the 18 Eurozone countries, investment and the start of banks' ability to repay LTRO loans, growth prospects remained at barely 1 percent. Under the austerity measures imposed by the bailouts, unemployment in the weaker economies remained between 15 percent and 25 percent, with much higher levels among 18 to 34 year olds. Although a significant increase in U.S. investment in EU companies and banks has spurred the recovery, economic competitiveness across the EU (excluding the United Kingdom) remains hampered by weak labor mobility, rigid labor laws, and a lack of reforms which would increase entrepreneurship and start-ups. For Greece, Spain, Portugal, and Ireland "the recession is over, but the crisis continues" (Mariano Rajoy, Prime Minister of Spain, quoted in Buck, 2013).

Resolution

In April 2014, only two years after it defaulted on its debt, Greece returned to global capital markets, easily raising €3 billion in a five-year deal. Although Ireland and Portugal have returned to the capital markets also and Spain has seen a return to growth for the past nine months of 2013–14, the recovery across Europe remains anemic and uneven. Germany is the exception, while growth is stagnant in France and is still negative in Italy. Overall, growth does not exceed 1 percent across the 28-member EU, and the region remains vulnerable to political and economic shocks.

Summary

In this chapter we have examined sovereign debt crises from the 1980s to present, their causes and their ramifications for international banking. In earlier decades, such crises were generally associated with emerging economies, and their resolution led by the IMF, in accordance with its original charter as lender of last resort to sovereign governments for temporary balance of payments adjustments.

The most recent sovereign debt crises, coming in the aftermath of the 2008 financial crisis, differ from previous crises in two important aspects. First, they affected OECD economies, considered to have in place strong governance and regulatory structures. Second, they brought to the surface the dangerous interlinkages, for developed economies also, between sovereign risk and the health of domestic financial systems.

Notes

1. See Mexico in 1995, Turkey in 2001, Argentina in 2002, Greece in 2009, and Spain in 2012.
2. See Iceland in 2008, Ireland in 2008, and Cyprus in 2012.
3. See Nordic countries in 1991, Japan in 1995, Republic of Korea in 1997, and the United States in 2008.
4. In 1995, at the Halifax Summit of the G-7, there was a proposal for the IMF to set up a new "Emergency Financing Mechanism", which would provide faster access to the Fund "with strong conditionality and larger up front disbursements in crisis situations" with a request for the G-10 to support this system (Truman 1996: 209). Following the sovereign debt crisis in Argentina in 2001, there was an IMF proposal to create a Sovereign Debt Restructuring Mechanism. However, due to technical and political difficulties these proposals were never fully enacted.
5. In spring 2011, Portugal required a €78 billion bailout, including €12 billion earmarked for recapitalizing the banking sector. Despite overexpenditure in the public sector and unsustainable debt, Portuguese banks had not speculated on the property bubble, unlike Spanish banks.

6 International bank regulation and supervision

Introduction

As discussed in Chapter 4, banks fail as a result of having assets insufficient to meet liability obligations. A decline in the value of the bank's asset base depletes capital and increases *leverage* – the gearing ratio expressing how much third party debt to shareholders' equity the bank holds. If large enough, the decrease in asset value may wipe out shareholders' equity, causing the bank to become insolvent.

Leverage is, therefore, a critical element to assess the risk profile of a bank. Equally important is the riskiness of the assets, the ability of the bank's funding to support short-term asset price volatility, and the reliability of the bank's internal risk measurement and management process.

The ability of a company to meet its debt obligations is a function of its leverage, the magnitude and volatility of the margins between revenues and production costs, and its ability to manage its balance sheet and properly protect itself against both known risks and unforeseen contingencies.

What makes the banking industry unique is that: (a) it is relatively prone to contagion – the risk that the market perception of financial troubles at one financial institution can quickly spill over to another and, possibly to the financial system as a whole; and (b) it is the fundamental conduit of credit to businesses and families – the jeopardizing of which, as amply illustrated in Chapter 4, has severe aggregate demand implications and social costs. The ultimate purpose of bank regulation is to establish prudential minimum standards that, if properly enforced by bank regulators, should prevent systemic financial crises.

In 1974, with the goal of ensuring international coordination of bank supervision, a standing committee of central bank governors was established, the Basel Committee on Banking Supervision (BCBS). Originally a forum of the G-10 countries (Belgium, Canada, France, Germany, Italy, Japan, the Netherlands, Sweden, the United Kingdom), and United States plus Luxembourg and Switzerland, BCBS membership was expanded in 2009 to include Argentina, Australia, Brazil, China, Hong Kong SAR, India, Indonesia, South Korea, Mexico, Russia, Saudi Arabia, Singapore, South Africa, and Turkey.

The permanent secretariat of the BCBS is headquartered at the *Bank for International Settlements* (BIS) in Basel, Switzerland. Founded in 1930, to manage German reparations from World War I (see Chapter 1), BCBS has no formal authority to enforce the guidelines established in the international accords. It is the responsibility of the domestic regulatory authorities to implement in their own jurisdictions the international guidelines agreed upon.

Domestic regulatory regimes

Before immersing ourselves in the complexities of international bank regulation, it is important to understand the fundamental aspects of domestic bank regulation.

Disruptions of credit flows can have severe effects on the economy as a whole, with widespread negative effects on businesses and people. As a result, all governments regulate banking. Bank regulation and supervision has two fundamental objectives:

(i) to ensure prudent practices at the individual bank level, through the imposition of capital standards and operational guidelines; and

(ii) to reduce systemic risk, through individual bank examinations and system-wide assessments.

Countries around the world have established government-backed agencies in order to mitigate the risk of system-wide runs – *deposit insurance agencies* funded by premiums paid by the banks themselves – to guarantee the safety of customers' deposits up to the same pre-established amount in all participant banks.

The United States was the first country to establish a formal institutional deposit insurance framework with the creation of the *Federal Deposit Insurance Corporation* (FDIC) in 1933, during the Great Depression, guaranteeing deposits up to US$2,500. In 2008, in response to the increasing risk of generalized bank runs as a result of the subprime mortgages meltdown, this limit was raised from US$100,000 (in place since 1980) to US$250,000.

Responsibility for support to a bank facing liquidity difficulties – rather than a solvency crisis – resides with a country's central bank, the *lender of last resort* to banks against acceptable collateral provided by the bank, such as high credit-standing securities.

The mission to intervene in a failing bank is typically reserved for the country's deposit insurance agency. In this capacity, the deposit insurance agency would take sole receivership responsibility for the troubled bank until a take-over by another healthier party can be arranged or, if this is not a viable option, final liquidation.

The combined effect of guaranteed bank deposits for bank customers (up to a certain well-established amount, as indicated above) and temporary liquidity support to banks by the central bank (against acceptable collateral) provides an unequivocal enhancement to peoples' trust in banks, a critical factor for the proper functioning of the financial system and the well-being of society as a whole. However, it also stimulates *moral hazard* – the tendency for economic agents to take higher risk than they otherwise might. Therefore, adequate prudential regulation and supervision of depositary financial institutions is absolutely critical to prevent both financial contagion from one institution to another and excessive risk taking by each.

A major additional challenge for bank supervisors is the potentially destabilizing effects of interconnectedness between depositary and non-depositary financial institutions, as evidenced in the U.S. subprime meltdown and ensuing global credit crunch in 2008. Country specific cultural, constitutional, and political considerations may lead to different institutional frameworks. However, what has become unquestionable around the world is the need for individual jurisdictions to have in place a supervisory framework that provides regulators with a real-time comprehensive understanding of any major threat to the stability of their financial systems, as well as the legal authority to act promptly if necessary.

A clear example of this was the establishment by the Dodd–Frank Act of the Financial Stability Oversight Council in the United States. This multi-agency committee with ultimate responsibility for the stability of the entire U.S. financial system is chaired by the Secretary of the Treasury and has as voting members the chairpersons of the Board of Governors of the Federal Reserve System, the Federal Deposit Insurance Corporation, the U.S. Securities and Exchange Commission, the Commodity Futures Trading Commission, and of the National Credit Union Administration Board, in addition to the Director of the Consumer Financial Protection Bureau, the Controller of the Currency, the Federal Housing Finance Agency, plus an independent member with insurance expertise appointed by the President and confirmed by the Senate.

Another noteworthy development in this regard was the enactment by the U.K. parliament of the Financial Services Act (2012), which extinguished the *Financial Services Authority* (FSA) as an independent regulatory and supervisory authority and transferred its responsibilities to two new bodies: the *Prudential Regulatory Authority* (PRA), as a division of the Bank of England, charged with the responsibility for prudential regulation and supervision of the entire financial system; and the *Financial Conduct Authority* (FCA), a separate body focused exclusively on business and market conduct.

These considerations aside, in order to better understand how a country's policy intentions with regard to its banking industry translate into governing legislation and, then, from legislation into a continuously improving rule-making and effective enforcement regulatory framework, it is useful to examine in greater detail a specific case: Canada, home to a financial system that in spite of its high degree of interconnectedness with those of the U.S. and Europe succeeded in weathering successfully the 2008 global financial crisis and credit crunch.

The case of Canada

Canada's central bank, the Bank of Canada, was established in 1934 by the Bank of Canada Act "to regulate credit and currency in the best interests of the economic life of the nation." Having opened its doors in March 1935 as a privately owned institution, with shares sold to the public, it became a 100 percent government-owned institution in 1938. As central bank, the Bank of Canada is the monopoly issuer of fiat money with legal tender in Canada, and is also the lender of last resort to banks operating in Canada.

The most important regulatory authority in Canada's financial system is the *Office of the Superintendent of Financial Institutions* (OSFI). Created by the OSFI Act of 1987, the OSFI is the regulatory agency responsible for the regulation and supervision of all federally chartered banks, insurance companies, trust and loan companies, and cooperative credit associations operating on Canadian territory. It was formed by the merger of the Office of the Inspector General of Banks (OIGB, in existence since the mid 1920s) and the Department of Insurance (formerly the Office of the Superintendent of Insurance).

The OSFI Act of 1987 also created the *Financial Institutions Supervisory Committee* (FISC), constituted by the Superintendent of Financial Institutions, the Governor of the Bank of Canada, the Deputy Minister of Finance, the Chairman of the Canada Deposit Insurance Corporation (CDIC), and the Commissioner of the Financial Consumer Agency of Canada (FCAC). The rationale for FISC was to enhance the exchange of information among its members on all matters related to the supervision of financial institutions and to strengthen the OSFI's "will to act" (*www.osfi-bsif.gc.ca*).

The OSFI works with the Basel Committee on Banking Supervision and is the party responsible for the incorporation of internationally agreed guidelines into Canada's body of domestic regulation, as well as its monitoring and enforcement. Two other mission-specific regulatory authorities complement the OSFI's supervisory responsibilities, the *Canada Deposit Insurance Corporation* and the *Financial Consumer Agency of Canada*.

The Canada Deposit Insurance Corporation was created in 1967 to provide deposit insurance for bank depositors (at end-2012, to a level of the first C$ 100,000 held in any bank). It relies mainly on the OSFI's examination reports of insured banks, but it has the authority to seek further clarification and to request to be appointed as receiver of a bank, if it believes that it will be called upon to make insurance payments to depositors of that bank.

The Financial Consumer Agency of Canada was established in 2001 to enforce the consumer provisions of the Bank Act, particularly with regard to disclosure of the terms of financial transactions and financial contracts. It has the authority to impose penalties on banks failing to comply with the principles embodied in the Act.

Minimum capital and liquidity requirements for banks operating in Canada are established by the OSFI, and are fundamentally the same as those proposed by the BCBS. Basel II guidelines had been put in place in Canada as scheduled by the BCBS (2007); full implementation of Basel III is expected well in advance of the 2019 deadline, according to the OSFI. Monitoring banks' compliance with capital adequacy guidelines is the principal mission of bank supervisors. Detection by the OSFI of a trend of deterioration in a bank's capital adequacy ratio triggers the demand for an immediate plan to address this weakness. The OSFI makes public its supervisory intervention program. As capital adequacy deteriorates, banks are assigned escalating stages of intervention, from additional reporting to restrictions on the business of the bank, including the requirement to cease the payment of dividends to shareholders.

If the OSFI believes that a bank is undercapitalized, it has the authority to direct it to increase its capital. That not being possible, the OSFI may take control of the assets of the bank or of the bank itself, to protect creditors and/or the system as a whole. The OSFI must report this action to the Minister of Finance, who could overrule it if he/she believed it not to be in the public interest. The OSFI may, then, proceed to request that the Attorney General apply to the federal court for the winding up – or liquidation – of the bank. The court, in issuing a winding up order, must appoint a liquidator, either a trustee licensed under Canada's Bankruptcy and Insolvency Act or, as is more likely, the Canada Deposit Insurance Corporation.

Once appointed as liquidator, the Canada Deposit Insurance Corporation can proceed with the winding up of the troubled bank or, if it believes a going-concern solution is possible, request an order to vest shares in the troubled bank prior to its sale to a new shareholder.

The CDIC can also seek the Minister of Finance's authorization to establish a bridge bank to absorb the liabilities and the good assets of the bank, the remainder assets to go into liquidation. This strategy, also known as the *good bank–bad bank solution*, is justified when the proceeds from a future sale to a third party of the bridge (or good) bank may lead to a lower final cost of the intervention than outright liquidation.

The Basel I Accord

The original accord (1988)

As indicated in Chapter 5, the 1988 Basel Capital Accord (Basel I Accord) was the international regulatory response to the threat to the stability of the global financial system posed by the 1980s Latin American debt crisis. Initially approved by representatives of the G-10 countries, then the only members of the BCBS, Basel I was eventually adopted by over 120 countries.

As outlined in Basel I, a bank's capital (K) should be at a minimum 8 percent of the sum total of the bank's assets, each asset weighted by its credit risk (TRWA), or K/TRWA >= 8 percent.

Negotiations between the Basel Committee and the banking industry – the latter seeking flexibility in the Basel I definition of capital – led to a hybrid numerator (K) with two components: Tier 1, or *core* equity, comprising issued and fully-paid common stock and *non-cumulative perpetual stock* plus retained earnings; and Tier 2, or complementary capital, comprising *cumulative perpetual preferred stock, subordinated term* debt with minimum maturity of five years, and undisclosed (or non-specific) reserves.

Banks were given until the end of 1992 to reach the minimum capital requirement. For many banks that meant issuing new common stock and/or reducing dividend pay-outs but, as a result of the flexibility provided by the Tier 2 definition of capital, prioritizing over the next two decades non-dilutive common shareholders' equity capital increased, such as non-cumulative preferred and subordinated debt issues.

Regarding the denominator, TRWA, Basel I distinguished very clearly Organisation for Economic Co-operation and Development (OECD) credit risk from non-OECD credit risk. As shown in Table 6.1 below, claims on OECD sovereign exposures commanded a much lower weight (0 percent) than non-OECD sovereign debt (100 percent), the same being true for over one year exposures to banks (20 percent for OECD versus 100 percent for non-OECD institutions). Basel I established also that mortgage loans – by definition, collateralized exposures backed by the home being financed – should command a significantly lower weight charge (50 percent) than general purpose private sector loans (100 percent).

The Basel I regulatory framework faced, from the start, four major criticisms from the banking industry:

(i)   It failed to properly differentiate between private sector credit risks (e.g. the same risk weight would apply to a large AAA corporation and a start-up business).
(ii) Its OECD/non-OECD distinction was arbitrary.
(iii) It failed to deal properly with important changes that had begun to take place in the structure of banks' balance sheets away from typically hold-to-maturity loans to securities traded in the secondary markets.
(iv) It failed to acknowledge the latest developments of modern finance, including the beneficial effects of diversification to risk mitigation being incorporated into banks' internal risk management models and techniques.

Items (i), (ii), and (iv) would be addressed only by The Basel II Accord, in 2004. However, a market risk capital charge for traded securities – more often than not

Table 6.1 Selected credit risk weights under Basel I

Risk Weight	Type of Asset
0%	Cash
	Claims on OECD governments
	Claims in national currency on non-OECD governments
20%	Claims on OECD banks and regulated broker-dealers
	Claims on non-OECD banks with maturity up to 1 year
50%	Residential mortgage loans
100%	Claims in foreign currency on non-OECD governments
	Claims on non-OECD banks with maturity over 1 year
	Claims on private sector borrowers and/or issuers

Source: Authors based on Bank for International Settlements 1988: 21

demanding a significantly lower charge than the corresponding credit risk charge for the same security – was incorporated into the Basel I Accord in 1996, through the Market Risk Amendment.

The Market Risk Amendment (1996)

The objective of the Market Risk Amendment to the Basel I Capital Accord was to explicitly acknowledge the risk of loss associated with asset-liability mismatches (e.g. foreign exchange, interest rate) in a bank's balance sheet, as well as to establish an explicit capital cushion for the risks arising from the price volatility associated with its trading in foreign exchange and interest rate contracts, along with fixed income and equity securities, commodities, and derivatives.

While representing a significant milestone in bank regulation, by explicitly addressing capital cushions for market risk, the Market Risk Amendment was, moreover, an affirmative nod by regulators to banks' demands that portfolios with secondary market liquidity deserve a different, and probably lower minimum capital charge treatment, than hold-to-maturity loan portfolios. As further detailed below, per the Market Risk Amendment, the capital charge to cushion a bank against market risk, should be a function of its total *value-at-risk (VaR)*.

The concept of VaR, originally developed by Bankers Trust in 1989, sought to estimate – with a degree of confidence of, say, at least 95 percent – how much the bank could lose on its entire trading book on a given day. The VaR methodology consisted of a mathematical formulation to apply historical observations to estimate future movements in securities prices relying on, fundamentally, two assumptions: (i) changes in securities prices, like most other natural phenomena, tend to follow a normal distribution; and (ii) price fluctuations at any time interval are independent events (e.g. tomorrow's price movement is independent from today's price movement).

Seeking to ensure a minimum degree of prudence, transparency, and consistency, the Market Amendment to Basel I approved by the Basel Committee on Banking Supervision for implementation beginning in 1996 allowed banks to use their in-house proprietary models to determine market risk, but required that: (i) the minimum capital charge for market risk should be the higher of the bank's previous day's value-at-risk, and three times the average of its daily value-at-risk for the preceding 60 days; (ii) the bank's VaR should be computed daily using a 99th percentile one-tailed confidence interval; (iii) a minimum price shock equivalent to a holding period of ten trading days should be used; and (iv) models should incorporate a minimum historical observation period of one year.

The guidelines for capital charges imposed by the Market Amendment to Basel I would remain essentially unaltered until after the subprime meltdown crisis and global credit crunch, when, under Basel III, incremental capital charges for market risk that explicitly factored in the liquidity horizon of individual positions or sets of positions and required stressed-VaR scenarios were imposed.

The Basel II Accord

In 1999, the Basel Committee on Banking Supervision presented a new accord that sought to connect capital requirements more closely to the actual risks incurred by banks, while providing incentives for banks to develop more sophisticated and robust internal risk management systems and practices consistent with the different characteristics and complexities of their individual operations. This proposal was put forward in the aftermath of the Southern Asian (1997) and Russian (1998) financial crises, when incidences of poor governance and inadequate disclosure were identified as important contributors to systemic contagion.

The Basel II Accord, introduced finally in 2004, consisted of three pillars intended to strengthen the safety and soundness of the financial system.

- Pillar 1, *minimum capital requirements* establishes guidelines for the minimum capital cushion banks should carry to protect against credit, market, and operational losses.
- Pillar 2, *supervisory review*, complements Pillar 1, setting out principles for the examination process that regulators should engage in to assess the quality of a bank's risk management procedures and internal governance, including board of directors' involvement and accountability.
- Pillar 3, *market discipline*, establishes guidelines for the external disclosure of a bank's overall risk position to depositors, counterparties, investors, and the public-at-large.

Pillar 1: minimum capital requirements

The Basel II Accord required banks to set aside capital cushions against potential *credit*, *market*, and *operational* losses. We will begin by examining the conceptual aspects surrounding the alternative methodological approaches banks may adopt to assess and quantify each of these three risk categories. We will then proceed to present the Basel II Accord formulation of minimum required *eligible regulatory capital* (ERC) to cushion a bank's potential total credit, market, and operational losses.

Credit risk capital

Credit risk is the risk of loss for a bank resulting from the inability of its borrowers to repay their loans in full and on time. Credit risk capital models attempt to quantify potential credit losses through statistical treatment of historical information and simulation, such that an appropriate capital cushion against such losses is always in place.

The Basel II Accord proposes three alternative approaches to determine credit risk capital: (i) the *Standardized Approach*; (ii) the Foundation Internal Ratings Based (*Foundation IRB*) approach; and (iii) the Advanced Internal Ratings Based (*Advanced IRB*) approach.

The Standardized Approach recommends that *external* credit ratings issued by *recognized* credit rating agencies (CRAs) should be utilized by banks in the determination of the weights of their credit exposures to publicly rated borrowers. The Basel Committee on Banking Supervision sets out certain criteria which ratings agencies should satisfy, but it is up to national regulators to formally *recognize* CRAs in their jurisdictions.

As previously indicated, under Basel I, loans to private sector borrowers had a 100 percent risk weight, regardless of the borrower's credit rating. Under Basel II, risk weights of loans to businesses can vary from 20 percent to 100 percent, as shown in Table 6.2 below, utilizing Standard and Poor's ratings.

Basel II's Standardized Approach acknowledges also that *collateral* – guarantees pledged by a borrower as security – can reduce the magnitude of the potential loss from a loan. For example, proposed risk weight for residential loans backed by a first mortgage on the property is 35 percent.

Foundation IRB and Advanced IRB allow banks to make use of their internal processes to assess the creditworthiness of borrowers and resulting estimated expected loss and required capital charges.

The IRB approaches are distinct from both Basel I and the Standardized Approach in that they introduce explicitly the concept of *unexpected loss*. Under the Internal Ratings Based approaches a bank must estimate both *expected loss* (EL) and *unexpected loss* (UL). Expected loss is a clearer statistical concept and, under Basel II, expected losses should be covered by banks from *current earnings* through the establishment of *loan loss provisions*. Unexpected loss is by definition – and as amply illustrated in Chapter 4 and Chapter 5 – much more difficult to predict.

While IRB credit risk capital models can become very mathematically-complex, they seek to reach robust estimates of potential losses through examination of the statistical relationships between five basic elements: *maturity* (M), *probability of default* (PD), *exposure at default* (EAD), *loss given default* (LGD) and *recovery rate* (RR).

It should be noted that, under the IRB approaches, banks are not required to specify risk weights for different types of loans, as estimation of *expected losses* (to be cushioned by provisions for loan losses), *and unexpected losses* (to be cushioned by capital) are generated by their internal models.

Under Foundation IRB only probability of default (PD) can be estimated internally by the bank; all other parameters are provided by the bank's supervisor. Under Advanced IRB, banks can use their internally generated information to

Table 6.2 Risk weights for corporates

Credit Assessment	AAA to AA−	A+ to A−	BBB+ to BB−	Below BB−	Unrated
Risk Weights	20%	50%	100%	150%	100%

Source: Bank for International Settlements 2001:8

estimate all the components of their credit risk capital models. Implicit in this distinction was an acknowledgement by bank regulators that banks with larger and more robust proprietary and more sophisticated internal credit rating models and risk management systems should be permitted to enjoy lower capital charges than those less able to estimate potential losses.

Market risk capital

Market risk is the risk of loss for a bank due to changes in interest rates, exchange rates, and the prices of securities and commodities.

The Basel Committee on Banking Supervision's first formal acknowledgement of concern with minimum capital requirements for market risk came about in 1996, through the issuance of the Market Risk Amendment to Basel I.

As discussed in Chapter 2, from the mid 1980s onward, banks had begun to change quickly from being, mainly, providers of hold-to-maturity loans to being increasingly also underwriters and traders of securities. Through securitization, they could transform loans into tradable assets. At the same time, market volatility pushed them to increasingly trade risk protection instruments, such as interest rate swaps and exchange rate forwards and, more recently, credit derivatives. Some banks have remained fundamentally end-users of derivatives; others would become market-makers in these instruments.

From Basel II, the first step in the determination of market risk is to allocate a bank's assets to its *banking book* or its *trading book*. Hold-to-maturity assets, such as loans, should be included in the banking book. Certain instruments used by the bank to hedge these assets (such as interest rate swaps) are allowed to be part of the banking book. Banking book assets are valued according to their historical cost.

Assets held with the intention to trade – or sell in the short-term – should be included in the trading book. These assets have to be *marked-to-market*, that is, valued at their *current market price*.

Unfortunately, this distinction, based on *intent*, between banking and trading book assets is less clear in practice. As indicated above, bets with derivatives – such as interest rate, foreign exchange, and credit default swaps, that can be construed as intended to mitigate credit risk and/or potential losses from asset/ liability mismatches imbedded in the banking book, can be carried also in the banking book. However, such *hold-to-maturity* positions can be reclassified as *available for sale* and migrate to the trading book, or vice-versa, at any moment in time.

For a number of banks, the majority of the losses arising from the U.S. subprime meltdown occurred in their trading books. This was due, in part, to *regulatory arbitrage*, the possibility for a bank to carry a position in the book that, at a particular moment, allows for a smaller capital charge. As we shall see, Basel III's market risk capital framework introduces the concept of an incremental risk capital charge for trading book assets, in effect curbing incentives to regulatory arbitrage between banking and trading books.

Under Basel II, as was the case under the Market Amendment to Basel I, banks are permitted to develop their internal market risk capital approach (MRA) to determine the minimum capital cushions for market risk.

Banks' MRAs typically consist of applications of VaR methodologies incorporating mathematical and statistical refinements to capture the effects of diversification, such as the beneficial effects of negative correlations, which make the total VaR of a set of portfolios smaller than the sum of the VaRs of individual portfolios. As indicated above, these guidelines were amended only in the aftermath of the subprime meltdown crisis and global credit crunch, when incremental capital charges for market risk, that took into consideration the liquidity horizon of individual positions or sets of positions and required stressed-VaR scenarios, would be imposed under Basel III.

In order to have their MRAs accepted by bank supervisors, a bank must demonstrate that it engages in regular stress-testing of VaRs, it maintains independent risk management and audit and control departments, and it integrates satisfactorily the measurement and the management, with the involvement of senior management and the board of directors as we will see under Pillar II, Supervisory Review.

Operational risk capital

Operational risk is the risk of loss as a result of failed internal processes due to human error or systems disruption, or external events. Examples of human failures include technical processing and control errors, including fraud. System failures include breakdowns in front-office functions, such as the settlement of transactions among customers, or between customers and the bank, or back office functions, such as the internal booking of transactions and reconciliation of accounts.

The larger the size, scope of activities, and degree of internationalization, the larger tends to be the operational risk carried by a bank, and imposed by this bank on the financial system as a whole. However, operational failures, from rogue trading events to computer system breakdowns, are too infrequent and varied in nature to allow for a generalized satisfactory statistical treatment.

Basel II offers three basic approaches for the determination of *operational risk capital*:

(i)   the Basic Indicator Approach, where operational risk capital should be at least 12.5 percent of the bank's operating income before tax;
(ii) the Advanced Measurement Approach, which allows banks to use their internal model to assess operational risk and quantify the necessary capital cushion; and
(iii) the Standardized Approach, which allows banks to determine the necessary capital charge under close supervision of regulators.

Minimum required eligible regulatory capital

As indicated above, the responsibility to approve and monitor a particular bank's approach to quantifying its credit, market, and operational capital at risk falls to national regulators. In line with the Basel II Accord, however, all agree that regardless of the jurisdiction, the minimum required *eligible regulatory capital* (ERC) imposed by any national regulator must not be less than 8 percent of a bank's potential (expected plus unexpected) loss, or, as we will see below, a bank's *total assets weighted for credit, market and operational risks*. Algebraically:

ERC/TRWA >= 8%, where

TRWA, *total risk-weighted assets*, is the sum of CRWA, MRWA, and ORWA;

CRWA, *total risk-weighted assets for credit risk* is determined by either the Standardized or the IRB approaches;

MRWA, *maximum expected loss for market risk*, is defined as 12.5 times the bank's market risk capital (MRC), in turn determined according to either the Standardized or the Internal Models approach;

ORWA, *maximum expected loss for operational risk*, is defined as 12.5 times the bank's operational risk capital (ORC), in turn determined according to the Basic Indicator, Standardized or advanced Measurement Approach; and

ERC, *eligible regulatory capital*, is – as it was under Basel I – Tier 1 capital plus Tier 2 capital minus Deductions.

Tier 1 (or core) capital is defined as common plus non-cumulative perpetual preferred stock, plus accumulated retained earnings, plus certain accrued and secured gains, such as tax credits for losses carry-forward.

Tier 2 capital comprises cumulative perpetual preferred stock, other forms of subordinated term debt with minimum maturity of five years, and undisclosed (or non-specific) reserves, such as asset revaluation reserves and excess loan loss provisions.

Capital items that must be deduced to determine regulatory capital include goodwill (the excess over book value paid upon the acquisition of a business) and stock the bank may hold in another bank.

Under the Basel II Accord, minimum required *Eligible Regulatory Tier 1 Capital* (ERT1C) remained unaltered from Basel I at no less than 4 percent of a bank's total risk-weighted assets for credit, market, and operational risks.

Pillar 2: supervisory review

Pillar 2 establishes guidelines for the process that regulators should engage in to assess the robustness of banks' risk measurement and management processes. Focused on internal governance procedures, it addresses also the importance of oversight by the board of directors of risk management policy and practice.

Specific capital adequacy aspects include continuous assessment of the risk of loss arising from credit concentration, asset-liability mismatches (typically interest rate and foreign exchange) in the banking book, and/or external events, such as sovereign debt crises and business cycles.

Pillar 2 calls on management to have in place an *internal capital adequacy assessment process* to quantify both *current* and *future* capital requirements. The Basel Committee on Banking Supervision views the supervisory review process as a continued dialogue between bank and supervisor, so that rapid action towards restoration of adequate capital cushion can prevent a bank run and/or its failure.[1]

Pillar 3: market discipline

Pillar 3 sets out the *disclosure* requirements on material capital information banks should make available to regulators, investors, and the public at large. In line with Basel II's *Market Discipline* guidelines, a piece of information is material if "its omission or misstatement could change or influence the assessment or decision of a user relying on that information for the purpose of making economic decisions."

As publicly-traded companies, most banks are subject to high levels of disclosure of business and financial information by the securities and exchange regulators of the jurisdictions in which their stocks are listed. Pillar 3 goes further, requiring that banks now not only develop policies and procedures formally approved by their board of directors for the disclosure of *material* information, but also that they must regularly reevaluate what information should, or should not be, disclosed in the future.

Specific themes requiring regular disclosure include capital structure issues (e.g. Tier 1, Tier 2, and eligible regulatory capital), quantitative information on major credit (e.g. industry and geographic concentrations, provisions, write-offs) and market (e.g. VaRs for different types of portfolios, including asset-liability mismatches in the banking book) risk aggregates, and qualitative assessment of operational risks.[2]

The Basel III Accord

The 2007–9 subprime mortgage meltdown in the United States and its devastating impact on financial institutions around the world brought to the surface the evidence of both failed internal risk measurement and management procedures, and external regulatory supervision.

In response to this evidence, the Basel Committee on Banking Supervision issued its new set of official guidelines for bank regulation globally, in June 2011. Entitled *Basel III – A global regulatory framework for more resilient banks and banking systems.*

Basel III represented a severe tightening of Basel II guidelines for pillars 1, 2, and 3. Furthermore, it imposed two new financial standards – *minimum liquidity* and *maximum nominal leverage* – to be met by all banks, and established the need for additional capital requirements for the so-called *systemically important financial institutions* (SIFIs).

Pillar 1: minimum capital requirements

Basel III brought a significant increase in minimum capital requirements by restricting the definitions of Tier 1 and Tier 2 Capital, and increasing the minimum requirement of Tier 1 Capital as a percentage of total risk-weighted assets. It added a *minimum capital conservation buffer* of 2.5 percent, comprised of Common Equity Tier 1 Capital (see definition below), on top of Basel II's minimum capital requirement of 8 percent of total risk-weighted assets. Finally, Basel III imposed stricter risk coverage through the imposition of higher capital charges for certain types of exposure, as well as the elimination of incentives for arbitrage between banking and trading books, thereby increasing the total amount of risk-weighted assets against which the minimum capital cushions should be set.

In addition to these adjustments, Basel III introduces the concept of a *counter-cyclical capital buffer* to be demanded at the discretion of national regulators. This buffer, ranging from zero to 2.5 percent of total risk-weighted assets, should be imposed in a particular jurisdiction when regulators perceive that excessive credit growth has resulted in an unacceptable level of systemic risk.

Minimum eligible regulatory capital

Under Basel III, total eligible capital is the sum of Common Equity Tier 1, Additional Tier 1, and Tier 2 capital, as defined below.

Eligible Common Equity Tier 1 Capital (CET1) includes common shares issued, retained earnings, and other accumulated income and disclosed reserves. Certain deferred gains, such as deferred tax assets (DTAs), to be realized as income in the future from tax loss carry-forward, or secured mortgage servicing rights (MSRs), and previously considered (CET1), must be excluded.

Eligible Additional Tier 1 Capital (ADT1) includes those categories of debt securities that are *subordinated* to *depositors*, *creditors*, and *subordinated debt* issued by the bank. They must have been fully paid-in and: (i) cannot be secured by any guarantee provided by any related entity of the bank; (ii) are perpetual, meaning that there is no maturity date and/or no incentives to redeem; (iii) are callable by the issuer only after a minimum of five years and cannot be redeemed; (iv) command a dividend distribution that is not sensitive to the bank's credit standing and is subject to the bank's full discretion, interruption of which cannot impose any restrictions on the bank, except in relation to distribution to common shareholders; and (v) no related party over which the bank exercises control or influence may make a purchase that has been funded directly or indirectly by the bank.

Eligible Tier 2 Capital consists of paid-in securities subordinated to depositors and general creditors of the bank that: (i) are not secured by any guarantee provided by any related entity of the bank; (ii) have minimum original maturity of five years and are subject to linear amortization on a straight line basis over the last five years before maturity; (iii) are callable by the issuer only after a minimum of five years; (iv) cannot have a credit sensitive dividend feature; and (v) no related party over which the bank exercises control or influence may make a purchase that has been funded directly or indirectly by the bank.

Provisions held against future presently unidentified losses qualify for inclusion as Tier 2 Capital; provisions ascribed to any asset deterioration identified trend cannot be included as Tier 2 Capital.

Table 6.3 below summarizes Basel III's minimum capital requirements as well as their scheduled phase-in through 2019.

Conservation buffer (CB)

Under Basel III, banks are required to build capital conservation buffers outside periods of stress to protect against waves of unanticipated losses. Banks will be permitted to continue to do business as normal when total Common Equity Tier 1 Capital falls below the minimum of 7 percent, but above the minimum of 4.5 percent (see 2019 in Table 6.3). They would, however, be subject to constraints on distribution of earnings to replenish the conservation buffer, as indicated in Table 6.4. Other forms of distributions implying depletion of Common Equity Tier 1 Capital (such as share buybacks, discretionary payments on Tier 1 securities, or discretionary bonus payments to staff) would also be restricted.

Countercyclical buffer

> Losses incurred in the banking sector can be extremely large when a downturn is preceded by a period of excessive credit growth. These losses can destabilise the banking sector, spark a vicious circle … contribute to a downturn in the real economy that then feeds back… (Basel III: A global regulatory framework for more resilient banks and banking systems, *BIS, June 2011*)

The countercyclical buffer is intended to ensure that minimum capital requirements take into consideration the prevailing macro-financial environment of the individual jurisdictions in which financial institutions operate. National regulatory authorities should continuously assess whether excessive credit growth may be

Table 6.3 Minimum capital requirements, Basel III

Capital/TRWA	2013	2014	2015	2016	2017	2018	2019
Min. Common Equity (Min CET1)	3.5%	4.0%	4.5%	4.5%	4.5%	4.5%	4.5%
Capital Conservation Buffer (CB)				0.625%	1.25%	1.875%	2.5%
Min CET1 + CB	3.5%	4.0%	4.5%	5.125%	5.75%	6.375%	7.0%
Min. Tier 1 Capital	4.5%	5.5%	6.0%	6.0%	6.0%	6.0%	6.0%
Min. Total Capital	8.0%	8.0%	8.0%	8.0%	8.0%	8.0%	8.0%
Min. Total Capital + CB	8.0%	8.0%	8.0%	8.625%	9.25%	9.875%	10.5%

Source: Bank for International Settlements 2010: Annex 4

Table 6.4 Capital conservation standards

Individual bank minimum capital conservation standards

Common Equity Tier 1 Ratio	Minimum Capital Conservation Ratios (expressed as a percentage of earnings)
4.5% – 5.125%	100 %
>5.125% – 5.75%	80 %
>5.75% – 6.375%	60 %
6.375% – 7.0%	40 %
>7.0%	0 %

Source: Bank for International Settlements 2010: 56

causing a build-up of systemic risk, in which case a system-wide countercyclical buffer should be imposed temporarily, to be released only when the cloud which triggered the buffer in the first place has dissipated.

The countercyclical buffer can range from zero to 2.5 percent of total risk-weighted assets and must be in the form of Common Equity Tier 1 Capital.[3] The countercyclical buffer, similarly to the capital conservation buffer, is to be enforced through restrictions on distributions for banks failing to satisfy the requirement. A decision by a jurisdiction to introduce or raise its countercyclical buffer requirement must be announced 12 months in advance of the date the requirement takes effect; a decision to decrease the level of the countercyclical buffer becomes effective immediately.

Internationally active banks would be subject to an overall countercyclical capital buffer requirement equal to the weighted average of the requirements imposed by the jurisdictions where they maintain credit exposures. Countercyclical buffer decisions by all jurisdictions will be made public by the Basel Committee on Banking Supervision on the BIS website in real time.

Risk coverage

> In addition to raising the quality and level of the capital base, there is a need to ensure that all material risks are captured… Failure to capture major on- and off-balance sheet risks, as well as derivative based exposures, was a key factor that amplified the crisis… (Basel III: A global regulatory framework for more resilient banks and banking systems, *BIS, June 2011*)

From a conceptual standpoint, there were three major types of adjustments brought about by Basel III to enhance risk coverage, thereby increasing the total amount of risk-weighted assets against which the minimum capital requirements would be set.

The first type of adjustment was the establishment of higher capital charges for securitization exposures as well as the elimination of the incentive to regulatory arbitrage between the trading book and the banking book through the leveling out of the capital charges for such exposures held in either book.[4] The second was the imposition of a capital charge for counterparty credit risk equal to the greater between the portfolio capital charge under current market conditions and the portfolio capital charge resulting from a stress calibration considering three years of historical information[5] – as opposed to one, under Basel II. The third type of adjustment, directed specifically at derivatives exposures, was the imposition of stricter margin requirement standards for large and illiquid derivatives exposures, in addition to an incentive for banks to migrate their derivatives exposures from the over-the-counter (OTC) market to central counterparties (CCPs), with exposure to the latter commanding a low risk weight (2 percent).

We will return to the discussion of capital charges and margin requirements for derivatives – including potentially diverging guidelines for swap regulation among different jurisdictions – in Chapter 10, Global Trends post-Crisis.

Maximum leverage

> One of the underlying features of the crisis was the build-up of excessive on- and off-balance sheet leverage in the banking system. In many cases, banks built up excessive leverage while still showing strong risk based capital ratios... (Basel III: A global regulatory framework for more resilient banks and banking systems, *BIS, June 2011*)

The main purpose of Basel III's *maximum leverage* requirement is to constrain the build-up of excessive leverage through a *non-risk based* backstop measure. The Basel Committee on Banking Supervision has, in principle, established that a minimum Tier 1 Capital leverage ratio of 3 percent will be tested between January 1, 2013 and January 1, 2017.

The transition to full implementation of Basel III's maximum leverage requirement encompasses three stages.

- Stage 1, *supervisory monitoring* period, begun on January 1, 2011, focuses on the development of the templates for the determination of non-risk based total exposure.
- Stage 2, *parallel run* period, runs from January 1, 2013 until January 1, 2017. During this period, banks will be required to calculate their leverage ratios according to the principles summarized below and to begin disclosure on January 1, 2015.
- Stage 3, consisting of final adjustments to the definition and calibration of the leverage ratio, will be conducted between January 1, 2017 and June 30, 2017, for formal migration to a Pillar 1 minimum capital requirement on January 1, 2018.

The following principles apply in the calculation of leverage ratios:

(i) The numerator – *capital measure* – for the maximum leverage ratio is Tier 1 Capital, as previously defined.

(ii) The denominator, *exposure measure*, is to be determined according to the following guiding principles:

    a.   on-balance sheet non-derivative exposures are to be considered net of specific provisions;

    b.   financial guarantees or collateral does not reduce on-balance sheet exposures;

    c.   on-balance sheet derivative exposures must combine the present value of the contract (typically zero at the outset but subsequently positive or negative depending of the performance of the underlying security) *plus an add-on for potential future* exposure, seeking to ensure that a derivative is converted into a potential loan amount; and

    d.   contingent off-balance sheet exposures – such as acceptances, standby letters of credit, liquidity facilities – command a 100 percent credit conversion factor; cancellable off-balance sheet commitments by the bank, even if unconditional at any time, must command a 10 percent credit conversion factor.

Minimum liquidity

> Strong capital requirements are a necessary condition for banking sector stability but by themselves are not sufficient. A strong liquidity base reinforced through robust supervisory standards is of equal importance (Basel III: A global regulatory framework for more resilient banks and banking systems, *BIS, June 2011*).

As evidenced by the 2008 financial crisis, rapid reversal in market conditions can cause liquidity to evaporate, which accelerates the fall in asset prices. Banks with adequate capital levels may experience severe funding difficulties, exacerbating significantly both the scale and credit risk of any intervention by central banks as lenders of last resort.

In response to this threat, the Basel Committee on Banking Supervision published a new set of guidelines for liquidity risk management in 2008 (Basel Committee 2008), providing specific, detailed recommendations to banks and bank supervisors on the measurement and monitoring of liquidity risk.

In December 2010, the Basel Committee on Banking Supervision proposed two minimum standards of liquidity, to undergo a period of observation beginning on January 1, 2011. These were:

- the *Liquidity Coverage Ratio* (LCR), aimed at ensuring banks' resilience to a short-term (30 day) stress scenario of eroded liquidity, to become a requirement on January 1, 2015; and,
- the *Net Stable Funding Ratio* (NSFR), aimed at limiting banks' over-reliance on short-term, and potentially unstable, funding, and inducing them to take adequate account of the liquidity risk associated with both on- and off

balance sheet positions, such as contingent liabilities, to become a requirement on January 1, 2018.

As shown in Table 6.5, different conversion factors were attributed to the various categories of assets and liabilities to undergo assessment and calibration by supervisors across all jurisdictions, during an observation period begun in 2011.

In January 2013, the Basel Committee issued its revised LCR requirement, providing banks some respite from the original December 2010 proposal, as summarized below:[6]

- The introduction of the LCR as a minimum requirement would be maintained as originally scheduled for January 1, 2015 but 'the minimum requirement will begin at 60%, rising in equal annual steps of 10 percentage points to reach 100% on 1 January 2019. This graduated approach is designed to ensure that the LCR can be introduced without disruption to the orderly strengthening of banking systems or the ongoing financing of economic activity.'

Table 6.5 LCR and NSFR conversion factors (sample of conversion factors under observation)

$$LCR = \frac{\text{Stock of highly liquid assets}}{\text{Net cash flow over 30-day stress period}} > 100\%$$

Highly Liquid Assets	Factor	Cash Outflows	Factor
Public sector bonds with 0% risk weight	100%	Stable deposits (retail)	7.5%
Corporate bonds w. rating AA- and over	80%	Institutional funding with operational relationships	25%
Corporate bonds w. rating A up to AA-	60%	Institutional funding w/o operational relationships	75%

$$NSFR = \frac{\text{Available amount of stable funding}}{\text{Required amount of stable funding}} > 100\%$$

Available Stable Funding	Factor	Required Stable Funding	Factor
Tier 1 and Tier 2 Capital	100%	Fully liquid s-t assets, < 1 year	0%
Long term funding >= 1 year	100%	Highly liquid assets, >= 1 year, 0% risk	5%
Stable deposits (retail < 1 year)	85%	Very liquid, corp. bonds >= 1 year, rating >= AA	20%
Less stable (SMEs < 1 year)	70%	Liquid, corp. bonds >= 1 year, rating >= A-	50%
Wholesale non-FIs < 1 year	50%	Less liquid, retail loans < 1 year	85%
Other liabilities	0%	Illiquid, receivables from FIs, other	100%

Source: Authors, from *Bank for International Settlements* 2009

- Amendments to the definition of high-quality liquid assets (HQLA, the numerator of the LCR) to allow for assets characterized as low-risk, easy to value, lowly correlated with risky assets and traded in a recognized exchange to be included as Level 2 assets in the HQLA calculation, provided that Level 2 assets do not exceed 40 percent of HQLA and that each Level 2 asset category commands a pre-defined haircut ranging from 15% to 50% of its market value.

Pillar 2 and Pillar 3

The 2007–9 U.S. subprime crisis and global credit crunch highlighted the failure of banks to put in place the necessary internal processes for firm-wide high standards of risk assessment and governance recommended by Basel II (Pillar 2), as well as to achieve the standards of disclosure of material information to regulators, investors, and the public at large (Pillar 3).

Regarding *risk management and supervision* (Pillar 2), the Basel III Accord requires banks to demonstrate to bank supervisors that they are fully capable of:

- capturing the risk of loss from off-balance sheet exposures and securitization activities, and properly assessing portfolio concentration risk;
- establishing and consistently maintaining incentives for the long-term alignment of risk and return, including adherence to sound compensation practices;
- stress-testing and properly accounting for financial instruments; and
- consistently operating under a high standard of internal governance, which includes the establishment of well-defined internal supervisory colleges and accountability.

Regarding market discipline (Pillar 3), Basel III specifically requires:

- enhanced disclosure of securitization exposures and sponsorship of off-balance sheet vehicles;
- enhanced disclosure of the components of regulatory capital with reconciliation to the reported financial statements, and a comprehensive explanation of how regulatory capital ratios are calculated.

Systemically important financial institutions

The 2008 financial crisis brought about the Basel III Accord, which, as detailed above, represented a most severe tightening of Basel II requirements for all internationally active banks. However, the political clamor against the huge cost to public coffers of government bail-outs of financial institutions, combined with the acknowledgement by legislators of the dangerous increase in moral hazard brought about by such interventions, caused governments around the world to engage in the debate on how to end *too big to fail*. How should they implement legislation to both minimize the risk of failure of *systemically important financial institutions* (SIFIs) and, when and if necessary, resolve in an orderly manner a failed SIFI at no cost to taxpayers?

The goal of further mitigation of the risk of failure by a systemically important bank is addressed also by the Basel III Accord, as described in Global Systemically Important Banks (G-SIBs) and Domestic Systemically Important Banks (D-SIBs), below. Measures regarding the regulation of non-bank financial institutions and the mechanisms being put in place by individual jurisdictions to end too big to fail are discussed under the sub-heading Beyond Basel, at the end of the chapter.

Global systemically important banks

As part of the Basel III guidelines for international bank regulation, the Basel Committee on Banking Supervision has already put in place additional require-ments for those institutions whose failure is considered not permissible because of a combination of their size, interconnectedness, non-substitutability, and/or complexity. The aims of these policies[7] are to reduce the probability of failure by globally systematically important banks (G-SIBs); and to reduce the impact of G-SIBS' failures through the establishment of resolution frameworks.

The minimum additional loss absorbency cushion required – 1 percent to 3.5 percent of total risk weighted assets, necessarily in the form of Common Equity Tier 1 Capital – is a function of the bucket into which that particular G-SIB falls in terms of the impact its failure would have on the global financial system (see Table 6.6).

The assessment methodology for determining into which bucket a G-SIB should belong entails an indicator-based measurement approach that gives equal weights to the following five characteristics: cross-jurisdictional activities, size, interconnectedness, substitutability, and complexity.

The cross-jurisdictional activity indicator seeks to capture the bank's activities (claims and liabilities) outside its home jurisdiction relative to the overall activi-ties of the other banks in the sample.

Size is measured using the same definition of total exposures that applies when determining the bank's leverage ratio, the score for each bank determined by the

Table 6.6 G-SIBs' buckets and minimum additional loss absorbency cushion stock of highly liquid assets

Bucket	Score Range	Additional Loss Absorbency Req.
5	D	3.5%
4	C-D	2.5%
3	B-C	2.0%
2	A-B	1.5%
1	A	1.0%

Source: Authors, based on *Bank for International Settlements*, 2011: 15

ratio between its total exposure and the sum of the total exposures of the other banks in the sample.

Interconnectedness is measured by the amount of intra-financial system assets and liabilities the bank carries on its balance sheet, and takes into consideration its wholesale funding ratio, defined as the ratio between total liabilities minus retail funding (retail deposits plus debt securities held by retail customers) and total liabilities.

Substitutability seeks to capture the bank's relative importance as a market participant and/or service provider, and is broken down into three indicators: assets under custody, payments cleared and settled, and values of underwritten transactions in debt and equity markets.

Complexity, finally, seeks to capture the greater cost and time required to resolve the failure of relatively more complex financial institutions. Three complexity indicators are considered in the calculation: (i) OTC derivatives notional value, that is, the ratio between the gross nominal value of the bank's total derivatives contracts not cleared through a central counterparty platform, and the total amounts for all the banks in the sample; (ii) Level 3 assets, that is, the amount of claims held by the bank for which only estimated value ranges can be produced as they cannot be determined using observable measures such as secondary markets and/or acceptable internal or external rating methodologies; and (iii) the value of held for trading and available for sale claims, as these assets are subject to much more severe and immediate loss of value than banking book assets under conditions of institutional or general market distress.

Individual jurisdictions are expected to maintain high quality data on the indicators selected, ensuring that the centralized data hub established is kept current, robust, and transparent to all participants.

The additional loss absorbency requirement for G-SIBs incorporates elements of Pillar 1 (consequences for the bank of failing to meet the additional capital requirement), and Pillar 2 (use of supervisory judgment for final allocation of individual banks to buckets). Regardless of whether it is understood as a Pillar 1 or Pillar 2 guideline, the additional loss absorbency requirement "sits on top of the capital buffers and minimum capital requirement, with a pre-determined set of consequences for banks that do not meet this requirement" (Bank for International Settlements, 2011: 21).

In November 2011, the Financial Stability Board (FSB) and the Basel Committee on Banking Supervision published an initial list of G-SIBs, and announced that the group of G-SIBs, with the possible inclusion of non-bank G-SIFIs, would be updated annually, based on new data published by the FSB. This first G-SIB list featured 29 financial institutions: Bank of America, Bank of New York Mellon, Citigroup, Goldman Sachs, JPMorgan Chase, Morgan Stanley, State Street, and Wells Fargo Bank (US); HSBC, Barclays, Lloyds Banking Group, and Royal Bank of Scotland (UK), Deutsche Bank and Commerzbank (Germany); BNP Paribas, Banque Populaire CdE, Group Crédit Agricole, and Société Générale (France); ING Groep (Holland); Banco Santander

Table 6.7 Indicator-based measurement approach

Indicator-based measurement approach

Category (and weighting) Weight	Individual Indicator	Indicator Weighting
Cross-jurisdictional activity (20%)	Cross-jurisdictional claims	10%
	Cross-jurisdictional liabilities	10%
Size (20%)	Total exposure as defined for use in the Basel III leverage ratio	20%
Interconnectedness (20%)	Intra-financial system assets	6.67%
	Intra-financial system liabilities	6.67%
	Wholesale funding ratio	6.67%
Substitutability/financial institution infrastructure (20%)	Assets under custody	6.67%
	Payments cleared and settled through payment systems	6.67%
	Value of underwritten transactions in debt and equity markets	6.67%
Complexity (20%)	OTC derivatives notional value	6.67%
	Level 3 assets	6.67%
	Held for trading and available for sale value	6.67%

Source: *Bank for International Settlements* 2011: 5

(Spain); UniCredit (Italy); Dexia (Belgium); Bank Credit Suisse and UBS (Switzerland); Nordea (Sweden); Mitsubishi UFJ FG, Mizuho FG, and Sumitomo Mitsui FG (Japan); and Bank of China (China). The second list, published in November 2012, no longer featured Dexia, Lloyds, and Commerzbank, but included two new banks, Standard Chartered and BBVA. Published in November 2013, the third list featured 29 banks, with the additional loss absorbency requirement imposed on each name (see Table 6.8).

Domestic systemically important banks

Upon endorsing the rules text for G-SIBS in November 2011, the G-20 leaders asked the Financial Stability Board and the Basel Committee on Banking Stability to develop a framework for *domestic systemically important banks* (D-SIBs), defined as banks that, while not likely to provoke significant cross-border negative externalities, can cause serious negative externalities to their domestic financial system and economy, with potential spillovers at the regional or bilateral levels.

The Basel Committee on Banking Stability's proposed principles to guide individual jurisdictions in the assessment methodology, and *higher loss absorbency* (HLA) requirements for D-SIBs were published on October 11, 2012 under the title *A Framework for dealing with systemically important banks* (Basel Committee 2012).

Table 6.8 Additional loss absorbency requirement for G-SIBs (as of November 2013)

Bucket	Minimum Additional Requirement	Banks
5	3.5%	
4	2.5%	HSBC, JPMorgan
3	2.0%	Citigroup, Deutsche Bank, Barclays, BNP Paribas
2	1.5%	Bank of America, Goldman Sachs, Morgan Stanley, Credit Suisse, UBS, Mitsubishi UFJ FG, RBS, Crédit Agricole
1	1.0%	Wells Fargo, Bank of New York Mellon State Street, Standard Chartered, Société Générale, Group BPCE, ING, Santander, BBVA, Nordea, Unicredit Sumitomo Mitsui FG, Mizuho FG, Bank of China, ICBC China

Source: *Authors from Bank for International Settlements 2013: 12, and company reports*

The D-SIBs proposed framework allows for national discretion to accommodate the structural characteristics of domestic financial systems, but it also encourages individual jurisdictions to go beyond the minimum suggested D-SIB loss absorbency requirement if the specific features of the country and its domestic banking sector make this necessary. In the United States, for example, bank regulators (Federal Reserve, Federal Deposit Insurance Corporation, and Comptroller of the Currency) announced on April 8, 2014, that eight bank holding companies[8] hold capital equal to at least five percent (as opposed to the minimum three percent proposed under the Basel III maximum leverage constraint discussed above).

In principle, the bank-specific characteristics identified as determinants of the impact of a D-SIB failure are the same as those for G-SIBs, excluding cross-jurisdictional activity. They are: size, interconnectedness, substitutability, and complexity (the latter including complexities from cross-border activities).

Regarding HLA, host authorities are expected to impose higher loss absorbency requirements on foreign banks identified as D-SIBS in their jurisdictions, and home authorities should impose the higher of the D-SIB or G-SIB HLA requirements in the case of a banking group that has been classified as both a D-SIB and a G-SIB.

Beyond Basel III

The 2008 financial crisis brought about a major revision of the regulatory framework for banks globally, as reflected in our examination of the Basel III Accord. Furthermore, it opened the door to intense questioning by society and concrete legislative proposals regarding: (i) curbing the scope of certain risky activities, in particular proprietary trading (e.g. Volcker Rule, United States; Ring-fencing, United Kingdom; and Separate Legal Entity, European Union); (ii) specific regulation and supervision for derivatives trading (swap regulation); and (iii) ending too big to fail; and, (iv) regulation and supervision of systemically important non-bank financial intermediaries, or shadow banks.

Curbing proprietary trading

Volcker rule (United States)

Named after Paul Volcker, former Chairman of the U.S. Federal Reserve System, the Volcker Rule is a provision of the Dodd-Frank Act, passed by the U.S. Congress in 2009, which curbs the ability of banks to engage in proprietary trading.

As defined in Chapter 2, banks engage in proprietary trading when they trade in securities and derivative contracts for their own account – as opposed to acting as intermediaries on behalf of customers, the ultimate holders of the position traded. The Volcker Rule's basic intent, to prevent vital banking services provided by a financial institution from being abruptly compromised as a result of risk taken by the institution in non-vital activities, is shared by the United Kingdom's ring-fence. However, it approaches the challenge in a very different way, and instead of requiring the erection of a protective wall around the financial institution's commercial banking activities, the Volcker Rule pushes outside of the banking entity this high risk and non-client oriented activity, typically part of the institution's investment banking platform.

The main definitional challenges for implementation of the Volcker Rule are determining exactly what constitutes an acceptable hedge position taken to protect the bank against losses in its banking book, and establishing very clearly where client-oriented securities underwriting and market-making activities end and proprietary trading begins. With regard to acceptable hedges against potential losses in the banking book, JPMorgan's London whale trade debacle of 2012 (resulting in a US$5 billion loss as described in Chapter 4) raised the question of whether it was a legitimate form of portfolio hedging or a speculative play on short-term price movements.

Regarding securities underwriting and market-making, regulators understand that in order to best execute these client-service oriented functions (see Chapter 2), banks must be able to carry positions. As such, the Volcker Rule establishes that: (i) activities that mitigate specific risks associated with the institution's other positions and do not give rise to new exposures qualify as hedging under the rule; and (ii) market-making and underwriting positions are to be allowed to the extent that they do not exceed the reasonably expected near-term demands of clients and the revenue they generate does not primarily accrue from appreciation of the positions' value.

A third area of the exclusion of positions considered proprietary trading under the Volcker Rule are those taken in conjunction with *bona fide liquidity management*. Again, however, the frontier between what is acceptable as necessary flexibility for a bank to conduct prudent asset-liability management and what becomes abuse in the form of proprietary trading remains to be clearly defined.

Ring-fence (United Kingdom)

In 2010, the U.K. Government established the *Independent Commission on Banking* (ICB) to re-examine all aspects of the 2008 financial crisis and propose banking reforms that would ensure the stability and competitiveness of the U.K. financial system.

The ICB's final report was published in September 2011 (ICB 2011), and served as the basis for the Banking Reform Bill presented to the U.K. Parliament by the Treasury in October 2012. This bill called for a dual approach: increasing banks' loss absorbency capacity (in line with the Basel III guidelines discussed above) and the *ring-fencing* of vital banking services.

The objective of the ring-fence is to protect those banking activities where the continuous provision of service is vital to a bank's customers and the economy from shocks caused by market volatility in non-vital risk-taking activities. Activities required to be within the ring-fence include the taking of deposits from and lending to individuals and small and medium enterprises in the European Economic Area (EEA). The United Kingdom's international treaty obligations establish the European Economic Area, rather than the United Kingdom, as the appropriate geographic scope for U.K. banks. Deposit taking from customers other than individuals and small and medium enterprises, and lending to large companies should be permitted – but not required – within the ring-fence.

Services should not be conducted within the ring-fence if they do not constitute provision of payment services to customers in the European Economic Area or intermediation between savers and borrowers within the European Economic Area's non-financial sector, or result in increased exposure by the ring-fenced bank to the global financial markets, or if they would significantly complicate the resolution of the ring-fenced bank in the case of a crisis.

Domestic retail banking services should be within the ring-fence; global wholesale/investment banking services, outside, and provision of straightforward commercial banking services to large non-financial companies can be within or without the ring-fence.

A bank's ring-fenced activities must be housed in a separate subsidiary, required to meet capital, liquidity and funding regulatory standards on a stand-alone basis. The ring-fenced subsidiary's relationship with other parts of its financial group must be conducted at arm's length and should be no greater than generally allowed by regulators with third parties.

The Independent Commission on Banking acknowledges that separation between ring-fenced and non-ring-fenced activities is not without cost for a bank. Operational costs may increase and flexibility to internally reallocate capital is curbed. However, the benefits of a universal banking-type business model are not compromised, with capital reallocation between ring-fenced and non-ring-fenced divisions possible (if minimum capital and liquidity standards of the ring-fenced activities are not violated), one-stop relationships for customers demanding both retail and investment banking services remain viable through internal agency agreements, information and expertise can be shared throughout the organization, and some operational infrastructure and branding benefits remain intact.

Separate legal entity requirement (EU)

In February 2012, the European Commission[9] established the *High-level Expert Group on Reforming the Structure of the EU Banking Sector*, to assess whether additional reforms targeting the structure of banks specifically would further reduce the probability and impact of bank failures, and better protect retail clients.

In its final report,[10] presented to the Commission in October 2012, the High-level Expert Group concluded that, in addition to the reforms already proposed – stricter capital and liquidity requirements, stronger risk management and governance standards, as well as disclosure requirements and the need for banks to have drawn up and made public effective recovery and resolution plans – proprietary trading activities should be assigned to an entirely separate legal entity (Liikanen et al. 2012).

These separated proprietary activities could still be carried out by an EU bank within the same banking group, but explicit and implicit guarantees carried by deposits would no longer support proprietary trading activities, as is also the intent of the Volcker rule in the United States and the ring-fence in the United Kingdom.

Swap regulation

On both sides of the Atlantic, legislators have gone beyond the Basel III imposition of higher capital requirements for OTC derivatives trading (Title VII of the Dodd-Frank Act in the United States; the European Market Infrastructure Regulation in the European Union) to require that a wide range of standardizable derivatives contracts be traded on organized exchanges and processed through *central counterparty clearing houses* (CCPs); and remaining OTC traded contracts face substantially higher capital and collateral requirements, in addition to stricter regulatory oversight. While moving derivative trading to central counterparty clearing houses mitigates the effect of a default by a clearing member, it gives rise to the emergence of an important new concern – the risk of clearing house failure.

The more complex and illiquid a derivative contract is, the more unpredictable its associated margin call, so that untroubled unwinding of the bet is guaranteed without causing a loss for the central counterparty clearing house. Therefore, the more complex the derivative trade, the less suited for centralized clearing it tends to be.

As of late 2013, regulators were still determining the types of contracts that would be required to migrate to central counterparty clearing houses, and the capital charges to impose and reporting requirements to centralized data repositories to demand for those remaining OTC derivatives. Nevertheless, swap dealers globally were already advanced in their preparations for the necessary additional investment in data management, compliance procedures, and infra-structure costs to comply with the new regulatory framework for derivatives trading.

By early 2013, 65 financial institutions, including several of the largest banks in the United States, United Kingdom, France, Germany, Switzerland, and Japan had already registered with the U.S. Commodity Futures Trading Commission (CFTC) as swap-dealers under the Dodd-Frank Act, which requires higher capital, collateral, and trading standards (Brush and Leising, 2013).

Regulation of shadow banking

The Financial Stability Board has defined shadow banking as "the system of credit intermediation that involves entities and activities outside the regular bank-ing system" (Financial Stability Board, 2012: 1). As of year-end 2010, the esti-mated size of the shadow banking system globally was US$60 trillion, approximately half of total bank assets.

In line with the Financial Stability Board's definition above, shadow banking encompasses all non-bank entities engaged in the following activities:

- accepting funding with deposit-like characteristics (such as *money market funds*— or *MMFs*, subject to massive redemptions);
- performing maturity and/or liquidity transformation (such as investment funds, securities entities, and special purpose vehicles that provide credit, including securities lending liquidity to counterparties through repurchase (repo) agreements); and,
- transformation of credit risk through the issuance of credit guarantees (such as insurance companies and reinsurance undertaking entities).

Shadow banking poses a number of risks to the global financial system, including runs on deposits, not unlike what may happen to banks, but without the corre-sponding protection mechanisms; the build-up of high and hidden leverage, thereby increasing systemic risk, including potential asset-liability mismatches due to the typical short-term nature of the funding of shadow banking entities. Furthermore, there is the risk of regulatory arbitrage, as the absence of minimum capital and/or liquidity constraints pushes credit provision away from the banking system and toward the shadow banking system, particularly during economic booms. Finally, the interconnectedness of the shadow banking system with the banking system through both direct credit exposure by and to shadow banking entities, and the systemic effect on asset prices of the potential massive sale of certain positions by shadow banking entities, only serve to increase risk.

In line with the Financial Stability Board recommendation, regulation of shadow banking is to be pursued globally along the following major dimensions:

(i)   regulation of banks' interactions with shadow banking entities (indirect regulation);

(ii)   regulatory reform of money market funds (MMFs);
(iii) regulation of other shadow banking entities (interconnectedness with the domestic and global financial systems a core consideration here);
(iv)   regulation of securitization (particular issues for attention here being the establishment of minimum retention requirements for originators and the transparency/standardization of products); and
(v)   regulation of securities lending and repos, with key aspects for consideration here being clear and stricter guidelines regarding collateral, margin requirements, and the strengthening of market infrastructure for clearing, settlement and reporting of repos.

Ending too big to fail

As indicated above, ending too big to fail requires that jurisdictions have in place a workable legal framework to effect the orderly – meaning without systemic disruption of credit flows and at no cost to taxpayers – resolution of a troubled SIFI, if that were to be necessary.

In the United States, Title II of the Dodd-Frank Act provides the legal framework for the resolution of "failing financial companies that pose a significant risk to the financial stability of the United States in a manner that mitigates such risk and minimizes moral hazard" (Sec. 204(a): 81).

Title II reaffirms the role of the Federal Deposit Insurance Corporation as the government agency charged with the orderly resolution of troubled financial institutions, and establishes the special powers that can be exercised by the Federal Deposit Insurance Corporation in the resolution of a troubled financial company.

Appointment of the FDIC as receiver

Section 203 of the Dodd-Frank Act establishes that only the Secretary of the Treasury (Secretary) can appoint the Federal Deposit Insurance Corporation as receiver for a systemically important financial institution.

A recommendation to the Secretary to place a SIFI into receivership must be made in writing by the Board of Governors of the Federal Reserve System (FED) and the Federal Deposit Insurance Corporation. If the failing SIFI is a broker-dealer, the recommendation must be made by the FED and the U.S. Securities and Exchange Commission, in consultation with the Federal Deposit Insurance Corporation; if it is an insurance company, by the FED, and the Federal Insurance Office, in consultation with the Federal Deposit Insurance Corporation.

The Dodd-Frank Act guarantees an expedited review process in case of objection to the Secretary's determination by the board of directors of the targeted SIFI: a hearing in a federal district court must decide the matter in 24 hours; failure by the court to do so confirms the Secretary's appointment of the Federal Deposit Insurance Corporation as receiver of the troubled financial company.

Special powers under Title II

There are five special powers granted to the Federal Deposit Insurance Corporation as receiver under the Dodd-Frank Act: (i) the ability to establish a bridge bank; (ii) the ability to transfer qualified financial contracts; (iii) the ability to obtain funding from the Department of Treasury; (iv) advanced distributions, and (v) advanced resolution planning authority.

The ability to establish a bridge financial company addresses the need to ensure continuation of the key operations of the firm as the orderly liquidation proceeds. The bridge financial company is a new federally chartered company owned by the Federal Deposit Insurance Corporation, to which assets and liabilities of the troubled SIFI may be transferred. Shareholders and creditors whose claims do not migrate to the bridge financial company remain in the receivership, to collect on their claims according to their priority of claims against the original troubled company. The bridge financial company will remain in existence until the troubled SIFI's operations are stabilized and appropriate buyers for its assets are found.

Under the bankruptcy code, creditors of qualified contracts with a debtor company can liquidate (or net out) such positions in case of bankruptcy. The ability to transfer such contracts into a bridge financial company allows for protection of the value represented by these contracts as market stability is restored. Since most of these contracts tend to be well collateralized, transfer of such contracts to the bridge financial company should not expose the receiver to undue risk and may prevent the precipitous deterioration in value that tends to prevail at the time of the SIFI failure.

Also key to the continuation of operations of a troubled SIFI is the availability of funding for the operations to be preserved. Under Title II, the Federal Deposit Insurance Corporation can borrow funds from the Department of Treasury to secure the continuing operations of the receivership. These funds are to be given a priority as amounts owed to the United States. In the unlikely event that the proceeds from the disposition of assets of the receivership fail to allow for full repayment of amounts owed to the United States, a subsequent assessment on the industry will be imposed to recover those amounts.

Advanced distributions refer to the authority given to the Federal Deposit Insurance Corporation to make advance dividend payments to unsecured creditors, provided that such advances are important for the continuing operations of the receivership and are in amounts less than the estimated value of receivership assets, so that no deficit to the receivership results from such distributions.

Another key prerequisite for the orderly liquidation of a SIFI is to have a resolution plan in place in advance of the moment when an intervention is deemed necessary. The Dodd-Frank Act enhances this ability by requiring that financial companies identified as SIFIs have a resolution plan – or living will – in place, and by granting the Federal Deposit Insurance Corporation on-site access to real-time data related to the businesses of those institutions.

EU evolution towards common rule

One final and critical obstacle of particular importance in the establishment of a globally consistent and enforceable framework for international bank regulation and supervision is the need for resolution of internal regulatory responsibilities within the European Union among EU, Eurozone, and national authorities.

In November 2010, the European Parliament established the *European Systemic Risk Board* to assume responsibility for the prudential oversight of the financial system within the entire European Union. The European Systemic Risk Board, headquartered in Frankfurt and chaired by the President of the European Central Bank (ECB), was established to work closely with the newly formed European Supervisory Authorities (ESAs), namely the *European Banking Authority* (EBA), the *European Insurance and Occupational Pensions Authority* (EIOPA), and the *European Securities and Market Authority* (ESMA), all represented by their respective chairpersons with voting rights on the European Systemic Risk Board.

Neither the European Systemic Risk Board nor the European Supervisory Authorities would, however, replace national supervisory agencies, as reflected in the public statement made on January 1, 2011 by Michel Barnier, European Commissioner for Internal Market and Services, announcing the creation of the European Supervisory Authorities. National authorities would retain the responsibility for daily surveillance while European authorities would be responsible for coordination, monitoring, contributions to harmonization of technical rules, and, if need be, arbitration between national authorities.

While significant in facilitating the establishment of the necessary consensus for regulatory reforms to become law throughout the European Union, this ruling fell short of allowing for the "transfer of sovereignty" necessary to "produce coherent and effective regulation for the entire region" (Ugeux 2012: 18).

In September 2012, the European Commission presented the proposal of a single supervisory mechanism led by the ECB for all euro area banks. This proposal was put forward simultaneously with the issuance of recommendations regarding changes to the London based European Banking Authority – seeking to ensure regulatory and supervisory consistency between euro and non-euro member States – and a communication calling for a "single rulebook, common deposit protection and a single bank resolution mechanism" for the entire European Union (European Commission, 2012).

Finally, in April 2014, the European Parliament approved legislation setting a common rulebook to ensure implementation of the European Banking in 2015. This body of legislation establishes a single resolution mechanism for dealing with troubled banks, a common fund to recover costs associated with such actions, a uniform guarantee to depositors (€100,000), and a single bank supervisor, the ECB, with oversight responsibility for over 6,000 EU banks.

Summary

The ultimate goal of international bank regulation is to provide the standards to be followed by banks around the world to ensure the stability of the global financial system.

While the main international accords on bank regulation – Basel I in 1988, Basel II in 2004, and Basel III in 2011 – have been reached in the aftermath of financial crises, permanent work is conducted by the Basel Committee on Banking Supervision, in conjunction with bank regulators around the world, to continuously refine the regulatory framework, through amendments to the prevailing accord, and to monitor implementation.

We began this chapter with a brief review of the rationale for bank regulation and the examination of the Canadian regulatory regime – internationally acknowledged as one of the world's more robust in the aftermath of the 2008 global financial crisis – as a means to illustrate the challenges of bank regulation even within the context of a single legal jurisdiction.

We proceeded to study the evolution of international bank regulation as reflected in the three major global accords to-date, namely:

- Basel I, reached in the aftermath of the Latin American sovereign debt crisis in 1988, establishing the first minimum capital requirement standards for internationally active banks, and complemented by its 1996 Market Risk Amendment, in response to regulated banks' demands that securities portfolios, with secondary market liquidity, deserve a different treatment than hold-to-maturity loan portfolios;
- Basel II, reached in 2004, after five years of debate among regulators and banks around the world on how to avoid a repeat of the internal risk management and market disclosure failures revealed by the Asian (1997) and Russian (1998) crises; and,
- Basel III, reached in 2011 – for gradual implementation until 2019 – substantially tightening Basel II demands by the imposition of higher minimum capital requirement and a stricter definition of eligible capital; greater weights for several types of credit, market and operational risk exposures; introduction of minimum short-term and liquidity standards; introduction of a maximum nominal leverage ratio; more explicit demands on top management and boards of directors regarding internal risk management processes (Pillar 2) and market disclosure (Pillar 3); and, for global systemically important banks (G-SIBs), an additional layer of capital requirements in the form of an additional loss absorbency capital cushion to range from 1 percent to 3.5 percent of total risk-weighted assets.

We then discussed additional prudential regulatory measures that go beyond the Basel III framework and seek to prevent the failure of SIFIs, banks and non-banks and, in case of a SIFI failure, from it having to be bailed-out at taxpayers' expense.

We concluded the chapter with a brief discussion of the evolution of the European Union toward the establishment of common rules and coordinated enforceability of bank regulation across national jurisdictions, an ongoing, essential, and critical piece for the construction of a globally consistent and effective prudential regulatory framework.

Notes

1. For a more detailed description of the practical steps undertaken by regulators in implementing the Supervisory Review process see Apostolik et al. 2009, pp. 208–15.
2. For a more detailed description of the practical steps for implementation of the Market Discipline guidelines see Apostolik et al. 2009, pp. 215–18.
3. For more detail see Basel Committee on Banking Supervision *Guidance for National Authorities Operating the Countercyclical Capital Buffer*. December 2010. *http://www.bis.org/publ/bcbs187.pdf*, last visited December 9, 2012.
4. These adjustments had been already put in place by the Basel Committee on Banking Supervision in July 2009, as detailed in the document *Enhancements to the Basel II Framework*, BIS, July 2009, also known as Basel II.5.
5. For more detail on the methodological guidelines for determination of capital charges for counterparty credit risk, see Section V. Internal Model Method: measuring exposure and minimum requirements, Annex 4, *Basel III: A global regulatory framework for more resilient banks and banking systems*, BIS, June 2011.
6. Detailed description of the proposed methodology for the revised LCR calculation can be found at *Basel III: The Liquidity Coverage Ratio and liquidity risk monitoring tools*, Basel Committee on Banking Supervision, Jan 2013, *http://www.bis.org/publ/bcbs238.htm*, last visited August 8, 2014.
7. These additional policy measures are outlined in the Basel Committee on Banking Supervision document entitled *Global systemically important banks: assessment methodology and the additional loss absorbency requirement*, Bank for International Settlements, November 2011. *http://www.bis.org/publ/bcbs207.htm*, last visited August 8, 2014.
8. Bank of America, Citigroup, Wells Fargo, JPMorgan Chase, State Street Corp, Goldman Sachs, and Morgan Stanley.
9. The executive body of the European Union, responsible for proposing legislation, implementing decisions, upholding the Union's treaties, and the day-to-day running of the European Union.
10. Known as the *Liikanen Report* after Erkki Liikanen, the Group's Chairman.
11. *http://ec.europa.eu/internal_market/bank/docs/high-level_expert_group/report_en.pdf*, last visited August 8, 2014.

7   Banking in emerging economies

Introduction

In this chapter we examine the workings of the domestic banking systems of a select group of emerging economies. The countries we analyze – all G-20 nations and, as such, members of the Basel Committee on Bank Supervision – are Mexico and Brazil (Latin America), China, India, and Indonesia (Asia), and South Africa, Russia, and Turkey (Europe, Middle East, and Africa (EMEA)).

Our primary objective is to explore how domestic macroeconomic conditions, political forces, and major external events have combined to shape the structure of each country's banking industry, in particular the dynamics of competition among public sector, domestic private sector, and foreign banks.

With this purpose in mind, the examination of each country's banking system is divided into three parts: a brief historical perspective through the early 1990s; the key elements of bank reform and industry restructurings between the mid 1990s and the early 2000s; and the most recent developments and leading players as of year-end 2013.

We have chosen not to use terms such as BRICS (Brazil, Russia, India, China, and South Africa), MINT (Mexico, Indonesia, Nigeria, and Turkey), and other acronyms that attempt to group developing countries without regard for distinct historical, cultural, geopolitical, and institutional characteristics that, as we will see, are critical for the understanding of the evolution of financial systems. We use, instead, the traditional term *emerging* for these countries, all sizable economies facing important institutional and/or operational challenges in instituting robust domestic credit and equity markets.

Since the countries selected are all voting members of the Basel Committee on Bank Supervision (as such, explicitly committed to full adherence to the Basel regulatory guidelines), we have refrained from adding a section on bank regulation and supervision for each. Country-specific Financial System Stability Assessment (FSSA) reports published by the International Monetary Fund (IMF) (www.imf.org) are a useful source for students interested in the evolution of economic, institutional, and/or operational matters delaying the maturation and deepening of domestic capital markets.

We conclude the chapter with a brief discussion of the prospects for the New Development Bank (announced on July 15, 2014 by the presidents of its five founding nations – Brazil, Russia, India, China and South Africa) in relation to other multilateral development banks, namely the World Bank Group and the regionally focused Inter-American Development Bank, Asian Development Bank, African Development Bank, and the European Bank for Reconstruction and Development.

Mexico

Sovereign default and the banking system (early 1980s to mid 1990s)

In August 1982, the Mexican government officially announced its inability to continue honoring its international debt obligations. As discussed in Chapter 5, the causes were declining oil prices (Mexico's main source of foreign exchange); large outstanding foreign debts (US$80 billion, 60 percent of gross domestic product (GDP)); and the increased cost of servicing this debt (in light of the sharp increase in the LIBOR rate that had followed the increases in the U.S. Fed funds after 1979).

The country's severe economic deterioration (a 5 percent decline in GDP and a 70 percent devaluation of the Mexican peso) had the effect of causing skyrocketing credit losses for domestic banks, also, for the most part, exposed to large asset-liability mismatches (borrowing at lower rates in US dollars to lend at higher rates in Mexican pesos).

Faced with the insolvency of the financial system, the Mexican government decided to nationalize 58 of the country's 60 commercial banks. The exceptions were Citibank, the only foreign bank with commercial branches in Mexico, and Banco Obrero, a small labor union-owned bank. A process of liquidation of failed institutions and industry consolidation followed, reducing the number of commercial and development banks in Mexico from 68 in 1982, to 29 in 1983, and finally 18 in 1988. Commercial banks were permitted to lend freely at market rates only up to 25 percent of their loan portfolios; the remainder of the loans had to be allocated to priority economic sectors as mandated by the Government (Hernández-Murillo 2007).

Mexico's sovereign default was to be formally resolved with the signing of the region's first Brady agreement in 1989. Following that – and in sync with the country's continuously improving macroeconomic conditions (low inflation, economic growth, and foreign exchange stability) and trade liberalization (the North American Free Trade Agreement (NAFTA) would be signed in 1994) – a faster path towards financial liberalization began, which included the elimination of controls on interest rates and the mandated sectorial quotas imposed by the government on commercial lending.

In 1990, three pieces of legislation were implemented with the objective of increasing the efficiency of the Mexican banking system: first, the establishment of FOBAPROA (Banking Fund for the Protection of Savings), a new deposit insurance institution with the authority to intervene in failing banks; second, a constitutional amendment permitting the privatization of the Mexican banking sector; and third, new banking legislation allowing the formation of financial groups (or universal banks).

Re-privatization of the Mexican banking system was conducted between June 1991 and July 1992, via public auctions open only to bids by Mexican nationals. As no traditional private commercial bankers remained active, leading broker-dealers (or bolseros), stimulated by the new universal banking legislation, became the most natural candidates for control of the country's leading financial institutions (Tschoegl 2006).

Tequila crisis and banking industry restructuring (mid to late 1990s)

Continuously improving overall macroeconomic conditions (low inflation, exchange rate stability, and economic growth) stimulated the risk appetite of lenders and borrowers. Between 1989 and 1994, bank credit to the private sector expanded from 20 percent to 47 percent of GDP (over 25 percent per annum), but non-performing loans grew even more rapidly (from 4.1 percent to 7.3 percent between December 1991 and 1993 (Hernández-Murillo 2007).

Risky lending was further encouraged by a lack of accounting standards (such as the requirement of consolidated financial statements for financial conglomerates) and of adequate regulatory supervision of lending practices (e.g. loans to interested parties such as affiliates, shareholders, and/or directors). In addition, FOBRAPOA's then prevailing guarantee of 100 percent of bank deposits regardless of size provided no incentive for market policing of banking practices.

In 1994, a delicate political transition process (exacerbated by the assassination of a presidential candidate in Chiapas, one of the country's poorest regions) combined with an up-swing in international interest rates to pressure the Mexican peso, eventually causing a massive loss of foreign exchange reserves, from US\$ 17.6 billion to US\$4.4 billion between October and December 1994. A 50 percent devaluation of the Mexican peso in December pushed estimated annualized inflation over 40 percent. This second sovereign debt crisis was dealt with swiftly. In February 1995, Mexico announced its commitment to a stringent adjustment program to be monitored by the IMF in exchange for a broad US\$48 billion international financial rescue package consisting of a US\$17.8 billion stand-by credit facility from the IMF, a US\$20 billion exchange-stabilization facility from the US Federal Reserve, and a US\$10 billion short-term credit facility from the G-10 central banks (www.imf.org/external/np/sec/pr/1995/pr9510.htm).

The impact of the Tequila crisis on banks' balance sheets, however, was dramatic. Past due loans, already at 17 percent of total loans at the end of 1994, reached 36.5 percent by December 1995, the result of the sharp economic slow-down (real GDP fell 6 percent in 1995) and the foreign exchange asset-liability mismatches throughout the banking industry.

The rescue of the banking industry combined liquidity support from the country's central bank, Banco de Mexico, with a recapitalization mechanism managed by the country's deposit insurance corporation. The 1995 rescue package for the banking industry included also a new law permitting foreign banks to acquire Mexican banks if the bank being acquired did not account for more than 6 percent of the total capital of the industry. More attractive to foreign investors was another aspect of the new law raising their maximum possible equity stake in Mexican banks from 9 percent (as established in the 1994 NAFTA agreement) to 25 percent.

A new regulatory framework imposing stricter accounting standards, capital requirements, and disclosure rules was formally implemented by Mexican bank supervision authorities in January 1997 and, in December 1998, Congress removed all restrictions on foreign ownership of Mexican banks.

Recent developments and leading players (2000–2)

In December 1998, five foreign banks acquired five of the six largest commercial banks in Mexico. In 2000, BBVA (Spain) acquired control of Bancomer (No.1 in total assets); Citibank (U.S.) acquired control of Banamex (No.2); and Scotia Bank (Canada) acquired control of Inverlat (No.6). In 2001, Banco Santander (Spain) took control of Banca Serfin (No.4); and in 2002, HSBC (UK) acquired BITAL (No.3). Only Banorte (No.3) remained under Mexican ownership and control.

In line with the IMF's latest Financial System Stability Assessment for Mexico (IMF CR12/65, March 2012), as of June 2011, credit to Mexico's private sector remained among the lowest in Latin America at 20 percent of GDP, compared with 72 percent of GDP for Chile, and 52 percent of GDP for Brazil).

Table 7.1 Mexico's largest domestic lenders (as of December 31, 2013)

Institution	Total Assets (pesos billions)	No. of Retail Branches
Public Sector		
1. BANOBRAS	354.3	infrastructure lender
2. NAFINSA	352.2	industrial development agency
3. BANCOMEXT	215.9	export-import bank
4. SHF	94.9	housing finance agency
Domestic Private		
1. Banorte	840.8	1,284
2. Inbursa	280.3	318
3. Banco de Bajio	122.2	283
Foreign		
1. BBVA Bancomer	1,502.00	1,793
2. BANAMEX	1,286.40	1,683
3. Santander	905.5	1,234
4. HSBC	560.6	987
5. Scotia	265.9	628

Source: Authors, based on data from Comision Nacional Bancaria y de Valores (1 USD = 13 Mexican Pesos)

Forty-seven commercial banks were in operation in Mexico at year-end 2013. The seven largest banks accounted for approximately 80 percent of total banking industry assets. Foreign BBVA Bancomer, Banamex, Santander, HSBC, and Scotia still held five of the top seven positions, with domestic private Banorte and Inbursa ranked No.4 and No. 7 by total assets respectively.

Four government agencies, all constituted as development banks and, as such, not competing for retail banking deposits in the market place, account for all public sector lending to businesses and families in Mexico. They are BANOBRAS, for infrastructure finance, NAFINSA, for SME lending, BANCOMEXT, for export financing, and SHF, for low-income housing.

Brazil

Oil shocks, inflation and the Brazilian financial system (late 1970s to early 1990s)

The embryo of hyperinflation, with its severe consequences for Brazil's political and economic stability and the organization of its financial system, can be traced to the 1970s oil shocks, which brought an end to the so-called Brazilian economic miracle.

As a result of the 1973 Organization of the Petroleum Exporting Countries' (OPEC) oil embargo, Brazil's import bill doubled to US$12.6 billion, and the country's current account deficit quadrupled to US$7.1 billion from 1973–4. Increased foreign borrowings allowed for the postponement of a domestic aggregate demand adjustment. By the end of 1994, GDP growth had dropped to 4.8 percent (less than half the average observed for the period between 1968 and 1973), inflation had more than doubled to 40 percent from 16 percent in 1973); and foreign indebtedness had tripled, reaching US$43 billion (Sotelino 2011: 260–2).

The second oil price hike in 1979 (from US$12 to US$36/barrel) set the Brazilian economy on a downward spiral. Monetary tightening and a reduction in government expenditures followed. The economy contracted 6 percent between 1980 and 1983. When the economy returned to growth in 1984 and 1985, inflation had already reached 200 percent per annum.

In February 1987, following a significant, but failed, economic stabilization attempt that shook domestic financial markets (the Cruzado Plan), the Brazilian government announced the suspension of interest payments on its debt to private sector lenders. Normal relations with the international banking community would only be reestablished in the early 1990s, following the Brady agreement for Brazil (see Chapter 5).

Brazilian private sector banks had, however, managed to remain profitable during this difficult period by avoiding excessive credit risk and asset-liability mismatches. They had learned, also, to benefit from inflation (or float revenues): the allocation of a good portion of negative real interest rate funding coming through the branch network to holdings of short-term inflation adjusted government bills. By year-end 1993, such float income accounted for over 35 percent of total commercial banks' revenues.

Plano Real, tequila crisis and restructuring of the Brazilian banking industry (mid to late 1990s)

Brazilian's society exhaustion with hyperinflation, running over 1,000 percent in 1993, created the political conditions for the enactment of Plano Real.

Approved by Congress in December 1993, Plano Real called for a period of monetary preparation (full price indexation for all goods and services, with no price controls of any sort), fiscal preparation (tax increases), and anchoring of expectations through the introduction of a shadow currency (the Unit of Real Value (URV)), adjusted daily to represent the same amount in domestic currency (cruzeiro) of one US dollar. This period of preparation lasted six months. On July 1, 1994, the new Brazilian currency, the real, was introduced at the rate of one real per URV, then 2,750 cruzeiros. Extremely tight monetary policy was put in place in conjunction with the introduction of the new currency with a target federal funds rate of 40 percent per annum under the expectation of annualized inflation of around 10 percent for the remainder of the year.

Plano Real met with astounding macroeconomic success. The inflation rate dropped from 46.6 percent per month in June to 2.5 percent per month in October, and 0.6 percent per month in December; aggregate consumption increased by 20 percent between June and December 1994; and GDP growth for the year was 5.9 percent. Banks, eager to compensate for the loss of float revenues that resulted from the sharp drop in inflation, began to lend more aggressively.

Unfortunately for Brazil, the Tequila Crisis erupted in Mexico in late 1994, bringing capital flight and a significant devaluation of the Mexican peso, and a similar threat for the Brazilian real (BRL). Seeking to protect its newborn real, the Central Bank of Brazil raised sharply its daily base rate from 50 percent per annum in January, to 70 percent per annum in March, and imposed lending restrictions (e.g. maximum 90-day financing for credit card dues).

While successful in preventing a major devaluation of the real, this severe monetary tightening caused grave problems for many banks, as non-performing loans began to escalate. After a few months it had become clear that a government-assisted restructuring of the Brazilian banking industry was necessary.

In November 1995, the Central Bank of Brazil announced the Program of Incentives to the Restructuring and Strengthening of the National Financial System (PROER), intended to stimulate the absorption of troubled private sector banks by healthier ones. Soon thereafter, the Program for Reducing the Presence of the State Public Sector in Banking Activity (PROES) was put in place, creating the necessary mechanisms for the recapitalization of federal banks and the clean up and subsequent privatization of state-owned banks. Finally, and as occurred in Mexico, Congressional approval was given for the removal of all restrictions on foreign ownership of Brazilian banks.

The largest PROER transactions were the absorptions of Banco Nacional by its local competitor, Unibanco, in 1995, and the absorption of Banco Bamerindus by HSBC (UK), in 1997. Under PROES, the largest transactions were the acquisitions of BANERJ (Banco do Estado do Rio de Janeiro) and BEMGE (Banco do Estado de Minas Gerais), by Banco Itaú, and of BANESPA (Banco do Estado de Sao Paulo) by Banco Santander, Spain. The total estimated cost of the PROER and PROES programs amounted to 9 percent of GDP (Goldfajn et al. 2003: 16).

Recent developments and leading players

Between 2000 and 2007, the Brazilian banking industry experienced a purely market-driven period of consolidation. Private sector banks proceeded to acquire many of their smaller competitors, as well as most of the country's largest independent finance companies (such as FININVEST, purchased by Unibanco; FINASA, purchased by Bradesco; and Losango, purchased by HSBC). The last transaction of this feverish period of industry consolidation was the absorption of ABN-Real by Santander-BANESPA, to form the then second largest private sector bank in Brazil.

An important new round of industry consolidation was triggered by the eruption of the global credit crunch in 2008, as relative bank valuations shifted in favor of institutions with more stable retail funding. In November 2008, Banco Itaú acquired Unibanco to form Itaú-Unibanco, then the largest bank in Brazil by total assets. A few days later, Banco do Brasil announced the acquisition of Sao Paulo state-owned Nossa Caixa and, in late 2009, of a 50 percent equity stake in Banco Votorantim, regaining its position as the largest bank in Brazil.

Ninety-six commercial banks were in operation in Brazil at the end of 2013. The seven largest banks – three public sector, two domestic private, and two foreign – accounted for over 90 percent of total banking industry assets. Government-controlled and publicly listed Banco do Brasil ranked No.1 by total assets; 100 percent government-owned CEF (No.1 mortgage lender) and BNDES (development bank) ranked No.3 and No.5 respectively. Private sector domestic

Table 7.2 Brazil's largest domestic lenders (as of December 31, 2013)

Institution	Total Assets (BRL billions)	No. of Retail Branches
Public Sector		
1. Banco do Brasil	1,218.5	5,417
2. Caixa Economica	858.5	3,176
3. BNDES	763.0	1
Domestic Private		
1. Itaú-Unibanco	1,027.3	3,895
2. Bradesco	776.7	4,706
Foreign		
1. Santander	495.4	2,633
2. HSBC	160.0	868

Source: Authors, from data available from Banco Central do Brasil (1 USD = 2.36 BRLs)

Itaú-Unibanco and Bradesco were ranked No.2 and No.4; with foreign controlled Santander and HSBC ranked No.6 and No.7 respectively.

India

Historical milestones

India's largest commercial bank, State Bank of India, traces its origin to the Bank of Calcutta (later, Bank of Bengal), established in 1806 as a joint-stock corporation (owned in part by the Government and in part by individuals) with the status of a presidency bank, that is, a bank granted the right by the Government to issue currency with legal tender.

In 1921, the Government formed the Imperial Bank of India (IBI) by merging Bank of Bengal with the only two other presidency banks in existence, Bank of Bombay and Bank of Madras. In 1935, still under British rule, the Reserve Bank of India (RBI) – India's central bank – was established.

Following independence on August 15, 1947, the Indian government took over IBI and, in 1955, merged it with other state-owned regional banks to form the State Bank of India (SBI), to date India's most important financial institution. Two further rounds of commercial bank nationalization resulted in government control of 91 percent of banking assets by 1980.

Balance of payments crisis and financial liberalization steps (early 1990s to mid 2000s)

Following a decade of increasing trade and fiscal deficits, financed in large part by increased external borrowings, a severe currency crisis – concurrent with the eruption of the First Gulf War – hit India in early 1991. In response to this balance of payments crisis, the Government began to engage in a series of reforms aimed at increasing the efficiency of the Indian economy. Measures directed at increased competition and the strengthening of the financial sector included deregulation of deposit and lending rates, easing of the licensing process for the establishment of new branches by existing private sector banks, lower entry barriers to new banks, and faster stock market listing for banks.

In the years that followed, several public sector banks became listed companies (such as SBI in 1994 and IDBI, formerly Industrial Development Bank of India in 1995), new domestic private sector banks were formed, and a small number of foreign banks began to expand their branch network and balance sheets.

By the eve of the 2008 global credit crunch, SBI's range of activities had expanded to include investment banking, asset management, housing finance, and investor services, becoming the country's leading universal bank. It faced, however, increased competition in the Indian domestic financial market from, by then, well-established financial institutions such as the private domestic ICICI and HDFC, and foreign Standard Chartered, Citibank, and HSBC, in addition to public sector Baroda, Punjab National Bank, and Bank of India.

Table 7.3 India's largest domestic lenders (as of March 31, 2013)

Institution	Total Loans (Rupees billions)	No. of Retail Branches
Public Sector		
1. SBI Group	13,793.2	21,301
2. Baroda	3,281.9	4,377
3. Punjab National	3,087.3	5,977
4. Bank of India	2,893.7	4,373
Domestic Private		
1. ICICI	2,902.5	3,134
2. HDFC	2,397.2	3,046
Foreign		
1. Standard Chartered	619.5	100
2. Citibank	520.3	43
3. HSBC	357.1	50

Source: Reserve Bank of India (1 USD = 55 Indian rupees)

Recent developments and leading players

The Indian financial system weathered the global financial crisis well, benefitting from strong profitability entering the crisis, proper capitalization under robust regulatory supervision, and timely actions by the central bank in support of adequate liquidity for the system as a whole.

Nevertheless, a global environment characterized by de-leveraging from the excesses that led to the crisis and much more selective capital allocation outside their home markets by international banks, has made foreign banks significantly more risk averse than domestic banks in most countries around the world.

As of March 30, 2013, total bank credit in India was distributed as follows: 76 percent for public sector banks, 19.5 percent for domestic private banks, and 4.5 percent for foreign banks. While there were 43 registered foreign banks in India (against 26 public sector and 20 domestic private), most foreign banks restricted themselves to trade financing, investment banking, and private banking activities.

As shown in Table 7.3 above, SBI remained India's leading provider of credit with total loans equal to over four times the second largest public sector bank (Bank Baroda), and the largest private sector bank (ICICI).

China

From single national bank to banking system (mid 1980s to late 1990s)

China began to reform its financial system in 1978, a gradual process that saw its first major structural development in 1984, when the People's Bank of China (PBOC) ceased to operate as both central bank and sole commercial lender and began to operate exclusively as its central bank. At the same time, four new government-owned *specialized* banks were formed to provide credit on a national basis: the Industrial and Commercial Bank of China (commercial banking); the China Construction Bank (infrastructure lending); the Agricultural Bank of China (agricultural lending and rural development); and the Bank of China (international trade financing).

In 1995, a new commercial banking law was passed to transform the four original specialized banks into commercial banks. Without abandoning their core purpose, these newly created state-owned commercial banks (SOCBs) (such as the internationally oriented Bank of China) would now have the mandate to access retail and institutional deposits nationwide, and lend across the full spectrum of business activities. Furthermore, the new law granted permission for the establishment of private sector commercial banks, the first of which was Minsheng Bank, founded in 1996. Prior to the enactment of this law, three new development (or policy) banks had been created: the China Development Bank; the Agricultural Development Bank of China; and the Export-Import Bank of China.

In 1998, China's Securities Law was enacted to provide the legal framework for primary issues and secondary market trading of securities, and empowering the newly formed China Securities Regulatory Commission (CSRC) as supervisor for the securities and futures markets.

Industry restructuring (late 1990s to mid 2000s)

Following their designation as fully-fledged commercial banks, the local currency equivalent of US$201 billion dollars was injected by the government into the four SOCBs: US$33 billion as fresh capital in 1998, and an additional US$168 billion via a swap of non-performing SOCB loans for government-backed bonds (the latter initially issued by government-owned asset management companies established for this purpose and, subsequently, by PBOC or the Chinese Treasury). Further industry restructuring efforts included capital injections and liquidity support by mergers among financial institutions at the provincial level.

Table 7.4 IPOs by major Chinese banks

Institution	Date	Offering Size (US$ billions)
Bank of Communications	June 2005	1.9
China Construction Bank	October 2005	9.0
Bank of China	January 2006	10.0
China Merchants Bank	September 2006	2.4
Industrial and Commercial Bank of China	October 2006	22.0
Agricultural Bank of China	July 2010	22.0
Minsheng Bank	November 2009	3.9

Source: Authors, based on Investor Relations website of respective companies

Benefitting from the enactment of securities legislation (1989), the four SOCBs had very successful initial public offerings open to minority participation by investors globally beginning in 2005. Other major public listings included Bank of Communications (the first to the market in June 2005, following the acquisition by HSBC of a 19.9 percent equity stake in 2004), and domestic private banks Minsheng Bank and China Merchants Bank.

Recent developments and leading players

The liberalization of China's financial system initiated in the years immediately prior to its accession to the World Trade Organization (WTO) in 2001, included two other dimensions in addition to the industry restructuring described above: interest rate liberalization and the opening up of the domestic financial services market to foreign competition.

Interest rate liberalization has been evolving gradually since the late 1990s, beginning with the liberalization of interest rates on money market and bond instruments (1996–8), and the elimination of lending rate ceilings and deposit rate floors (but not ceilings) in 2004. As of year-end 2013, loan and deposit rates remained clustered around benchmark guidance rates put forward by the PBOC.

The process of opening up China's domestic financial services market to foreign competition has evolved gradually since the country's accession to the WTO. Initially, foreign banks were permitted to offer local currency services to foreign clients, and the domestic wholesale market was opened to foreign competition.

After 2006, barriers to foreign competition in retail banking were removed progressively, with restrictions on the establishment of new retail branches eased, and greater freedom granted to foreign banks to offer banking services in domestic currency to clients, including Chinese households. As of year-end 2013, however, foreign ownership of Chinese banks remained capped at 20 percent for a single investor, and at 25 percent maximum for all foreign investors combined, as China's WTO commitments do not include permission for foreign banks to acquire Chinese banks.

The most recent IMF Financial System Stability Assessment for the People's Republic of China (IMF CR 11/321, November 2011), shows that public sector banks held approximately two-thirds of total banking industry assets and foreign banks under 2 percent at year-end 2010.

By the end of 2013, the four original specialized banks, established in 1984 and made state-owned commercial banks in 1995, and which became government-controlled publicly listed and traded companies between 2005 and 2010, remained much the largest banks in China.

Bank of Communications, whose largest shareholders are the Ministry of Finance and HSBC, was ranked No.5. Private domestic China Merchants Bank and Minsheng Bank were ranked No.6 and No.8 by total assets, with China CITIC Bank (a banking subsidiary of the state-owned investment company China International Trust and Investment Corporation) ranking No. 7.

Table 7.5 China's largest domestic lenders (as of December 31, 2013)

Institution	Total Assets (RMB billions)	No. of Retail Branches
Public Sector		
Industrial and Commercial Bank of China	18,917.8	18,023
China Construction Bank	15,363.2	14,925
Agricultural Bank of China	14,562.1	23,547
Bank of China	13,874.3	46
Bank of Communications	5,960.9	155
China CITIC Bank	3,649.2	780
Private Domestic		
China Merchants Bank	4,016.4	400
Minsheng Bank	3,226.2	419

Source: Authors, based on 2013 annual reports from respective companies' websites (1 USD = 6.06 RMBs)

Indonesia

Historical milestones

The first bank to operate in Indonesia – then the Dutch colony of Dutch East Indies – was De Bank van Leening, established in Java in 1746. In 1828, and with Indonesia still under Dutch rule, the first bank authorized by the Government to issue fiat money, the De Javasche Bank (DJB), began operations.

Dutch East Indies banking activities were halted during the Japanese occupation of 1942 to 1945. With the end of World War II, banking activities were to be reestablished, but with the domestic banking system divided in two, with on one side DJB and other Dutch banks, under Dutch rule, and on the other Bank Negara, Indonesia's first state-owned bank (established in 1946 by the revolutionary government) and Jajasan Poesat Bank.

In 1949, after four years of civil war and intermittent negotiations with the involvement of the United Nations (UN), the Netherlands finally agreed to cede sovereignty over the entire Indonesian territory. An initial parliamentary democratic period was followed by the authoritarian regime of President Sukarno (1957–64), during which time DJB was nationalized and, subsequently renamed Bank of Indonesia.

In 1967, under President Suharto, Indonesia undertook a series of economic and banking reforms. Under the new Basic Banking Law, promulgated in 1967, Bank of Indonesia became the country's sole central bank (monopoly issuer of the country's fiat money, with no commercial lending authority), and Bank Negara became exclusively a commercial bank, without the fiat money issuing capacity it had enjoyed previously.

The Basic Banking Law broke Bank Negara into seven state-owned banks with specific sectorial focuses. It permitted the establishment of private sector domestic banks and allowed foreign banks to establish branches and/or representative offices (not to incorporate a bank) in Indonesia.

In addition to acting as central bank for the financial system as a whole, Bank of Indonesia was responsible for controlling interest rates on loans and deposits, and setting credit limits for state-owned banks.

An initial round of liberalization had taken place in 1983, with the abolishment of Bank of Indonesia's control over interest rates on deposits and loans, the elimination of credit ceilings for state-owned banks, and the end of the practice of government liquidity funding of public sector banks (Bennett 1995: 459).

In 1988, the Indonesian government adopted a series of measures aimed at transforming the Indonesian banking system from one dominated by a small number of state-owned banks to one where competition among public and private sector banks was encouraged. These measures resulted from the need to increase the ability of the banking system to spur economic growth, particularly in light of the weakening of the Indonesian economy resulting from the decline in oil export revenues beginning in 1980.

The 1988 reform, known as PAKTO '88, eased restrictions on domestic expansion by foreign banks (e.g. foreign banks with offices in Jakarta were allowed to open branches in the country's other seven largest cities); permitted the establishment of joint-ventures between foreign and domestic banks (provided export credits would reach at least 50 percent of total loan portfolio after one year); lowered minimum capital requirements for newly formed private sector domestic banks; and removed restrictions for expansion of branch networks by both private and public sector banks. Reductions in compulsory reserve requirements further stimulated the expansion of the banking system.

Between 1988 and 1992, the number of private sector banks grew from 63 to 134 and the total value of loans outstanding doubled, with the market shares of private sector domestic banks growing from 23 percent to 47 percent, while that of public sector banks declined from 71 percent to 53 percent. Foreign and joint-venture share also grew from 6 percent to 9 percent, while remaining oriented toward wholesale corporate business, in large part credit support to international companies operating in Indonesia.

Asian crisis and the Indonesian banking system (late 1990s)

As it turned out, the 1988 bank liberalization reform revealed itself too fast and too sweeping in light of the prevailing lack of prudential supervision. The government bail-out of Indonesia's banking industry was a critical piece of the country's sovereign debt structuring agreement with the IMF in the aftermath of the 1997–98 Asian crisis (see Chapter 4).

The framework for intervention was provided by newly promulgated banking legislation (1998 Banking Act), and conducted under close IMF supervision. It involved the clean-up and recapitalization of eight private sector banks, the liquidation and/or government take-over of private sector banks for future privatization, and a major restructuring and recapitalization of government banks, which included the absorption by Bank Mandiri, the country's largest, of four other state banks. The 1998 Banking Act also raised the maximum foreign ownership share in Indonesian banks from 51 percent to 99 percent.

It is estimated that capital injections from public and private sources amounted to approximately 60 percent of Indonesia's GDP (Greenville 2004: 17). Between 2000 and 2004 15 banks, representing over 70 percent of total industry assets, were privatized. By year-end 2004, foreign controlled banks accounted for 42 percent of total industry assets (Goeltom 2006: 2).

Recent developments and leading players

The Indonesian banking industry weathered well the 2008 global market turmoil, benefitting from relatively high levels of capital adequacy and stable funding (bank deposits accounting for 78 percent of total liabilities). As of September 2009, 121 commercial banks were in operation, accounting for 98.6 percent of total industry assets. The remaining 1.4 percent of industry assets was distributed among 1,765 small rural banks under the supervision of the Bank of Indonesia. Government-owned banks accounted for 45.2 percent of total industry assets, foreign banks, 30 percent, and Sharia banks, 1.8 percent. The top three government-owned banks accounted for over one-third of total deposits and loans (IMF CR 12/335, 2012: 5).

As shown in Table 7.6 below, as of September 2013, four of the 10 largest banks in Indonesia were public sector banks, one was private domestic, and five were either foreign controlled or had a foreign bank as major shareholder.

Table 7.6 Indonesia's largest domestic lenders (as of December 31, 2013)

Institution	Total Assets (IDR trillions)
Public Sector	
Bank Mandiri	733.1
Bank Rakyat Indonesia	606.4
Bank Negara Indonesia	386.7
Bank Tabungan Negara	131.2
Private Domestic	
Bank Central Asia	496.3
Bank Danamon	184.2
Panin Bank (PNBN)	153.2
Foreign Control	
Bank CIMB Niaga (CIMB Group)	218.9
Bank Permata (Standard Chartered)	144.3
Bank Internasional Indonesia (Maybank, Malaysia)	140.6

Source: Authors, based on 2013 financial statements from companies' websites (1 USD = 12,171 Indonesian rupiah)

South Africa

Historical milestones

Paper money was first introduced in 1782 into Cape Town in the Cape Colony, then a governorate of the Dutch East India Company. Unable to secure adequate coinage from the Dutch Republic and without a printing press available to him, the paper money was handwritten by the colony's treasury under Governor Van Plettenberg. The first bank to operate in South Africa was the Lombaard Bank, a state bank founded in 1793, which closed its doors in 1883, forced out of business by private sector competition.

The British seized the Cape of Good Hope area in 1806, pushing the Dutch settlers to establish their own communities to the north. Discoveries of diamonds and gold led to intensification of the economic exploration of the hinterlands. Between the late 1830s and 1900, over 30 new private sector banks were formed, all printing their own paper money. Toward the turn of the century, three newly formed Cape Town-based banks of British origin, supported by significant capital, began aggressively to open branches and take over private banks throughout the colony (see South African Reserve Bank, n.d.).

In 1910, following British victory in the Second Boer War (1902), the Union of South Africa was formed, granting South Africa nominal independence. At that time, four private sector banks remained capable of issuing paper money for circulation in the country. The Reserve Bank of South Africa, the country's central bank, opened its doors in 1922.

The Union of South Africa became fully independent from England in 1934. In 1961, as the Rand became the currency of the newly-formed Republic of South Africa, the South African Reserve Bank began to replace pound sterling notes with banknotes of the new currency.

1990s bank reform

Three pieces of legislation enacted between 1989 and 1993 combined to provide the legal framework for financial services in South Africa: the South African Reserve Bank Act of 1989, the Banks Act of 1990, and the Mutual Banks Act of 1993. Responsibility for the supervision of banks operating in the country falls with the Office for Banks, a department of the Reserve Bank of South Africa.

In 1994, after almost half a century, the institutionalized apartheid regime that legally protected and enforced preferential treatment of whites over blacks ended, and the first multiracial elections took place.

Recent developments and leading players

Strong bank supervision combined with domestic-led expansion of the South African financial sector allowed the country to weather the 2008–9 global financial crisis (see IMF CR 10/353, 2010). As of December 2013, 20 commercial banks were

Table 7.7 South Africa's largest domestic lenders (as of December 31, 2013)

Institution	Total Assets (Rand billions)	Ownership Control
Standard of South Africa	979.9	Private domestic, 20% ICBC-China
First Rand	785.4	Private domestic
ABSA	777.8	Foreign (Barclays Bank PLC)
Nedbank	658.2	Private domestic
Subtotal	**3,201.4**	
Total	**3,843.2**	

Source: Reserve Bank of South Africa (www.resbank.co.za) (1USD = 10.5 rands)

in operation in South Africa, of which six were subsidiaries of foreign banks. In addition, 14 foreign banks maintained a local branch and 42 a representative office.

As shown in Table 7.7 above, four full-service banking franchises, ABSA, Firstrand, Standard of South Africa and Nedbank accounted for 83.3% of total banking industry assets.

Russia

Historical milestones

The Central Bank of the Russian Federation (CBR or Bank of Russia), created in 1990, had its roots in the State Bank of the Russian Empire, founded in 1860. The State Bank of the Russian Empire was established originally as a commercial bank, designed to strengthen the Empire's payments system through the discounting of bills of exchange, the buying and selling of gold and silver, and buying government securities for its own account. A monetary reform launched in 1895 introduced the gold standard in Russia, and granted the State Bank the right to issue currency.

By 1914, the State Bank had become one of the strongest financial institutions in Europe, with gold reserves averaging over 100 percent of deposits, while also acting as a major lender to industry and trade. With the eruption of World War I, the State Bank became the primary financier of Russia's war effort, in the process transforming its asset portfolio from primarily private sector commercial exposure to treasury bills and causing a substantial decline of its gold reserves.

The Bolshevik Revolution of 1917 led to the establishment of a state monopoly on banking. All credit institutions were nationalized and merged with the State Bank to form the People's Bank of the Russian Federative Socialist Republic (People's Bank). In 1920, the People's Bank had its banking charter abolished upon transfer of its reduced banking functions to the Central Budget and Settlements Administration of the Ministry of Finance.

As Russia launched its New Economic Policy in 1921, aimed at faster development of industry and agriculture, the State Bank was reborn, with a mission to expand credit, improve money circulation, and facilitate trade. It was then granted the right to issue currency and full control over foreign exchange and commodity trading transactions within the Union of Soviet Socialist Republics (USSR).

The New Economic Policy brought about the establishment of sectorial-specialized banks and mutual loan societies. These newly-established financial institutions were initially granted relative autonomy to perform their functions, including the ability to provide short-term credit to their respective constituencies. In the early 1930s, inflationary pressures led the Soviet Government to revert to a much more centralized control over the credit supply. Over the next few years, mutual commercial credit was abolished, specialized banks were made long-term lenders and subsidiaries of the State Bank, making the State Bank the single central agent for the planned provision of credit to the economy, the management of money in circulation, and the settlement of foreign exchange transactions.

Between 1987 and 1991, the Soviet banking system underwent significant transformation. The State Bank of the USSR (Gosbank) was dissolved, and its assets and liabilities transferred to the newly created Central Bank of the Russian Federation (Bank of Russia). In turn, this was divided into a central bank (Bank of Russia), and five sectorial commercial banks (or spetsbanks): Agromprombank (agriculture); Promstroibank (industry and construction); Zhilsotsbank (housing and social development); as well as the old Soviet foreign trade bank and savings bank (Sberbank), that remained as subsidiaries of the Bank of Russia.

With the dissolution of the Soviet Union in 1991, an informal and fragmented process of bank privatization began. Managers of individual spetsbanks branches were given freedom to form small banks and combine into larger banks. By 1997, 1,675 banks had been licensed, most of them former Sberbank branches.

Russian crisis and industry restructuring (late 1990s)

Between 1992 and 1998, these private sector successors of the spetsbanks became highly profitable, intermediating central bank funds to state-owned enterprises and dealing in foreign exchange and commodities. They failed, however, to serve as a significant source of finance to private firms and households (see Berkowitz, Hoekstra, and Schoors, 2013).

As discussed in Chapter 5, continuously falling oil prices, combined with the Duma's refusal to accept the conditions of an IMF loan agreement, triggered the Russian sovereign debt crisis and default of 1998. Massive capital flight and a decline in GDP of almost 5 percent caused hundreds of banks to fail, and required strong actions by the Bank of Russia and the Treasury of the Russian Federation.

The Government's initial reaction was to provide liquidity support through the Bank of Russia to the troubled banking system. That quickly proved insufficient, despite the improvement in Russia's external accounts and the economy as a whole, brought about by a major devaluation of the ruble and the upward reaction of oil prices.

As elsewhere through history, government response to the banking crisis occurred on two fronts: improvements to the institutional framework, and prompt engagement in the clean-up and restructuring of the banking system.

On the institutional front, a bank restructuring agency (ARCO) was established, with authority to intervene, liquidate, and/or induce mergers among banks,

Table 7.8 Russia's largest domestic lenders (as of December 31, 2013)

Institution	Total Assets (rubles billions)
Public Sector	
Sberbank	18,210
VTB / Bank of Moscow	8,769
Gazprombank	3,647
Rosselhozbank (Russian Agricultural Bank)	1,305
Private Domestic	
Alfa Bank	1,592
Nomos Bank	1,379
Promsvyazbank	738
Foreign	
Unicredit (Unicredit, Italy)	889
Rosbank (Société Générale, France)	748
Raiffensenbank (RZB, Austria)	718

Source: Authors, from 2013 financial statements from companies' websites (1 USD = 32.73 rubles)

and the Bank of Russia embarked on a review of regulatory and supervision policies and procedures so as to gradually incorporate best global practices, including accounting standards.

Recent developments and leading players

The domestic banking system would be tested further in the aftermath of the U.S. subprime meltdown and ensuing global credit crunch, which also caused a sharp decline in oil prices. In response to a 7.75 percent GDP contraction in 2009, Government authorities put in place an immediate and major fiscal stimulus as well as a blanket Bank of Russia liquidity support to the banking system. Capital injections in the form of equity and/or subordinated debt were provided to government-owned and private sector banks in the amount Rub505 billion, or 1.3 percent of GDP, and Rub904 billion, or 2.2 percent of GDP, respectively.

Improved overall liquidity conditions brought about by the restoration of confidence in the banking system and strong GDP growth of 4 percent, led to some early prepayments of subordinated loans in 2010, such as Rub200 billion by Sberbank. Post-crisis consolidation, however, reduced competition by strengthening mainly large state-owned banks (IMF CReport 11/291 2011: 8–16).

Turkey

Historical milestones

In the mid 1800s, as the Ottoman Empire began to approach its final decline, its rulers, seeking to reduce the Empire's dependency on borrowings from European capitals, began to grant licenses primarily for banks, primarily foreign-owned, to open in Ottoman territory.

The first bank of the Ottoman Empire, the Ottoman Bank, was a British–French joint-venture partnership established in 1856. Much later it became part of Garanti Bank, and at year-end 2013 it was Turkey's third largest bank.

In 1863, Bank-1 Osmani was granted the right to print money, effectively becoming the central bank of the Ottoman Empire. Also in 1863, credit cooperatives were given permission to be formed. In 1888, these credit cooperatives were incorporated into a newly founded state bank, Ziraat Bank, Turkey's largest bank by deposits and number one agricultural lender, by 2013.

In 1923, as the Turkish Republic was formed from the remnants of the collapsed Ottoman Empire, credit was not only extremely scarce – in light of the dismal economic conditions inherited – but almost entirely dependent on foreign-controlled banks. In 1924, Turkiie Is Bankasi, the first private-sector domestic bank under the new regime was formed. At the end of 2013, it remained the largest bank by total assets in Turkey. The establishment of two government-owned development banks followed: Sanayi ve Maadin for industrial development; and Emlak ve Eytam for construction. In 1930, a congressional act established the Central Bank of the Turkish Republic (CBTR).

Between the end of World War II and the late 1980s, Turkey – as did many other non-communist emerging economies – oscillated between more market-oriented and more centralized-planning regimes, with a predominance of the latter. Economic optimism in the aftermath of World War II led to the establishment of new private-sector banks, the expansion of branch networks, and rapid credit growth. Erosion of fiscal discipline, however, brought inflation, increasing political tension and, in 1960, a military coup that put in place a centrally-planned import substitution model regime. By the early 1980s, export-led growth and economic liberalization initiatives began to take hold, including elimination of lending quotas and interest rate controls, the establishment of the Istanbul stock exchange in 1986, and the liberalization of capital flows in 1990.

Economic liberalization was not, however, matched by fiscal discipline. As a result, the inflation rate climbed from 60 percent in 1990, to over 100 percent in 1994, remaining high and volatile for the rest of the decade. The share of domestically-held foreign exchange deposits increased from 20 percent to 43 percent between 1990 and 1999, and interest payments on domestic public-sector debt grew from less than 20 percent of tax revenues in 1989, to over 75 percent by 1999. Turkey's fragile fiscal situation proved unsustainable as the world witnessed the Asian (1997) and Russian (1998) crises. Foreign capital inflows began to fall sharply, and the country endured a 5 percent drop in GDP in 1999 (Akyuz and Boratav 2002: 5–9).

Turkish twin crises and the restructuring of the banking industry

In December 1999, the Turkish government announced – with the explicit support of the IMF in the form of a US$3.8 billion stand-by agreement – a major stabilization program that sought to bring inflation down to single-digit levels in 2002 and beyond.

The stabilization effort was anchored on a pre-announced crawling-peg exchange rate regime (in place from January 2000 to June 2001), and a fiscal adjustment (tax increases, government spending cuts, pension reform, and privatization initiatives) robust enough to produce credible primary fiscal surpluses from 2000 onward. The hope was that an orderly return to a flexible exchange rate regime through progressive widening of the foreign exchange band would be possible, beginning in July 2001.

The 1999 stabilization program gave the economy a boost, with GDP growth of 7 percent in 2000). However, foreign exchange denominated deposits by Turkish savers continued to rise, and net foreign capital inflows continued to be concentrated in public- and private-sector debt issues, as foreign direct and equity portfolio investments declined. Additionally, an important systemic fragility had been building in the banking system in the form of direct foreign exchange asset-liability mismatches, as well as credit outstanding to borrowers highly exposed to exchange rate risk.

The inflation target established for year-end 2000 (25 percent) was about to be missed by almost 15 percentage points when, in December 2000, a supplemental IMF stand-by credit facility in the amount of US$7.5 billion was announced (IMF Press Release 00/80 2000:1–6).

The stability brought about by this renewed IMF support was short lived. In February 2001, facing massive flight from the Turkish lira that drove overnight rates to over 5,000 percent, the government decided to break the crawling peg, which led to a 30 percent devaluation of the currency in a single day. Accelerated deterioration of banks' balance sheets ensued. In September 2001, similarly to Mexico in 1994, a new stand-by credit support facility (raising the IMF's exposure to Turkey to US$30 billion) was announced, incorporating measures directed at resolving both the sovereign debt and imminent systemic banking crises (Akyuz and Boratav 2002: 22–4).

Between 2001 and 2003, the Turkish Banking and Regulatory Agency embarked on the implementation of a bank rehabilitation program that involved recapitalization of public sector banks, liquidation and/or clean up and privatization of banks that had been placed under receivership by Turkey's deposit insurance agency, the Savings and Deposit Insurance Fund (SDIF), while also allowing for the take-over of Turkish banks by foreign investors.

Recent developments and leading players

At the end of 2010, the total number of banks operating in Turkey was 49, down from 59 at the beginning of the decade. Domestic private banks held 52 percent of total banking industry assets, public sector banks held 32 percent, and foreign banks held 17%. Between 2003 and 2011, credit expanded at over 20 percent per annum on average, with a contraction in 2008–9 rapidly compensated for in higher growth in 2009–10. According to the IMF (IMF CR 12/261 2011: 7–13),

Table 7.9 Turkey's largest domestic lenders (as of December 31, 2013)

Institution	Total Assets (Turkish Lira billions)
Public Sector	
Ziraat Bankasi	207.5
Halk Bankasi	141.5
Vakif Bank	139.3
Private Domestic	
Garanti Bankasi	217.7
Is Bankasi	210.5
Ak Bank	195.5
Yapi ve Kredi Bank	160.3
Foreign	
Denizbank (Sberbank, Russia)	79.7
Finansbank (National Bank of Greece)	66.0
Turk Ekonomi Bankasi (BNP Paribas (France)	53.4
HSBC Bank AS (HSBC, U.K.)	36.3
ING AS (ING, Netherlands)	34.9

Source: Authors, from 2013 financial statements from companies' websites (1 USD = Turkish lira)

this strong recovery in the aftermath of the 2008 global credit crisis had been, in large part, externally financed, leading to an overvalued real exchange rate and current account concerns for the years to come.

Multilateral development banks and the BRICS New Development Bank

On July 15, 2014, the leaders of Brazil, Russia, India, China, and South Africa announced the creation of the New Development Bank (NDB), with the goal of providing financing for infrastructure and sustainable development projects. Initial capital commitment (still pending approval from the respective parliaments at the time of writing) was US$10 billion per country, totaling US$50 billion. No one founding member can increase their share of capital without the agreement of the other founding members. New members are permitted, provided that the combined share of the founders does not fall below 55 percent.

In conjunction with the announcement of the creation of the NDB, the BRICS leaders agreed to establish a Contingent Reserve Arrangement (CRA) in the amount of US$100 billion for temporary balance of payments support to its members. China committed US$41 billion; Brazil, India, and Russia each committed US$18 billion; and South Africa committed US$5 billion.

As amply reported by the media, the leaders of Brazil, Russia, India, China, and South Africa, used the opportunity to make clear that the NDB and CRA were born in part as a result of dissatisfaction with the relative power of emerging economies in the governance of the World Bank and the IMF. Nevertheless, the leaders of the World Bank and the IMF were quick to welcome the formation of, and suggest close cooperation with, the NDB and the CRA in the goals of sustainable economic development and financial stability globally.

A few additional considerations are in order. In its effort to provide coordinated multilateral support to economic development, the NDB joins not only the World Bank Group (including the IFC, its private sector development arm), but other regional multilateral development agencies also, such as the Inter-American Development Bank (IDB, 1959), African Development Bank (AFDB, 1964), Asian Development Bank (ADB, 1966), and the European Bank for Reconstruction and Development (1991).

These multilateral development banks are characterized by a clear distinction between lenders (typically Organisation for Economic Co-operation and Development (OECD) member-countries), and borrowers (typically emerging economies, including the BRICS). While all members contribute some capital, poorer nations tend to be the larger borrowers (as of 2013, China, India, Brazil, and South Africa are among the World Bank Group's largest borrowers). The same has not been true for the IMF, where, since 2008, temporary balance of payments imbalances have been more evenly distributed among members from the EU, the former Soviet Union, and poorer nations.

However, the governance of all these multilateral institutions is conducted by an executive board formed by representatives of the member countries, to which the operational departments, including credit and treasury functions report, and to which full disclosure of project lending (for the development banks) and balance of payments lending (for the IMF) is made available for ultimate decision-making regarding credit exposure.

Looking ahead, important challenges face the NDB, namely to implement and maintain governance principles, operational procedures, and a credible professional team that can earn the trust and confidence of investors, so that the initial capital commitment (US$50 billion over seven years) will increase such that it constitutes a truly material addition to the funding already available from other multilateral organizations and the market at large for investment in infrastructure and sustainable development projects.

Summary

In this chapter we have explored how macroeconomic conditions, political forces, and major external events have combined to shape the structure of the banking industries of eight selected large emerging economies.

The countries selected, all G-20 nations and, as such, members of the Basel Committee on Bank Supervision, were Mexico, Brazil, India, China, Indonesia, South Africa, Russia, and Turkey.

As we saw in Chapters 2 and 3, the 1990s was a decade of re-invention for banks and the banking systems of developed economies, a transformation driven fundamentally by the forces of financial liberalization on both sides of the Atlantic, rapid technological change, and resulting explosive growth of securities markets globally.

As discussed in this chapter, the 1990s was also a decade of profound transformation in the banking systems of leading emerging economies. In these economies, however, the market forces mentioned above operated in a context of significantly more intense political change, with major policy decisions often having to be made in the context of imminent banking crises (see Chapter 4), sovereign debt crises (see Chapter 5), or both – ironically, situations the developed world seemed long rid of, but would again face beginning in 2008.

While monetary regimes, bank regulation frameworks, and financial institutions' internal governance practices have converged substantially over the past 20 years across the sample of countries examined, at the end of 2013, their domestic industry profiles remained rather varied with regard to ownership control of leading financial institutions.

As we have concluded herein, at the end of 2013, public sector banks remained dominant in Russia, China, and India; foreign banks in Mexico; domestic private-sector banks in South Africa; and a more nuanced balance of market power among domestic private, public sector, and foreign banks prevailed in Brazil, Turkey, and Indonesia.

Finally, we have suggested that the BRICS' NDB, to be established with an initial capital commitment by its members of US$50 billion over seven years, can become an important additional source of funding for infrastructure and sustainable development projects of emerging economies around the world. Nevertheless, important challenges remain, namely to implement and maintain governance principles, operational procedures, and the professional team that can earn the credibility of investors, so that the initial capital commitment can grow to represent a truly material addition to the funding already available from other multilateral organizations and the market at large for investment in infrastructure and sustainable development projects.

8 Financial fraud, corruption and illegal activities

> Related to the ideas of money, credit, trust and confidence is the true rule of law.
>
> (David Landes, Wealth and Poverty of Nations, 1998)

Introduction

In this chapter, we will examine financial practices and institutions that have violated both domestic and international laws, rules of conduct, and sound business practices. We will examine the resolution of these cases, including new levels of fines, penalties, criminal liability, and the potential repercussions, specifically for foreign banks in the United States. Between 2006 and 2013, financial institutions in the United States have incurred more than US$7.5 billion in Anti-Money Laundering (AML) and Office of Foreign Assets Control (OFAC) violations. In 2014, the amounts rose dramatically, as BNP was fined $8.9 billion for money laundering related to dollar transactions with Iran and Sudan from 2002 to 2009 (Protess and Silver-Greenburgh 2014: B1).

The losses incurred by money laundering, tax evasion or by specific frauds (including rogue traders and Ponzi schemes) can be quantified, but, since 2008, banks and financial markets have also been accused of unethical, but not necessarily illegal behavior. According to the Financial Crisis Inquiry Commission, the global financial crisis of 2008 was also a "systemic breakdown in accountability and ethics … we witnessed an erosion of standards of responsibility and ethics that exacerbated the financial crisis" (Financial Crisis Inquiry Report, 2011: xxii) As Judge Jed S. Rakoff noted, "it can be hard to prove criminal intent, particularly against people several levels removed from those who constructed and marketed the securities" (Norris, 2013). In 2012, fines in the United States exceeded US$25 billion, which included fines for fraudulent mortgage backed securities transactions (JP Morgan, Bank of America, Goldman Sachs, and UBS); tax fraud (Credit Suisse); manipulation of LIBOR (Barclays, Rabobank, and RBS).

Documented manipulation of the London Interbank Offered Rate (LIBOR) and foreign exchange market (FOREX) rates was prosecuted as a direct violation of traders' obligation to provide accurate rate information to global markets. Yet it often remains unclear whether banks are liable under civil or criminal law, or if this was part of a widespread culture which, before 2007, encouraged or turned a blind eye to these practices. Criminal and illegal activity, even when prosecuted, punished, and brought to public attention, has long lasting repercussions as it severely erodes the fundamental bond of trust between banks and civil society. Since 2013, banks and regulators have begun to examine the longer term repercussions of these actions: loss of shareholder value, loss of reputation, loss of confidence in the institutions and in the financial sector by civil society.

Even more than bank or sovereign debt failures (see Chapters 4 and 5), financial criminal activity implicates different branches of governments and the judiciary as well as banks and civil societies. Long after institutions or individuals are legally forced to cease activity or face penalties, the repercussions can last for decades based on renegade individuals, undisclosed accounts and cross-border criminal linkages: the case of Banco Ambrosiano (1970s to 1982) resonated decades later in the Vatican Bank money laundering probe of 2012 to 2013. The collapse of Crédit Lyonnais (1995) was in part attributed to the fraudulent loans to former Bank of Credit and Commerce International (BCCI) associates (1970s to 1990).

The global institutional and management structures of international banks post-2000 have allowed banks to be held accountable outside of their home country jurisdiction. The home/host country arrangements established in the 1980s, and to which institutions must adhere, are facing serious challenges in matters of tax violations. U.S. and German governments have rejected UBS and other Swiss banks' claim of distinction under Swiss law between permissible tax avoidance and illegal tax evasion and tax fraud; banks that have faced accusations and penalties due to money laundering charges in violation of U.S. sanctions against rogue or designated terrorist regimes include Standard Chartered, HSBC, and BNP for the transfer of monies to Iran and Sudan. Most often rogue trader fraudulent activities and losses have occurred in foreign subsidiaries: Baring in Singapore, Allied Irish and Sumitomo in the United States, UBS and JP Morgan in the United Kingdom.

The broader jurisdiction of the United States

Globally, "[t]he United States authorities hold enormous sway over dollar clearing because such transactions ultimately clear in the United States, even when they are initiated overseas. The United States government itself plays a hugely important role in processing payments through the Federal Reserve's Fedwire Funds Service system" (Eavis 2014: B6). Therefore, in both setting rules and enforcing sanctions, the United States has led the charge in exposing these activities and imposing the harshest penalties and fines. Since 2013, the European Commission and the United Kingdom have followed suit in light of tax fraud and the manipulation of LIBOR and FOREX rates. As systemically important financial institutions, or institutions termed too big to fail, earn over one third of their profits from foreign subsidiaries outside of the home country, and as global transactions are most often conducted in dollars, the United States has the leverage to threaten closure of bank branches and operations if their rules and laws are violated.

Historical overview: speculation, counterfeiting, and insider trading

We will examine illegal, criminal, and fraudulent activity by international and domestic banks on behalf of international clients and their holdings, including BCCI (incorporated in Luxembourg, with headquarters in London and Pakistan, Banco Ambrosiano (Italy), the Vatican Bank (Vatican City), and Riggs Bank (United States), as well as money laundering in violation of political sanctions (Standard Chartered and BNP), and drug-related criminal violations (HSBC).

Financial fraud and fraudulent schemes are not confined to the modern era. They began in the 1700s in England and France, with the issuance and distribution of paper notes, shares, and the start of a gold/paper speculative market. A surge in speculative activity between 1704 and 1715, conducted "by small time sharks, back street usurers" (Rudé 1971: 547), in paper to gold transactions, created a vast unregulated market that fed on rumors of convertibility of paper into gold, silver, and even copper coin, as confidence in paper notes fluctuated on a daily basis. Even when notes issued by the Bank of England were recognized as fully backed by gold, the British economist Adam Smith, a defender of banknotes, stipulated that if paper had to replace coinage, "a Law indeed might lay restraints and threaten Penalties, but it can't change Men's minds, to make them think a piece of paper is a piece of Money" (Smith, 1776). In 1809, the German poet and philosopher Goethe, having personally observed the failure of the French Revolution's assignats (paper shares backed by confiscated church property) never trusted paper issuance in Germany, comparing it to a new form of alchemy, in which paper replaces gold as a means of paying expenses and canceling debts (Goethe 1879).

In the United States, politicians, journalists and authors, including Mark Twain, Ralph Waldo Emerson, and Washington Irving, saw in paper deviousness, corruptibility, and a lack of clarity and accountability. Since the Great Depression of the 1930s, fear of speculation is associated with loss of paper value in stocks and bonds, which translates into loss of real value.

Counterfeit, from the Latin, contra facto, against the fact, and defined by the French term faux monnayeurs, specifically references those who create false or fake money violating the basic trust between buyer and seller. The fear of counterfeiting first applied to coinage, which was reputed to be verifiable by the ring of the coin, and the hardness of the metal if bitten down on. In the United States, the first nation to issue paper currency (1785), counterfeit notes were a persistent problem for the new nation's economic health. During the Civil War (1861–5), there was an urgent need to fund the Union, and paper currency had to be printed in order to supplement the dwindling supply of gold reserves. Stephan Mihm (Mihm 2007) described how, without a central bank and one issuing authority, the proliferation of banks issuing paper money rose from 200 in 1815 to over 300 in 1830. By the 1850s, more than 10,000 different kinds of paper currency circulated across the states and territories, making it extremely difficult to differentiate real from fake.

As the country grew and demand for goods and capital expanded, these notes were accepted and circulated. "Many people in the business of banking viewed counterfeiting as a small price to pay for a system of money creation governed not by the edicts of a central bank or the fiscal arm of the state, but by insatiable private demand for credit in the form of bank notes" (Mihm 2007: 15). By the 1880s, the first financial sheets, including the Dow Jones newsletter, offered daily warnings where and which bills and notes were genuine or counterfeit. These practices stopped once the dollar became a convertible currency from 1905, and under the note-issuing monopoly granted to the Federal Reserve Bank in 1913.

Insider trading

Increased deregulation and greater self-regulation in the United States and United Kingdom, and a surge in competitiveness, coupled with new instruments in the 1980s and 1990s, gave rise to corporate white collar crime. Although the U.S. Securities and Exchange Commission (SEC) had strict rules prohibiting insider trading (defined as the exchange of confidential information on prior knowledge of corporate transactions, mergers and buyouts), these activities began to proliferate in the 1980s. The indictment and trial of California financier Ivan Boesky in 1986 became the first prosecution for insider trading (see Bruck 1989 and Stewart 1991). In 1989, the prestigious Wall Street firm of Drexel Burnham Lambert collapsed after the indictment and conviction of its top trader Michael Milken, known as the junk bond king. The next manifestation, linked to new high technology companies and the dot.com boom, was the scandal around the actions of Wall Street analysts. From the mid 1990s to 2002, top stock analysts at Salomon Smith Barney (the investment banking arm of Citigroup), Morgan Stanley, and Merrill Lynch provided false and misleading information to their clients, as investment houses garnered vast returns based on a "fraudulent system where [the analyst] was expected to help her company make hundreds of millions of dollars underwriting stocks and then issue 'objective' research on the same companies..." (Gasparino, 2005: 9). Among the firms most highly touted by Citigroup analysts were WorldCom and Global Crossing in telecommunications, and Enron in energy sales, brokerage, and online trading.

Created in 1985,[1] Enron became the largest seller of natural gas in North America. Considered until 2001 by the markets and rating agencies as one of the best run U.S. companies, Enron expanded its services to include casualty and risk management services to power plants and energy providers. Its financial strategy also included setting up long-term contracts, which needed to be hedged due to fluctuations in future energy prices. Although a 750 percent increase in revenues was reported between 1996 and 2000, there were large unreported losses siphoned off into special purpose entities. These offshore shell corporations were created with the aid of Arthur Anderson, one of the five largest global accounting and auditing firms, who also audited Enron's balance sheet. Arthur Anderson understated the liabilities, and falsified mark to market accounting fraudulently, inflating the share price. Until 2002, as Citicorp, JPMorgan Chase, and Merrill earned huge amounts in fees for their underwriting activities related to Enron, their analysts pushed Enron as a top stock pick. Within months of September 11, with U.S. markets still in shock, the stock listed at US$90 in 2000, fell to US$1 in November, 2001, after a last attempt to secure a US$2 billion bridge loan failed. Enron filed for bankruptcy in December 2001. In 2002, Enron collapsed with US$23 billion in liabilities, followed by WorldCom, revealing collusion and fraudulent complicity between corporations, banks, rating agencies, and accounting firms.

The investigation by the SEC and New York Attorney General's office lasted six years. The chairman and Chief Executive Officer (CEO), Chief Operating Officer (COO), and Chief Financial Officer (CFO) were indicted on bank fraud, false statements, securities fraud, wire fraud, money laundering, and insider trading charges. Shareholders filed a US$40 billion lawsuit. The firm was dissolved, the executives sentenced to long prison terms and Arthur Anderson, accused of obstruction of justice, shredding documents and falsifying accounts, lost its Certified Public Accountant (CPA) license in 2002. After Congressional investigations in July 2002, the Sarbanes-Oxley Act was enacted, which included the creation of the Public Company Accounting Oversight Board (PCAOB). The PCAOB's supervisory functions included enhancing corporate responsibility and financial disclosures in order to combat corporate and accounting fraud. Furthermore, it made directors of publicly traded companies potentially financially accountable for institutional failures related to misrepresentation of relevant information. It required strict firewalls between accounting, auditing, and advisory functions. Intended to be applied to all publicly-traded companies, domestic and foreign, by 2003, foreign corporations and banks, however, asked for and received exemptions in order not to incur the prohibitive costs of complying with U.S. standards.

In 2009, the New York Attorney General's office began investigations into insider trading activities in hedge funds, specifically at the Galleon Group, culminating in indictments and long prison sentences for its employees and CEO, Raj Rajaratnam.

Money laundering

"Money laundering is the art ... of converting illegally secured cash into legitimate assets. It involves criminals ... transferring their ill-gotten gains through networks of agents and international financial institutions into investments ... in the names of organizations and individuals with no known criminal ties" (Vogl 2012: 233). The methods used include placement of funds through deposits of cash; layering, which involves movement of funds from institution to institution in home or host countries; integration of funds into the financial system for investment, thereby eliminating all traces of origination of funds.

Post-2001, the G-20 recognized the scope of the problem associated with corruption and illegal flows of funds across borders, which are often linked to terrorist regimes' need to use "sophisticated cross border money laundering devices such as secret numbered bank accounts, off shore financial havens" (Vogl 2012: 111). Emerging markets, including China, Russia, Mexico, Saudi Arabia, Malaysia, Kuwait, Nigeria, Venezuela, Qatar, Guinea, and Gabon, with weak controls and regulation, but vast commodity, oil, and gas assets have the highest level of illicit financial outflows. After September 11, and the enactment of the USA PATRIOT Act, money laundering became directly correlated with flows of terrorist funds or funds from countries designated as sponsors of terrorist activities.

The KPMG Global Anti-Money Laundering Survey in 2011 reported over US$1 trillion per year of money from financial crimes, drugs, arms, and rogue states, circulating in the international financial system. In volatile political regimes there can be government–bank collusion through private banks or even central banks in the illegal transfer of funds, specific and indirect money laundering through subsidiaries, affiliates, and correspondent banks. These activities are often abetted by offshore accounts and shell institutions sanctioned by sovereign states in locations such as the Cayman Islands, Antigua, Bermuda, Luxembourg, Liechtenstein, and Andorra, or aided by bank secrecy laws which allow tax evasion or avoidance, in the cases of Switzerland, Luxembourg, and Liechtenstein.

After September 11, U.S. counterterrorism officials were given permission to examine banking transactions routed through the Society for Worldwide Interbank Financial Telecommunication (SWIFT) data base in Belgium. One of the most notorious cases was the Afghanistan Bank of Kabul, associated with and run by the ruling Karzai family. An investigative report by Kroll revealed massive cash inflows from the United States were diverted, shipped to Dubai, or the money funneled from the Bank back to the families (Rosenberg 2012).

Abetted by new technologies, money laundering allegations have surfaced in the realm of virtual currencies (egold in 1999, bitcoin in 2013), as non-government backed, unregulated transactional tools are prone to be used for the transfer of monies obtained from illegal activities. Bitcoin, created by computer code by an anonymous individual or group of traders in Japan, is a non-asset based, borderless, unregulated, electronic currency with computers located in Iceland and other undisclosed locations. In 2014, the U.S. Government shut down Silk Road, an online marketplace for illegal drugs using bitcoin, followed by the collapse and bankruptcy of Mt Gox, the largest bitcoin-based exchange, which handled 80 percent of all transactions. The U.S. Department of the Treasury called for bitcoin exchanges to monitor accounts, adhere to anti-money laundering procedures, and apply the "know your customer" due diligence and identity checks for all transactions. Foreign central banks, including China and Russia, as well as Sweden and Estonia, which were instrumental in advocating online banking, refused to consider the currency as an alternative to legitimate currencies.

Banco Ambrosiano

Banco Ambrosiano, a domestic Italian bank created in 1896, expanded into a Luxembourg holding company in 1963, with direct patronage and capital from the Vatican. Roberto Calvi, promoted to chief executive officer in 1971, began aggressively buying offshore companies in the Bahamas and South America, selling stakes to Italian businessmen, and intersecting with a French offshore clearing house, Clear Stream. In 1978, after an investigation into Clear Stream implicated

French and Italian politicians, the Bank of Italy opened an investigation into Banco Ambrosiano's complex and interlinking connections with the Vatican, Masonic Lodge, and Mafia. By 1982, it was discovered that the bank had lost or siphoned off US$1.2 billion. Calvi fled to London, where he was found hanged from Blackfriars Bridge on June 18, 1982. The ensuing scandal and investigations into fraud and possible murder remained active for over two decades. Banco Ambrosiano was dissolved and investigations prompted the Italian banking sector to begin to consolidate and slowly attempt to unravel incestuous linkages between the world of finance, the Italian Government, and the Catholic Church. The funds were never fully recovered, and connections with the failed bank resurfaced in the dissolution of BCCI, the Crédit Lyonnais scandal in 1995, and allegations made against the Vatican Bank of money laundering, in 2012. Banco Ambrosiano was completely restructured into Nuovo Banco Ambrosiano and merged into Banco Ambrosiano Veneto in 1989, becoming part of one of the four major regional Italian banking conglomerates.

BCCI

To understand the pervasive geographic scope and political ramifications of large-scale money laundering we must examine the actions, illegal activities, collapse, and resolution of BCCI. BCCI facilitated widespread criminal activity covering almost all violations of money laundering, support of terrorism, bribery of government officials, arms trafficking, tax evasion, and smuggling. It was described as "the largest case of organized crime in history", and the first instance of a United States Congressional investigation into the closing and prosecution of a foreign-owned bank (Kerry and Brown 1992: 50).

Founded in Pakistan in 1972, with capital from the United Arab Emirates, Saudi Arabia, and Pakistan, BCCI was incorporated in Luxembourg, conducted operations out of London, through various subsidiaries and a bank within the bank known as ICIC. After the oil crisis, BCCI proclaimed itself a counterweight to Western European banks, offering more culturally compatible services to developing economies and Muslim leaders seeking discrete banking services. Between 1973 and 1977, it expanded from 19 branches in five countries with assets of US$200 million, to 146 branches in 43 countries with assets of US$2.2 billion. By the mid 1980s, it was operating in 73 countries with a balance sheet of close to US$22 billion. It provided secret loans to autocratic regimes across Africa and Asia, including to Saddam Hussein. Bank of America was an initial investor, but divested in 1978, following a critical report by the Office of the Comptroller in 1978, though it continued to serve in an advisory capacity. By 1980, ICIC holdings were transferred to the Cayman Islands. In 1985, the head of Luxembourg's Institut Monétaire Luxembourgeois asked Price Waterhouse auditors to review trading activities, which revealed untraceable losses of over US$849 million. By 1991, auditors found that the bank had unrecorded deposits of US$400 million.

BCCI functioned through layers of holding companies, affiliates, and subsidiaries, all providing support for arms trafficking, smuggling, terrorism, and other criminal activity. Receiving siphoned deposits from central banks and political payoffs, it had contacts around the world, from Panama, to Pakistan, and from India, to the United States.[2]

Through Bert Lance, President Carter's Director of the Office of Budget and Management, and close friend, "… BCCI developed a plan to infiltrate the U.S. market through secretly purchasing U.S. banks while opening branch offices of BCCI throughout the U.S., and eventually merging the institutions", in return for paying off Director Lance's loans (Kerry and Brown, 1992: 5). By fraudulently purchasing Georgia's Financial General Bank shares and later contributing over US$8 million to Carter's foundations, BCCI implicated the National Bank of Georgia, prominent politicians, former Secretary of Defense Clark Clifford, and Bank of America. Despite being in clear violation of money laundering and U.S. banking laws, the U.S. Department of Justice pursued only a limited case in Florida and individual bankers were held accountable rather than the institution.

For the first time in its history, the Bank of England was indirectly involved in criminal activity when, cognizant of the problems, it allowed the reorganization and recapitalization of BCCI to proceed through Abu Dhabi, with the implicit agreement of Price Waterhouse, which had proven negligent in reporting auditing, accounting, and regulatory violations. In 1990, Abu Dhabi promised to commit funds to recapitalize the bank with the implicit promise that evidence of criminal activity would be suppressed. The Bank of England had failed to act on endless red flags and offered only limited cooperation with the U.S. investigation. The full Sandstorm report[3] was released only in 2011.

In 1989, Robert Morgenthau, Manhattan District Attorney, took over the case when an investigation into the purchase of the American bank revealed huge losses, lack of compliance with state or federal disclosure rules, and political bribery charges. Despite resistance from the U.K.'s Serious Fraud Office, Morgenthau proceeded with an indictment in July 1991, accusing BCCI of paying bribes and kickbacks and using bank secrecy in Luxembourg and the Cayman Islands to avoid regulation. BCCI left US$10 billion in losses with 760,000 valid claims in 69 countries which were never recouped.

BCCI's U.S. and U.K. operations shut down in 1991. The ensuing investigation implicated the Central Intelligence Agency (CIA), departments of Justice, and Treasury, and the highest levels of the U.K., U.S., and governments of developing countries for their lack of transparency in sharing information with regulators, and in particular weak oversight in the United States at both state and federal levels in allowing BCCI to acquire U.S. banks, and the Bank of England for withholding information.

In response to the BCCI scandal, the Foreign Bank Supervision Enhancement Act of 1991 was enacted, requiring far more stringent oversight of foreign banks in the United States. The executive summary of the 1992 Congressional report focused on the mishandling of the case by the U.S. Department of Justice, Customs Service, and Treasury. It stated that "BCCI's accountants failed to protect BCCI's innocent depositors and creditors from the consequences of poor practices at the bank of which the auditors were aware for years" (Kerry and

Brown, 1992: 7). The complexity of its multi-layered operations and extended global network of branches and affiliates meant that the ramifications of the BCCI collapse dragged out for decades with interlinked accounts and connections with Banco Ambrosiano, Crédit Lyonnais (see Chapter 4), the Vatican Bank, and banks across the Middle East.

In 1996, the implementation of U.S. Government-imposed financial sanctions was reinforced by the Helms-Burton Act which extended the trading embargo against Cuba to all foreign companies with U.S. affiliates or subsidiaries. Under pressure these limitations were waived for EU companies in 1999.

Riggs Bank

Riggs National Bank, a Washington, DC institution, was created before the Civil War. From the 1960s, a major part of Riggs' profits derived from a special section of its private banking arm, Embassy Banking, where the majority of foreign missions and embassies in Washington, D.C. had accounts with Riggs. As a state bank, chartered in the District of Columbia, Riggs was supervised by the OCC. From January 1987, the OCC required each bank under its supervision to establish and maintain a Bank Secrecy Act (BSA) compliance program, which provided internal controls, independent testing, and designation of individuals responsible for the coordination and monitoring of day-to-day compliance. The implication of Riggs Bank in the Enron scandal led to an investigation of its clients and depositors in the Washington diplomatic and political community, which found that "Riggs willfully violated the suspicious activity and currency transaction reporting requirements of the BSA and its implementing regulations, and that Riggs has willfully violated the anti-money laundering program" (Financial Crimes Enforcement Network 2005: 1).

A 2004 Report by the United States Senate, noted that despite a U.S. freeze on Chile's former head of state, Augusto Pinochet, Riggs Bank was the principal agent in laundering Pinochet funds through 2002. The bank operated offshore shell corporations in direct violation of the interdictions on foreign shell companies in the USA PATRIOT Act. In addition, Riggs was implicated in Saudi accounts and movement of funds post-September 11, in violation of the USA PATRIOT Act. The bank had a nonexistent or "dysfunctional AML program". Furthermore there were failures on the part of the OCC, who despite being aware of the failings at Riggs "failed to take any enforcement actions" (United States Senate Permanent Subcommittee on Investigations, 2004: 5). This investigation highlighted the deep inconsistencies and loopholes in "the ability of U.S. financial institutions with foreign affiliates to get key due diligence information about accounts opened and managed by their foreign affiliates" (ibid: 6).

Riggs, "without admitting or denying either the facts or determination", paid the civil penalty imposed by FinCEN of US$25 million (Financial Crimes Enforcement Network 2005: 1). The entire fines were $41million in total civil and criminal penalties, for dealings with the governments of Chile and Equatorial Guinea. Riggs was merged with PNC Financial Services Group of Pittsburgh.

Vatican Bank

The Commission for Works of Charity was created in 1887 as an administrative entity to fund religious works. In 1942, it became a bank, the Institute for Religious Works, commonly referred to as the Vatican Bank. Following the collapse of Banco Ambrosiano in 1982, the Vatican was revealed to have been the bank's largest shareholder (Sanderson, 2013). During the Cold War, the Bank had quietly funded anti-Communist movements in Catholic countries from Cuba to Poland.

Located in Vatican City, officially known as Vatican City State, the Bank benefitted from the sovereignty of this independent city state. Responsibility, however, fell on Mario Draghi, Governor of the Bank of Italy from 2006 to 2011. Under initial investigations it was revealed that the Institute for Religious works reported 33,000 accounts and €5 billion in assets. The Vatican Bank claimed as its sole purpose the funding of the works of the Catholic Church. However, in the wake of the financial crisis of 2008, major U.S. and EU banks began to scrutinize their correspondent banking relationships with the Vatican, correspondent banking relationships "which gave the Vatican access to foreign financial markets ... and moved as much as €2 billion a year from the Vatican's bank to other accounts across the globe" (Sanderson, 2013).

The Vatican Bank's principal clients were the Holy See, religious orders, and clergy, but a percentage of the clients were loosely identified as having "some affiliation to the Catholic Church" (ibid). That "as much as 25 per cent of the bank's business is done in cash", (ibid) with monies coming from donations and charities with numerous proxy holders, did nothing to relieve the opacity surrounding the Bank's transactions, or the potential for abuse. The bank did not observe any of the compliance requirements imposed on EU countries. It lacked clear checks and balances on record and public disclosure.

With the onset of the financial crisis, the OECD, Financial Stability Board, and Financial Task Force began an investigation into an arm of Unicredit which showed undocumented dealings with the Vatican Bank, with unnamed holders of accounts. In 2010, Italian regulators froze €23 million of the Bank's assets, flagging its noncompliance with anti-money laundering regulations by attempting to make transfers to unidentified beneficiaries for unstated purposes. Although the Bank of Italy had no authority over the Vatican Bank, it nevertheless warned that it was no longer on the white list of banks in compliance. Despite probes into criminal activity in Italy tied to the Vatican's diverse holdings, the bank continued to resist disclosure, forcing the Bank of Italy to freeze assets and apply notification of noncompliance.

In 2012 to 2013, the Vatican Bank was implicated in a money laundering scandal reaching into the top echelons of the Vatican hierarchy, the Patrimony of the Apostolic See. The opacity of the Bank's operations, the lack of mechanisms for due diligence and risk management forced other EU banks to demand transparency for fear of being implicated. The Vatican reluctantly created a new position of financial supervisor, but pressure mounted from the Council of Europe's Anti-Money Laundering Committee. The first financial supervisor, former head of Santander in Italy Gotti Tedeschi, a highly respected conservative banker, was forced out in 2012, unable to crack the culture of opacity and internal corruption. The unwillingness of the Bank to comply with anti-money laundering and newly-strengthened tax evasion rules and regulations rules threatened the reputation of major correspondent banks. In March 2012, JPMorgan closed the account it held for the Bank for lack of information required by regulators. "We would say, 'We need to answer the regulator on this matter.' They would say, 'We answer to God'" (ibid). Finally, when the Bank of Italy ordered Deutsche Bank to close the accounts of the Vatican Bank, including its ATMs in Vatican City, the Vatican was forced to act. Pope Benedict appointed a new financial regulator and a new bank chief.

In February 2013, a unique and historic change occurred when Pope Benedict announced his resignation. His successor, Pope Francis, free of any European or Italian financial affiliations, finally began to overhaul the accounts and practices of the Vatican Bank, insisting on reform of the entire institutional framework. Peter Sutherland (Goldman Sachs) was brought in to explain the need for transparency. An American global risk control group specializing in regulatory and compliance issues, Promontory Financial, was hired to conduct a complete review of all account holders, with the result that hundreds of accounts have been closed to date. For the first time in its history, the Vatican is bringing on board regulators and auditors, and has created a new supervisory board, sharing information with regulators internationally. Pope Francis has shown extraordinary openness and condemned the secrecy and opaque transactions of banks, stating that "whether it's a bank, a fund, a whatever, it should be based on transparency and honesty" (ibid). Finally, in June 2014, Pope Francis named four new members, including three non-Italian members, to the board of the Financial Information Authority, the regulator overseeing the Vatican Bank. He noted that "Economic administration calls for honesty and transparency."

Barclays' Qatar connection

After the collapse of Lehman at the height of the financial crisis, a number of European banks sought and received emergency funding from Middle Eastern and Asian investors in order to shore up capital and avoid nationalization or large government aid. Barclays surprised the markets when it chose not to participate in the October 2008 recapitalization by the U.K. Government. Barclays, which needed to boost its reserves by GB£10 billion by issuing equity, selling assets and slashing the dividend, insisted that it could raise the money privately.

Allegations of money laundering arose in February 2013, when the U.K. Financial Services Authority and Serious Fraud Office launched an investigation into whether or not Barclays gave a loan to Qatar to fund the bank's cash call in order to avoid a state bailout. It was revealed that Qatar Holding was one of two Qatari investors that participated in these transactions in 2008, both related to the royal family. Credit Suisse engaged in the same type of operations in October 2008. Although these loan transactions may not be illegal, the issue remains as to why these transactions were neither reported nor publicly disclosed.

HSBC and Mexican drug deposits

For nearly a decade up to 2012, bank officers at HSBC in Mexico facilitated the transfer of US$881 million on behalf of Mexican drug cartels, usually accepting vast cash only deposits. The subsequent U.S. Senate investigation revealed that "HSBC was a conduit for drug money, had clients with alleged ties to terrorism and stripped details from transactions that would have identified Iranian entities" (Rathbone 2012). Following its MXN1.1 billion acquisition of Grupo Financiero Bital in 2002, HSBC had more branches in Mexico than Britain. From 2007 to 2008, US$7 billion in cash was transferred to HBMX, the HSBC affiliate in Mexico, but no accounts were closed nor flagged. HSBC was accused of stripping information from wire transfers to circumvent U.K. controls. In 2012, HSBC was fined US$1.92 billion. Other banks involved in drug money wire transfers in Mexico included the U.S. Wachovia bank (acquired by Wells Fargo in 2008).

Iran sanction violations

The D'Amato-Kennedy Act of 1996 implemented sanctions against investment in Iran and Libya and against foreign investors in the energy sector. Although the Act was supposed to expire in 2006, it was extended to 2011. Since 2006, more than a dozen international banks have been fined in connection with this act: in 2012, ING was fined US$619 million for altering records and transferring more than US$2 billion for entities trading with Iran. In 2013, corruption investigations in Turkey implicated Halkbank, the largest state-owned bank, in transactions with Iran, which were legal until July 2013 when the United States increased sanctions which included all banks dealing with or acting as intermediaries in gold or currency movements with Iran. The Chinese bank Kunlun was accused of providing hundreds of millions of services to Iranian banks and barred from any business with the U.S. financial sector. In 2012–14, allegations of money laundering were brought against Standard Chartered (United Kingdom) and BNP (France).

Standard Chartered

Standard Chartered prided itself on having withstood the financial crisis when a U.S. Government investigation into Iranian sanction breaches, led by the New York State Department of Financial Services, accused Standard Chartered in August 2012 of "hiding $250billion of transactions with the Iranian government" (Jenkins and Goff, 2012). Accused of being a "rogue institution" which had forged records and conducted "wire stripping" (removal of key information), Standard Chartered faced losing its US dollar clearing license and a large fine.

BNP: 2014 – a new penalty benchmark

France's largest bank by market value, BNP Paribas, was among the least exposed in the subprime mortgage crisis and in the sovereign debt crisis. Prior to the crisis in 2007, the Manhattan District Attorney's office was notified of possible sanction violations in BNP's energy and commodities finance unit in Geneva. The bank conducted its own internal inquiry, and in 2011 claimed that it had "identified a significant volume of transactions that could be considered impermissible", from 2002 to 2009 (Fitch Ratings 2014). These transactions were cleared in dollars and unauthorized dollar payments were made on behalf of the bank to Sudanese or Iranian entities. However, as Christian Noyer, Governor of the Bank of France, stressed, "We have verified that all transactions conformed with European and French laws and rules." "None were broken" (Deen 2014). The bank had set aside US$1 billion for payment of fines, but the duration and extent of the transactions with Iran and Sudan, the lack of cooperation and timely disclosure, and an ever increasing scale of fines imposed on foreign banks raised the fine to almost US$10 billion. The immense discrepancy between the fine imposed on BNP Paribas and those imposed on Standard Chartered (US$667 million) and Credit Suisse (US$536 million) for assisting Iranian, Libyan, and Sudanese clients violate U.S. sanctions provoked an unprecedented political and diplomatic fall-out. Although BNP Paribas was privatized in 1993, the French government continues to exert influence over its banks (see Chapter 1). The unforeseen consequences of the fine on the French banking sector and the stability of the barely recovering EU banking sector (prior to the ECB stress tests of October 2014) meant that French ministers, and even President Hollande, intervened.

The bank would agree to a guilty plea provided that U.S. regulators would not bring criminal charges or revoke the bank's license (the same conditions as set out by HSBC in 2012). However, the threat remained that the New York State Superintendent of Financial Services could "temporarily suspend the bank's ability to transfer money through New York branches on behalf of foreign clients". As of July 2014 BNP's COF had been fired and the bank agreed to plead guilty and pay a $8.9billion penalty (Protess and Silver-Greenburg, 2014).

Global regulation around money laundering

The legislation in place to prevent money laundering is extensive and includes the following:

- Bank Secrecy Act of 1970, requiring all cash transactions in excess of US$10,000 to be reported.
- Money Laundering Control Act (1986), enacted in the wake of the Marcos regime.
- Financial Action Task Force, created in 1989 and pooling the G7 money laundering expertise.
- Foreign Bank Supervision Enhancement Act (1991), enacted following Congressional hearings on BCCI.
- Annunzio-Wylie Anti-Money Laundering Act (1992), following the report of the BCCI Bank Secrecy Act Advisory Group.

- Basel I Committee: *Minimum Standards for the Supervision of International Banking Groups and their Cross Border Establishments.*
- Money Laundering Suppression Act (1994).
- Money Laundering and Financial Crimes Strategy Act (1998).
- USA PATRIOT Act (2001): The most stringent measures implemented to curb terrorist financing, the Act called for: the criminalization of terrorism financing; the strengthening of customer identification; prohibiting financial institutions from engaging in business with foreign shell banks; due diligence on all foreign accounts; sharing of information between financial institutions and the U.S. Government; increased penalties; requiring federal banking agencies to consider anti-money laundering record when reviewing bank mergers and acquisitions.
- Intelligence Reform and Terrorism Prevention Act of 2004, requiring the reporting of cross-border electronic transmittals of funds (in the wake of the investigation into Riggs Bank).
- China's new Anti-Money Laundering Law (2006).
- The Vatican's new Anti-Money Laundering Law (2011), enacted in response to money laundering through the Vatican Bank in 2010, this law requires all transactions in excess of €10,000 to be declared.

Tax evasion and tax fraud

UBS

In 2012, the G-20 recognized the scope of tax evasion through international banks. Since the 1930s, Switzerland, politically neutral and economically sound, was the leading destination for global wealth assets. In 2007, prior to the crisis, Swiss banking assets totaled CHF3.5 trillion. The banking sector, dominated by UBS and Credit Suisse, employed 3 percent of the country's workforce. From 2000 to 2007, UBS invested in the U.S. mortgage market, its high level of exposure bringing the bank close to collapse in October 2008, and causing the Swiss Government to intervene. "In the fall of 2008, the Swiss National Bank (SNB) undertook to acquire securities held by UBS in an amount of up to 60 billion US dollars to relieve UBS's balance sheet" (UBS Transparency Report 2010: 1). The losses severely affected the Global Asset Management sector, as allegations of UBS abetting U.S. clients' tax evasion were revealed.

In 2007, an American working in the Geneva office notified the U.S. Department of Justice that UBS "had tolerated, in numerous instances, the violation of SEC restrictions … and there had been circumvention with respect to clients subject to US taxation" (ibid, 8). U.S. Department of Justice documents revealed that, between 2000 and 2007, 11,000 to 14,000 U.S. clients did not report taxable income totaling approximately US$20 billion in assets held in offshore shell companies set up by UBS bankers.

In its defense, UBS offered that Swiss bank secrecy laws allowed the bank to shield U.S. taxpayers. The case was transferred to the Internal Revenue Service

(IRS), which demanded that UBS produce all records of U.S. taxpayers with UBS accounts who had sought to engage in tax evasion.[4] The crux of the problem was that tax evasion services sought by clients were not equated with tax fraud in Switzerland.

In February 2009, the U.S. Department of Justice signed a Deferred Prosecution Agreement with UBS, allowing the bank to avoid criminal indictment, which would have forced the closure of all the bank's U.S. operations and revocation of its banking license in the United States, by paying a fine of US$780 million and disclosing the names of 250 clients concerned. Within a year, Germany and France brought similar accusations against UBS and Credit Suisse, in which the banks had to provide the names of thousands of French and German nationals who had also benefitted from the tax evasion loopholes. In August 2009, UBS settled with the IRS by providing information on 4,509 accounts. By 2010 that number had increased to 7,500, and although the details of the full 52,000 account holders were not provided, the number increased again in 2010 until it was finally resolved in November 2010.

In response to a request from the Swiss Parliament, UBS published the *UBS Transparency Report by the Board of Directors to Shareholders* on May 30, 2010. In the Report, UBS claimed that the restructured bank had regained profitability, reorganized its governance and risk management structures, and brought in new senior management, in addition to implementing extensive legal, due diligence, and risk assessment training to achieve a new corporate culture. UBS carefully distinguished individual employee culpability from that of the bank, asking "Did UBS or employees of UBS actively participate in tax fraud committed by their clients? The SFBC Cross-Border Report concludes that this cannot be excluded" (ibid, 39).

In the fourth quarter, after shedding assets, UBS posted a net profit and its "core wealth-management business drew in net new money of 5.8billion francs" (Letzing, 2014).

Credit Suisse

In 2014, Credit Suisse was called to testify before the Senate Homeland and Governmental Affairs Investigations Subcommittee, and was subsequently proven to have engaged in the same activities as UBS. On May 20, 2014, Credit Suisse pleaded guilty to "extensive and wide reaching conspiracy" to help U.S. clients evade taxes, and agreed to pay US$2.6 billion in fines, a vast increase over the US$780 million that UBS was fined (U.S. Department of Justice, 2014). The Department of Justice received US$1.8 billion in fines and restitution; New York State Department of Financial Services received US$715 million, and the Federal Reserve received US$100 million. Although Credit Suisse pleaded guilty, its investor advisor license to do business in the United States was not revoked. Brady Dugan, a Credit Suisse career banker and CEO since 2007, sought to mitigate the fine and penalties but the U.S. Department of Justice refused a Deferred Prosecution Agreement, which would have spared the bank criminal charges.

Credit Suisse was found guilty of failure to cooperate, delays in turning over documents, deletion of emails, and keeping indicted employees on the payroll. More importantly, like UBS, the bank was not required to turn over the names of its U.S. account holders, then forbidden under Swiss law, and the CEO, Brady Dugan, refused to step down.

The Declaration on Automatic Exchange of Information in Tax Matters, adopted on May 6, 2014, requires all countries to "collect and exchange information on bank accounts, the beneficial ownership of companies and other legal structures, such as trusts" (Houlder 2014). It has been signed by approximately 44 countries, including Switzerland, the world's largest offshore financial center, the Cayman Islands and Jersey.

London Interbank Offered Rate manipulation

The London Interbank Offered Rate (LIBOR) was created in 1969, when a group of European banks extended a loan to Iran and had to set a rate to "... represent the cost of unsecured funding in the open market for the largest financial firms [...] LIBOR was designed to reflect the rates at which the large banks borrowed money from one another each day; these rates were the foundation for what they would then charge their customers" (Rose and Sesia 2013: 2).

The products involved covered a vast range of financial transactions, including "on the Chicago Mercantile Exchange, over US$564 trillion of futures contracts tied to the value of LIBOR traded in 2011" (ibid). In 1986, the British Bankers Association took over management of setting LIBOR in three currencies: US dollar, Japanese yen and the pound sterling. By 2012, however, LIBOR was produced for 10 currencies with 15 maturities for each: 150 rates each business day. For the US dollar, 16 banks, including Barclays, submitted rates each day between 11:00 and 11:10AM. There was a similar process for the Euro Interbank Offered Rate (EURIBOR), in which 40 to 50 leading banks submitted rates, with the process overseen by the European Banking Federation.

In September 2007, rumors began to circulate about the validity of the process amid concerns that the "Dollar LIBOR rates submitted by contributing banks, including Barclays, were too low and did not accurately reflect the market" (United States Department of Justice, 2012). In June 2008, the President of the Federal Reserve Bank of New York, Timothy Geithner (Treasury Secretary from 2008 to 2013), and the Governor of the Bank of England, Mervyn King, expressed doubts and sought to enhance the accuracy and credibility of LIBOR. Neither the Bank of England nor the U.K. Financial Services Authority, accountable to Treasury and Parliament, were directly responsible for the process.

Investigations conducted in 2012 revealed that between 2005 and 2009, Barclays, UBS, Rabobank, and other banks had submitted incorrect LIBOR rates "thereby benefitting their respective derivatives trading positions and either increasing their profits or minimizing their losses" (CFTC 2012). Lowballing is the practice of "deliberately underestimating a price to deceive the market"

(Binham, 2012). UBS rate submitters were reporting artificially low benchmark interest rates to make the bank seem stronger during the financial crisis.

Barclays

In September 2008, Barclays acquired Lehman's U.S. business for US$1.75 billion (Rose and Sesia 2008), having previously been sought as a white knight during Lehman's collapse. However, in the wake of the U.K. Government's partial nationalization of Lloyds and RBS in October 2008, Barclays elected to raise additional capital privately rather than accept taxpayer monies. In order to maintain the pretense of greater liquidity, Barclays traders began to systematically manipulate LIBOR. Neither its risk management and control systems nor its compliance unit addressed these issues. The determination of costs in borrowing currencies was set by its Money Market Desk, located on the same trading floor with derivative traders. These traders requested rates or adjusted rates, improperly using the rates to benefit their trading positions. By October 2009, the Bank of England began to question why "Barclays was always toward the top end of the LIBOR pricing" (Masters and Binhan 2012).

Although the first allegations of LIBOR manipulation occurred in U.K. banks, specifically Barclays, the investigation was spearheaded by U.S. regulators, specifically the Commodity Futures Trading Commission (CFTC). As LIBOR was used in derivative contracts traded in the United States, authorities there had regulatory jurisdiction, and the U.K. Financial Services Authority worked in concert with the U.S. Department of Justice. Barclays settled with U.S. and U.K. regulators, agreeing to pay US$450 million in fines, and "admitted and accepted responsibility for its misconduct" (U.S. Department of Justice 2012). Pursuing this inquiry, in April 2014, the U.K. Serious Fraud Office charged three Barclays traders with conspiracy to defraud. Between 2007 and 2009, during the financial crisis and global credit crunch, Barclays "made dishonestly low LIBOR submission rates to dampen market speculation and negative media comments about the firm's viability during the financial crisis" (Clayton and Sesia 2013).

UBS, Rabobank

In February 2012, the Swiss Government undertook an investigation of 12 major banks, including Citibank and Deutsche, which led to charges against former UBS traders. Rabobank, a Dutch lender, admitted that dozens of its traders manipulated LIBOR over a period of six years, working with traders in other banks to manipulate LIBOR and EURIBOR for the US dollar, Japanese yen and pound sterling interest rates, for the benefit of the bank's traders and at the expense of its counterparties.

The LIBOR settlement between the implicated banks and U.S. and U.K. regulators, by October 2013, had reached US$1.5 billion for UBS, US$450 million for Barclays, and US$615 million for Rabobank. A further 20 banks are under investigation including Deutsche Bank, UBS, Credit Suisse, and Rabobank (Clayton and Sesia 2013). Moreover, the LIBOR scandal has forced banks to set aside additional capital to cover litigation costs. Swiss regulators ordered UBS to increase by 50 percent the amount of capital held against compliance and operational risk, and litigation costs, and Deutsche Bank set aside an additional €1.2 billion to meet litigation costs.

Finally, investigations into rate manipulation are not confined to LIBOR. In 2014, investigations were conducted into rate manipulation in foreign exchange currency markets (FOREX), including the US$5.3 trillion spot market, implicating Deutsche Bank, UBS, Citigroup, RBS, and Barclays; and the Bank of England had to conduct an internal inquiry which concluded that the Bank was not implicated (Strauss et al. 2014).

The Wheatley Review by the U.K. Financial Services Authority (since 2013, the Financial Conduct Authority) concluded that LIBOR could not remain self-regulated. It set out a series of recommendations to reform the setting of bench-mark rates such as LIBOR and EURIBOR. These recommendations included ending self-regulation, and bringing LIBOR under a new regulatory regime under the supervision of the U.K. Financial Conduct Authority. There will be a new code of conduct governing LIBOR submission by banks, with civil and criminal penalties imposed in instances of abuse.

Rogue traders

Société Générale: home office losses

The case of Jerome Kerviel, like that of Nick Leeson discussed in Chapter 4, offers a further example of extravagant positions taken, vast amounts of the bank's money made available to a junior trader, collusion between the back office and the trading floor, the creation of fictitious accounts, and benign complicity on the part of management. However, where Barings failed or turned a blind eye to the doings of profitable traders in their Singapore office, Société Générale's lack of oversight was part of a larger cultural and historical hierarchy in which Jerome Kerviel was culprit as well as scapegoat.

Kerviel, an inexperienced junior trader was moved from the firm's back office to the elite Delta Desk, where he dealt in complex derivative hedging transactions. He began to generate losses in 2007, but despite more than 74 warnings from internal audits and counterparties, his line of credit was neither reduced nor curtailed. In order to hide his losses, he created fictitious reports or claimed that errors had occurred. In January 2008, losses reached € 4.9 billion and could no longer be hidden. When caught, he averred that in this business model of derivative trading "[i]t is impossible to generate that much profit with small positions, which leads me to say that so long as I was in profit, the superiors closed their eyes to the way I did it and the amounts I took on" (Clark and Bennhold 2008).

Kerviel did not personally benefit from his trades, but rather sought to impress his superiors with his trading strategies. In a volatile market, Société Générale sought to unravel these trades without notifying the Bank of France or Treasury. Nevertheless, his trial in 2010 and appeal in 2013 placed the blame on the trader, ordering him to repay the €4.9 billion lost, and exculpating the bank. Although Kerviel's appeal in 2014 failed, it no longer required him to make total restitution, and Société Générale was accused of lax risk management and poor supervisory controls. Kerviel was given a three-year sentence and jailed in May 2014. In September 2014 a French higher court ordered Kerviel's sentence reduced to probation and electronic monitoring. He was freed after 100 days in jail.

UBS

Kweku Adoboli joined the UBS London back office in 2003, and within three years was promoted to trader on the exchange traded funds desk, and then to associate director. In 2008, he began placing unauthorized trades, betting on stock markets. As his losses grew, he maintained an "umbrella account" to hide evidence of his trades, through the creation of phony counterparties. When the losses of over $2 billion were discovered, he confessed to having used the profits in part to cover gambling debts. He was found guilty of fraud and abuse of position, and sentenced to seven years in jail. UBS was fined GB£29.7 million by the U.K. Financial Services Authority for "seriously defective" risk management controls (Ugeux 2011).

JPMorgan: the London Whale

JPMorgan, judged a paragon of sound management during the financial crisis of 2008–9, has, since 2012, been the subject of civil and criminal litigation, and seen penalties imposed in connection with its credit card debt procedures, and its mortgage and foreclosures practices.

In 2012, the bank incurred a US$6.2 billion loss as a result of a huge proprietary position held by the London arm of its Chief Investment Office (CIO). The "London Whale" name was attached to the senior trader, Bruno Iksil, responsible for building the enormous synthetic credit portfolio. Iksil's strategy was originally described as a hedge to reduce exposure to deteriorating credit conditions. However, as the portfolio declined in value and losses accumulated, in order to cover the losses, bank officials resorted to "fudging the valuations" and changing the models for valuing these credit derivatives (Norris 2013: B1). When required by the OCC to provide accurate information on these transactions, the bank hid losses of hundreds of millions of dollars and continued to insist that the trades were proper.

In June 2012, CEO Jaime Dimon dismissed the losses as only US$2 billion, a fraction of JPMorgan's immense balance sheet of US$2.4 trillion. The Senate Committee hearings conducted on the losses proved that the bank's proposals: "encompassed multiple, complex credit trading strategies, using jargon that even the relevant actors and regulators could not understand" (ibid)). The Senate investigation led to the conclusion that "[t]his weak valuation process is all the more troubling given the high-risk nature of synthetic credit derivatives, the lack of any underlying tangible assets to stem losses, and the speed with which substantial losses can accumulate and threaten a bank's profitability" (ibid). Actual losses exceeded US$6 billion. JPMorgan's Chief Investment Officer, Ina

Drew, was forced to retire, Bruno Iksil was fined, but not jailed, and JPMorgan incurred penalties and fines of over US$2 billion. Yet in 2014, the Board gave a vote of full confidence to Jaime Dimon and increased his compensation.

The cases of Société Générale, UBS and JPMorgan reflect the comment made by Eric Holder, Attorney General of the United States, who claimed that banks cannot be criminally prosecuted as such a prosecution under U.S. law would mean the loss of their banking license, which would have "a negative impact on the national economy, perhaps even the world economy" (Holder 2013).

From Ponzi to Madoff

In his economic modeling, American economist Hyman Minsky "attached great importance to the behavior of heavily indebted borrowers, particularly those that increased their indebtedness in the expansion to finance the purchase of real estate or stocks or commodities for short term capital gains" (Kindleberger and Aliber 2011: 22). Minsky judged that an exogenous shock would initially provoke expansion and feed into these asset bubbles. However, once the economy slows, or there is a negative shock, firms involved in this type of behavior quickly fall into increased speculative activity to offset losses, or outright Ponzi schemes if the firm does not have operating income sufficient to meet its obligations. Speculative pyramid schemes originating in the 1720 Mississippi Bubble became known in the twentieth century as Ponzi schemes. The original scheme was based on speculation in postage stamps, in which Charles Ponzi, who ran a small loans company in Boston in the early 1920s, promised to pay depositors interest of 30 percent a month (the annual rate of return on bank deposits was 5 percent). After three months, however, the inflow of cash from new depositors was smaller than the interest payment promised to the initial investors. When suspicious investors began to demand their money back, the entire scheme collapsed.

In December 2008, Bernard L. Madoff, former Vice Chair of NASD and founding member of NASDAQ, confessed to having run a Ponzi scheme on a grand scale for almost 15 years. Madoff promised his investors steady returns of 12 to 15 percent, despite any and all market fluctuations. By December 2008, in the wake of the financial crisis, Madoff faced US$7 billion in redemptions. With the financial crisis, it was impossible to maintain the "exponential increase in the number of participants … required at each level" and the entire scheme collapsed (SEC). His clients, including universities, major sports teams, and countless foundations and individuals, lost investments totaling US$65 billion.

With the funds never actually invested, Madoff had to create fictitious accounts, audits, and involve real counterparties and banks. In each case it became easier, and then necessary, to pay investors with other investors' money. Although the scheme largely affected American investors and institutions, Madoff had connections with smaller banks and investors in other countries, but he required the services of a major bank to allow him to move monies between different accounts, as well as it offering additional prestige and cover for his fraudulent activities. In January 2014, five years after the collapse of Madoff's scheme, JPMorgan was penalized and fined for failing to report suspicious activity in the Madoff accounts. "Suspicions were there, but so were the profits and the profits seemed to have outweighed any other concerns" (Norris 2014, B1). However, it is impossible to know who was responsible, as each transaction went through so many layers of "turf wars and incompetence" (ibid). While compliance requirements did exist, in reality compliance was lax, and just a few months after Madoff's arrest, his JPMorgan client relationship manager was asked to certify that the client was in compliance with all legal and regulatory policies.

In 2007, JPMorgan's Chief Risk Officer refused to increase exposure to Madoff from US$100 million to US$1 billion after "Mr. Madoff had made it clear that he would not allow JPMorgan to perform due diligence on what he was doing with investors' money" (ibid). Madoff kept investigators at bay by allowing rumors having advance knowledge of stock movements to benefit his investments. In reality, there were no actual investments, the monies in the accounts never went into securities, but simply moved from investors to repay investors. Between 1990 and 2008, despite warnings and red flags in London and New York, check kiting operations continued in which Madoff's securities firm and one of his largest clients, Bankers Trust, moved checks for tens of millions between the two accounts "allowing Mr. Madoff to inappropriately collect interest on the "float", or the time it took the cash balances to get transferred between accounts, according to Tuesday's settlement" (Fitzpatrick 2014). JPMorgan withdrew most of its funds in October 2008, limiting its actual losses to US$40 million. Nevertheless, a series of settlements with the U.S. Department of Justice required it to pay US$2.6 billion, used in part to compensate victims and creditors. Madoff was sentenced to serve 150 years in prison and, as of 2014, barely one third of his victims have been compensated.

Concluding remarks

As this chapter demonstrates, systemically important financial institutions have been among the worst offenders in terms of money laundering, tax evasion, rogue trading, misrepresentation, and fraudulent dealings. The situation has worsened since the financial crisis of 2008.

Public admission of guilt

The cascade of scandals and violations has forced CEOs to acknowledge their institutional shortcomings in annual reports, public statements, and speeches. At HSBC, "The Board is determined to adopt and enforce the highest behavioral and compliance standards in HSBC. For well documented reasons, the last two years have been extremely damaging to HSBC's reputation and our perception of ourselves" (HSBC 2013). Jaime Dimon, CEO of JPMorgan, included in the Annual Report 2012 the letter sent by the Operating Committee stating that "[t]here is no piece of business, no deal, no revenue stream that is more important than our obligation to act responsibly, ethically and within the rules. [...] Compliance isn't just the province of our Compliance Department ... it is everyone's responsibility" (Dimon 2013). Of the London Whale debacle, Dimon stated that "[t]hese problems were our fault and it is our job to fix them. In fact I feel terrible that we let our regulators down" (ibid). Like HSBC and UBS, JPMorgan has vowed to "mak[e] our control agenda priority #1" (ibid).

Provisions to cover legal costs

In 2014, Deutsche Bank posted losses of a €1 billion after settling lawsuits over fraudulent mortgage securities and alleged manipulation of EURIBOR. JPMorgan paid fines of almost US$20 billion to resolve the London Whale incident and mortgage bond sales misrepresentation. LIBOR settlements to authorities in the United States, United Kingdom, and the Netherlands have included $1.5 billion (UBS); $1 billion (Rabobank); $450million (Barclays); and $615 million (RBS). These massive fines have required financial institutions to set aside significantly larger reserves to cover litigation costs: Deutsche Bank's litigation provisions, for example, were set at up to € 4.1 billion. Fines imposed on financial institutions in the United States since 2012 exceed US$25 billion. This includes penalties for fraudulent activity on mortgage backed securities (JPMorgan, Bank of America, Deutsche Bank, and Goldman Sachs); tax fraud (Credit Suisse and UBS); defrauding investors (Citibank); LIBOR manipulation (Barclays and RBS).

New Risk management, monitoring and oversight bodies

In the wake of these scandals many financial institutions have established new risk management and oversight bodies. Deutsche Bank and UBS have reduced their investment bank activities, improved risk management supervision, revamped their boards of directors, and established ethics and conduct oversight committees. An independent monitor at HSBC will now report directly to authorities in the United Kingdom and United States. In addition, HSBC has created the Financial System Vulnerabilities Committee, to provide "governance, oversight and policy guidance" on any exposure "to financial crime or system abuse" (HSBC 2013).

Compliance with domestic and global regulations

All financial institutions acknowledge pressure in complying with the increased regulatory requirements introduced in the aftermath of the financial crisis, including the almost 400 rules required by the Dodd-Frank Act, as well as new capital requirements introduced under Basel III, and stress tests.

Despite the generic admissions of responsibility and public relations rhetoric, the public perception of banks and bankers remains unchanged, as shareholders continue to grant bankers and traders exorbitant remuneration: "The Dodd-Frank Act, the Volcker Rule, the increased capital requirements and the rest have done next to nothing to change the fundamental fact that bankers and traders are still being rewarded to take imprudent risks with other people's money in order to get big bonuses. That's the Wall Street reality" (Cohan 2014).

Since the 1980s, the fundamental culture of financial institutions remains unchanged. It is profit driven, with a constant need for innovation driven by technology and competition. The criteria for remuneration and bonuses is short term rather than multi-year. The less rigorous risk management criteria applied to investment, trading and derivative sectors (especially in foreign subsidiaries) have remained prevalent. New regulatory requirements will impose stronger disclosure, accountability, and compliance. Yet, once a financial institution passes the stress tests, absorbs the large fines and penalties, and returns to full profitability, what incentives will or can motivate these institutions to change profoundly, or will they simply be very careful to avoid making the same mistakes, but be all too ready to assume new risks in the name of profits, remuneration, and expansion until the next scandal, fraud or crisis? It is interesting to note that in 2012, HSBC's market capitalization increased from USS136 billion to US$194 billion (HSBC 2013). UBS, JPMorgan, and RBS all enjoyed strong growth in 2013.

In 2014, there is a new awareness of the importance of redefining corporate governance and institutional culture, as well as the severity of the costs in terms of reputational damage. For the first time, there is a concerted effort from public figures, boards, and regulators to find the means to assess risk culture, to quantify the conditions that foster this and indicators that predict or measure it, and from this a desire to create custom metrics that facilitate risk culture assessment.

Summary

We introduced this chapter with a historical overview of past speculative schemes and banking frauds, which led us to examine the Bernard Madoff case involving U.S. investors and both domestic and foreign financial institutions. We proceeded to analyze violations of the U.S. Securities and Exchange Act, specifically the Enron case (2002), and its ramifications.

In the next section, Rogue Traders, we examined trading scandals at Société Générale (2008), UBS (2011), and the JPMorgan London Whale (2012). The section on money laundering considered the definition of money laundering, and delved into key precedents – BCCI, Riggs Bank, and Banco Ambrosiano, as well as more recent examples including Barclays, HSBC, and the Vatican Bank. In these cases we referred also to implications for other institutions and increased levels of scrutiny and jurisdictional authority granted to the United States to take the lead in investigating these civil and criminal violations.

We have detailed the major anti-money laundering measures in place, led by the United States. The dominance of the United States in this domain is explained by the fact that any leading financial institution that conducts business in the United States requires a New York State license. Since 2011, New York State has increased its regulatory authority through the creation of the New York Department of Financial Services, which replaced the New York State Banking Department and New York State Insurance Department. By September 2014, this new department "claims jurisdiction over 1,900 such companies" (Farrell 2014).

In the next section we considered the violation of U.S. sanctions, dealing with institutions charged with direct violation of U.S.-imposed sanctions under the Helms-Burton and D'Amato-Kennedy Acts, as well as sanctions imposed since on regimes designated as terrorists. We examined in detail the cases of Standard Chartered and BNP.

We then proceeded to issues of tax evasion and fraud, specifically UBS and Credit Suisse. The final section examined the 2012–14 LIBOR rate manipulation scandal and the ongoing FOREX currency benchmark rigging allegations. These allegations implicating Deutsche Bank, Goldman Sachs, RBS, and UBS, which together account for 43 percent of the largely unregulated US$5.3 trillion a day foreign exchange market, is still in process.

These scandals and violations of best practices, conduct, and public trust have inflicted significant damage to the reputation of financial institutions and resulted in direct loss of share valuation, and provisions for legal costs and fines. Since 2012, banks in the United States have incurred large fines in relation to misconduct and fraudulent activities undertaken both during and after the U.S. subprime mortgage crises. We ended this chapter by looking at new measures undertaken by global banks to impose a set of ethical standards, and bring about a shift in culture and a reevaluation of best practices in the international banking industry at large.

Notes

1. This was just three years after the massive bankruptcy of Penn Square Bank (United States) on falsified oil and gas leases, see Chapter 4.
2. Other countries in which BCCI had contacts included: Nigeria, Cameroon, Senegal, Congo, Lebanon, Saudi Arabia, the United Arab Emirates, Kuwait, and Iraq.
3. This report was prepared for the Bank of England by Price Waterhouse, who referred to BCCI as Sandstorm.
4. Since the late 1990s, the IRS has in place the Qualifying Intermediary System, clarifying the legal framework allowing U.S. citizens to hold accounts in foreign banks.

9 International banking trends and challenges

Introduction

In this chapter, we begin with a brief re-examination of the key determinants of the fast process of internationalization by most leading Organization for Economic Co-operation and Development (OECD) banks between the late 1980s and 2008 (see Chapters 1, 2, 3, and 7).

We then examine the consequences of governments' reactions to the U.S. subprime crisis and ensuing global credit crunch as well as the nature of private sector responses (see Chapters 4, 5, and 6), and proceed to discuss the political, cultural and monetary implications, particularly from 2011 onwards of financial fraud by leading financial institutions (see Chapter 8).

We conclude with the outline of a conceptual framework that captures the fundamental challenge faced by boards of directors of banks around the world with regard to the scope and reach of their institutions' international offering: how to accurately assess their companies' strengths and weaknesses vis-à-vis those of their stronger competitors, across the full spectrum of their financial services offerings, in each geographic arena under consideration, so that acceptable and sustainable returns on capital to each initiative in each jurisdiction can be achieved (Sotelino and Bermudez 2014).

Market-driven internationalization: mid 1980s to 2008

Between the late 1980s and early 2000s, banks were forced to redefine themselves in order to compete effectively for the business of international clients. As discussed in Chapter 2, the main drivers of this process were regulatory reform, including deregulation that reduced the barriers-to-entry by banks into new jurisdictions, technological change, and, in conjunction with these changes, the explosive growth of securities markets. The role of government as controlling shareholder in major banks waned as banks, especially in continental Europe, were denationalized and privatized.

On the regulatory front, the Financial Services Action Plan[1] in the European Union (EU) formalized a series of measures to implement a single wholesale financial market and a more open retail market, completing a process of gradual reduction of the barriers to cross-border financial intermediation, first established with the EU Second Banking Directive of 1989. In the United States, over six decades of regulatory firewalls limiting interstate and universal banking were removed. The Riegle-Neal Interstate Banking and Branching Efficiency Act of 1994 revoked restrictions on interstate mergers among banks put in place by the McFadden Act (1927). The Gramm-Leach-Bliley Act of 1999 completed the elimination of regulatory constraints on the securities underwriting activities of commercial banks, introduced by the Glass-Steagall Act in 1933. These major regulatory reforms opened the door to a wave of mergers and acquisitions in the United States and Europe that resulted in the creation of a group of important international universal banks or financial supermarkets.

On the technological front, an acceleration of paper-to-digital operations revolutionized how financial information was assembled and disseminated, credit risk assessed, priced and provisioned against, large volumes of loans classified, bundled and securitized, contractual obligations established and monitored, and trades conducted and settled.

Deregulation and technological change combined to facilitate the explosive growth of securities markets, putting downward pressure on the spreads that commercial banks could earn from loans, and pushing them into capital market activities and higher-margin consumer finance endeavors, at home and abroad.

Finally, as discussed in Chapter 3, stricter enforcement of legislation against tax evasion, particularly after 2000, further accelerated a shift in priority by high net worth individuals away from the discrete protection of wealth towards yield.

The stage was set for banks to become more universal (in terms of scope of activities) and/or more international (in terms of geographic reach). A fundamentally market-driven expansion of the scope of activities and the broadening of geographic reach by leading OECD banks followed.

However, this accelerated process of internationalization came to a halt in 2008, as the U.S. subprime crisis, the ensuing global liquidity crunch, and threat of a major economic recession forced governments to come to the rescue of many of their major banks.

Governments' responses to the global financial crisis of 2008

Under the threat of collapse of their financial systems, governments responded with a combination of (i) increased government backing of bank deposits; (ii) liquidity assistance by central banks to financial institutions in their jurisdictions; and (iii) wherever necessary and in addition to central bank liquidity support against acceptable collateral, direct recapitalization of severely affected major banks by national treasuries at taxpayers' expense.

As described in Chapter 4, emergency government assistance to troubled banks in 2008 to 2009 took three main forms:

- Capital infusion by Treasury with *de facto* take-over of management control by government at least in the short term. This was the case with Fannie Mae,

Freddie Mac, and AIG in the United States; Royal Bank of Scotland, Lloyds Bank, and HBOS in the United Kingdom; Allied Irish Bank, Bank of Ireland, and Anglo Irish Bank in Ireland; and Kaupthng, Glitnir, and Landsbanki in Iceland.

- Capital infusion by Treasury without government take-over of management control. This was the case with Citibank and Bank of America in the United States; UBS in Switzerland; ING in the Netherlands; and Commerzbank in Germany.
- Government-assisted absorption of the troubled financial institution by a healthier institution, typically via extended liquidity support against collateral negotiated by the acquiring institution with the central bank. This was the case with Bear Stearns and Washington Mutual by JPMorgan Chase, and Countrywide and Merrill Lynch by Bank of America in the United States; Dresdner Bank by Commerzbank in Germany; HBOS by Lloyds Bank in the United Kingdom; and Fortis by BNP Paribas in Belgium.

However, public recognition that excessive leverage, over-reliance on short-term funding and inadequate supervision by bank regulators had been at the root of the quasi collapse of the financial system led to a major overhaul of bank regulation. In June 2011, the Basel Committee on Banking Supervision put forward the Basel III Accord, embodying a set of standards that severely tightened capital adequacy requirements in relation to those prevailing under Basel II, and introduced new quantitative specific guidelines for minimum short-term liquidity and medium-term stability of funding. As discussed in detail in Chapter 6, Basel III called for the gradual, but full, implementation by 2019 by all jurisdictions of a minimum common equity ratio in relation to total risk-weighted assets more than three times greater than what was required under Basel II (from 2–3 percent to 7–9.5 percent); higher risk-weights for derivative trading and off-balance sheet exposures (resulting in larger total risk-weighted assets for the denominator of the minimum common equity ratio required); newly introduced minimum short-term liquidity and medium-term stability of funding requirements; newly introduced maximum leverage constraints through a requirement of minimum common equity of at least 3 percent (later raised to 5 percent in the United States) of total notional assets, defined as total nominal credit risk exposures without weighing for risk; and last but not least, an additional loss absorbency requirement of up to 3.5 percent of total risk-weighted assets for systemically important financial institutions (SIFIs). These institutions would be identified annually by the Basel Committee on Banking Supervision based on an examination of five measures of the financial institution: size, cross jurisdictional activity, interconnectedness, substitutability, and complexity.

In the United States, United Kingdom, and European Union, legislators have gone beyond the proposed Basel III guidelines to put in place additional measures directed at curbing excessive risk-taking by banks in their jurisdictions. These measures include swap regulation, to push derivative trading from the over-the-counter market (where counterparties assume one another's credit risk) to central

counterparty clearing houses (for greater transparency and adequate collateraliza-
tion of trades), as well as restrictions on proprietary trading by banks, as proposed
by the Volcker Rule in the United States, the Ring Fence in the United Kingdom,
and the Separate Legal Entity in the European Union.

Full implementation of the European Banking Union has been scheduled for 2015.
On April 16, 2014, the EU Parliament enacted three pieces of legislation defining
the functions and objectives of this new supervisory and oversight body, namely:

- Bank Recovery and Resolution Directive, giving all 28 EU states a common
  rule book for handling failing banks and obliging creditors (like bondholders)
  to take losses of up to 8 percent of a bank's total liabilities before state money
  can be used;
- Single Resolution Mechanism, establishing a common fund of €55 billion (to
  be built over 8 years) to cover the costs of resolving troubled banks;
- Guarantee of all bank deposits up to €100,000.

In conjunction with the establishment of the European Banking Union, the
European Central Bank (ECB) has expanded its mandate to assume supervisory
authority over 6,000 EU banks, a daunting challenge that will certainly require
extreme degrees of transparency and cooperation among national authorities and
the ECB.

Since 2008, central banks have seen an increase in their scope of supervisory
activities and authority to monitor the stability of financial systems. It is now
established and accepted practice for central banks to conduct intensive stress-
testing of the capital adequacy of the most important banks in their jurisdictions,
as well as the obligation for such banks to submit living wills providing regulators
with a roadmap of how a financial institution can be liquidated without disruption
to the financial system. In addition, orderly liquidation authority (OLA) legislation
is being put in place in jurisdictions around the world to empower regulators to
intervene in a SIFI, oust its management and board, wipe-out its equity holders,
and liquidate the institution according to the debt holders' hierarchy of rights.

While final implementation of these measures is still in process, the consequences for financial institutions, particularly those considered domestically and/
or internationally of systemic importance, are clear: substantially higher capital
requirements overall, and for securities trading in particular; stricter funding
constraints; regulatory restrictions on proprietary trading; and, last but not least,
much greater regulatory scrutiny and supervision.

Private sector response to the global financial crisis of 2008

The private sector response to the crisis occurred in two stages. The first stage
(2008–9) was characterized by immediate emergency measures, particularly for
those more exposed to institutional as opposed to retail funding, and opportunistic
take-overs of weakened banks by healthier ones, often with some sort of government

assistance, such as liquidity support from the central bank and/or treasury-backed guarantees for bad assets.

In the United States, two of the five largest investment banks, Goldman Sachs and Morgan Stanley, obtained important capital infusions from Berkshire Hathaway (U.S.) and Mitsubishi-UFJ (Japan) respectively. These institutions changed their legal status from broker-dealers to bank holding companies, becoming eligible for Federal Reserve liquidity support and subject to Federal Reserve supervision. Bear Stearns and Merrill Lynch were absorbed by universal banks JPMorgan Chase and Bank of America; and Lehman Brothers collapsed. Among U.S. private sector mortgage lenders, the two largest, Countrywide and Washington Mutual, were absorbed by Bank of America and JPMorgan Chase respectively; and Wachovia Bank, which acquired the mortgage lender Golden West in 2006, was acquired by Wells Fargo. In Europe, Dresdner Bank was acquired by Commerzbank in Germany, HBOS by Lloyds Bank in the United Kingdom, and Fortis (Belgium) by BNP Paribas (France).

The second stage (2009–11) was characterized by market driven initiatives to restore capital adequacy, primarily through asset sales, including the divestment of non-core business activities, often overseas. Examples include Citigroup's sale of its consumer finance operations in Germany to France's Crédit Mutuel, and of its credit card franchise in Brazil (Credicard) to Itaú-Unibanco; ING Groep's sale of its ING-Direct U.S. operations to Capital One and U.K. operations to Barclays; and HSBC's sale of its U.S. domestic credit card business to Capital One, and its retail banking operations in Russia, Poland, Japan, and Thailand to domestic competitors. When viable, banks also turned to the public markets to raise capital, as evidenced by Banco Santander's stock exchange listings of its Brazilian (Reuters 2009) and Mexican subsidiaries (de la Merced 2012). Through these offerings, Banco Santander managed to raise over US$12 billion in fresh equity without loss of ownership control of these operations.

Cultural implications and challenges

In 2004, when asked about Citi's corporate culture, Sandy Weil, Chief Executive Officer, responded that "culture is for yoghurt" (Finel-Honigman 2009: viii). During the highly profitable years 1998 to 2007, with expansion, mergers and acquisitions, institutional culture was considered as non-quantifiable and, therefore, largely irrelevant to a bank's performance, valuation, competitiveness, or reputation.

However, in the aftermath of the financial crisis of 2008, banks have been forced to assume legal, civil, and even criminal responsibility for their practices and operations, which has led to ever-larger fines and penalties under U.S. and U.K. jurisdictions.

As we describe in Chapter 8, these behavioral failures have included manipulation of LIBOR and FOREX rates, the violation of U.S. sanctions, tax fraud, mortgage transaction abuses, money laundering and incidences of rogue traders. The level of fines imposed in response to such behavior has hurt profitability and caused reputational damage, bringing the reexamination of individual and corporate culture to the forefront of the debate at the highest levels of management.

In 2013 and 2014, the term *corporate culture* appeared in the Liikanen High Level Expert Group Report on EU Bank Reform (October 2013), and in the Capital Requirement Directive IV, Article 98.7 and Article 91.8 refer to "corporate culture and values". The specific focus is on risk culture, with Deputy Comptroller for Operational Risk at the Office of the Comptroller of the Currency, Carolyn Duchene, stating that "it is an organization's risk culture that most determines success in identifying and mitigating risk" (DuChene 2013). European Banking Authority guidelines on internal governance specify that institutions must foster "an integrated and institution-wide risk culture", mentioned also in the U.K. Corporate Governance Code.

In 2014, Deutsche Bank imposed a new institution-wide code of conduct, which extends to the internal behavior of traders, with an emphasis on "to do what is right – not just what is allowed" (Ewing 2014: B4). Since 2012, Deutsche Bank has held "mandatory seminars on ethical leadership for top managers and added hundreds of compliance enforcers" (ibid.) and has shifted the compensation structure toward rewarding long-term results.

The extreme level of fines imposed on BNP reflected the fact that the Swiss subsidiary board, where the largest number of sanctions violations were approved, included the head of compliance at BNP. And even FBI Director, James Cooney, noted that "(u)ntil shareholders demand from their boards that those boards choose leaders who understand what it means to create a healthy culture of compliance, the money will keep walking out the door…" (Davidson and Prior 2014).

The complex challenge is how to promote a system of values throughout the institution, not only shared but practiced by the board and all levels of the management hierarchy, while maintaining competitiveness and profit-focused operations.

A framework for strategic decision-making

In the aftermath of the global financial crisis of 2008, merger and acquisition activity among financial institutions was fundamentally intra- (as opposed to inter-) jurisdictional, leading to greater concentrations of domestic banking industries around the world and, for the United States, accelerating a trend toward universal banking.

Stricter capital, liquidity, and disclosure requirements are here to stay, as well as regulators' strengthened abilities to monitor banks' activities and to impose severe penalties for financial misconduct.

Furthermore, society at large has become much more aware of the huge costs of financial system collapses and much more demanding of institutional corporate responsibility. As acknowledged by Jürgen Fitschen and Anshu Jain, co-chairs of Deutsche Bank, in the bank's March 2014 management board meeting, "[r]estoring the bond of trust with society is top priority for the banking industry" (Fitschen and Jain 2014).

These factors should lead financial institutions to a much more rigorous and continuous examination of their businesses. Internal methodologies for the assessment of performance of business units (RAROC methodologies, focused on individual business units' return on capital adjusted for risk) must be assiduously and thoroughly revisited so that capital allocation and compensation decisions are made in a way that credit, market, and operational risks (including the monetary costs and reputation damages) are clearly accounted for, are transparent to boards of directors, and can be translated into solid reporting to regulators. This process will require incorporation of rigorous stress testing of capital needs, liquidity consequences and overall profitability implications for variations in key credit, market and operational aspects affecting the performance of the particular business unit, as well as cross-divisional contributions to stable growth of earnings and good reputation of the company as a whole.

Table 9.1 presents a panel designed to help frame the strategic decision-making process faced by a major bank with international ambitions, with regard to the allocation of capital and human resources to different businesses and geographic regions. The panel brings together, in the format of a decision tree, the three core components of a bank's business strategy: *scope of activity*, *geographic reach*, and actual or desired *market share*. In doing so, it pushes decision-makers toward a thorough assessment of strengths and weaknesses across the full spectrum of its existing and/or potential financial services offering compared with those of their stronger competitors in each geographic arena under consideration, so that acceptable and sustainable returns on the capital allocated to each initiative in each jurisdiction can be achieved. Or, more simply put, how to have in place an organization capable of achieving and sustaining strong market positions and enjoy a solid reputation, with virtually assured acceptable profitability in all it chooses to do.

The core categories listed for *scope of activity* choices are *retail commercial banking, wholesale banking, wealth management* (or private banking), *asset management* and *insurance*. These major categories can be broken down further; for example, under *retail commercial*, two categories: *individual* and small- and medium sized enterprises (SME) commercial banking.

The core categories listed for *geographic reach* range from *domestic* to *global*, with intermediate categories labeled *regional* and *international* (overseas presence that goes beyond a regional focus). Here again, the nomenclature proposed can be revisited to better reflect the particular characteristics of the financial institution in question, such as adding the category multi-regional to reflect a situation of overseas presence in two selected regions, Latin America and Central Europe for example.

Finally, the core categories listed for *market share* (or, alternatively, *scale*) range from *participant* to *leading*, with intermediate categories labeled as *significant* and *important*. Once again, the nomenclature can be refined and the specific borders between them debated by management and boards. Still, at the end of the day, the nomenclature chosen must reflect the company's contemplated ability to exercise market power as implied by the term chosen.

For the sake of illustration, let us consider the specific cases of a few selected banks mentioned in previous chapters of this book, namely: Citibank, HSBC, Banco Santander, Deutsche Bank, UBS, BNP Paribas, Unicredit, Mitsubishi-UFJ, and RBC. If we were to plot these banks' business strategies and market positions (as reflected in their 2013 annual reports) into Table 9.1, we would probably agree that, as of year-end 2013:

- Citibank was a leading domestic (U.S.) universal bank, a leading regional commercial bank (as it owns Banamex, the second largest bank), a leading global wholesale (corporate and investment bank), and an important global private bank;
- Morgan Stanley (U.S.) was a leading global investment bank and an important global private bank;
- HSBC was a leading domestic (U.K.) universal bank, an important to leading international commercial bank (leading in Asia, important in Latin America), an important global wholesale bank, and an important global private bank;
- Banco Santander was a leading domestic universal bank (Spain), an important international commercial bank (EMU, United Kingdom, Latin America, and United States), an important international wholesale bank (EMU and Latin America), and an important international private bank (EMU, United Kingdom, Latin America, and United States);
- Deutsche Bank was a leading domestic universal bank (Germany), a leading global investment bank, and a significant global private bank;
- UBS was a leading domestic universal bank (Switzerland), an important global investment bank, a leading global private bank and a significant global asset manager;
- BNP Paribas was a leading domestic universal bank, an important regional commercial bank (Italy, Belgium, Luxembourg), a leading regional (EU) and important global wholesale bank, and an important global private bank;
- Unicredit was a leading domestic universal bank (Italy), an important regional commercial bank (Central Europe), an important international wholesale bank

Table 9.1 Strategy panel

Scope of Activities	Geographic Reach	Market Share or Scale
Retail Commercial Banking		Participant
	Domestic	
SMEs Commercial Banking		Significant
	Regional	
Wholesale (or Institutional) Banking		Important
	International	
Private Banking (or Wealth Management)		Leading
	Global	
Asset Management		Dominant

Source: Authors

(EMU and Central Europe) and a significant international private bank (EMU and Central Europe);

- Mitsubishi-UFJ was a leading domestic universal bank (Japan), an important international commercial bank (Asia and United States), an important global wholesale bank, and an important regional private bank (Asia and United States);
- RBC was a leading domestic universal bank (Canada), an important regional commercial bank (United States and Caribbean), an important global wholesale bank, and an important global private bank.

As we weigh up all the considerations discussed in this chapter, we conclude that unless international (if not global) leadership in a major category of activities can be maintained (such as in investment banking), the leading publicly traded financial institutions from all jurisdictions around the world should remain committed to the universal banking model at home, as cross synergies from businesses with strong market shares tend to be more easily realized; but they will most likely be compelled to become increasingly selective regarding the international reach of their chosen financial services offering.

Global financial institutions are essential components of domestic, regional, and global economic health. Since 2008, however, governments and civil societies have suffered the consequences of excessive risk-taking and fraudulent practices, and lending has remained anemic.

In the next decade, banks will continue to expand, merge, and take on new functions in light of new technologies and financial innovation. Financial institutions from China, Brazil, India, and other emerging powers will join the ranks of G-SIBS. Nevertheless, these institutions, like the existing G-SIBs, must work hard, and with humility, to restore society's trust and prove their economic and social viability as engines for sustained economic growth.

Note

1. First introduced in 1999, with its gradual implementation to be completed by 2005.

References

Ahearne, A. "Political-Economic Context in Ireland." N.p. Proceedings of Paper Prepared for Resolving the European Debt Crisis, a Conference Hosted by the Peterson Institute for International Economics and Bruegel, Chantilly, France. 2011.

Akyuz, Y. and Boratav, K. *The Making of the Turkish Financial Crisis*, UNCTAD Discussion Paper No. 158, April 2002. Web. 2 Feb. 2015. <http://www.networkideas. org/feathm/oct2002/boratavyilmaz.pdf>.

Apostolik, R., Donohue, C. and Went, P. *Foundations of Banking Risk: An Overview of Banking, Banking Risks, and Risk-based Banking Regulation*. Hoboken, NJ: John Wiley, 2009.

Bagehot, W. *Lombard Street: A Description of the Money Market*. New York: Scribner's Sons, 1897.

Banco, S. "Santander 2010 Annual Report." Report. April 2011. Web. 27 Feb. 2015. <http:// memoria.santander.webfg.com/2010/index.php?sec=informes&lang=en>.

Banco, S. "Santander 2013 Annual Report." Report. March 2014. Web. 15 May 2014. <http://www.santanderannualreport.com/2013/en.html>.

Bank for International Settlements. "BIS 71st Annual Report." 9 June 2001. Web. 26 June 2012. <http://www.bis.org/publ/arpdf/ar2001e.htm>.

Bank for International Settlements. *Basel III: A Global Regulatory System for More Resilient Banks and Banking Systems*. Rep. N.p., n.d. Web. 3 Mar. 2014. <http://www. bis.org/publ/bcbs189.pdf>.

Bank for International Settlements. *Enhancements to the Basel II Framework*. Basel: Bank for International Settlements, 2009. Web. 3 Feb. 2013. <http://www.bis.org/publ/bcbs157. pdf>.

Bank for International Settlements. *Global Systemically Important Banks: Assessment Methodology and the Additional Loss Absorbency Requirement*. Rep. N.p., Nov. 2011. Web. 21 Jan. 2013. <http://www.bis.org/publ/bcbs207.pdf>.

Bank for International Settlements. *International Framework for Liquidity Risk Measurement, Standards and Monitoring*. Rep. N.p., Dec. 2009. Web. 27 Mar. 2014. <http://www.bis. org/publ/bcbs165.pdf>.

Bank for International Settlements. *Statistical Release: OTC Derivatives Statistics at End-December 2012*. Monetary and Economic Department. Rep. May 2013. Web. 12 Feb. 2015. <http://www.bis.org/publ/otc_hy1305.pdf>.

Bank of America. "Bank of America to Exit International Credit Card Businesses." Press Release. 15 Aug. 2011. Web. 27 Feb. 2015. <http://investor.bankofamerica.com/ phoenix.zhtml?c=71595&p=irol-newsArticle&ID=1596320#fbid=uGeXwCrRL3T>.

Basel Committee on Banking Supervision. *A Framework for Dealing with Domestic Systemically Important Banks*. Rep. Oct. 2013. Web. 12 Feb. 2015. <http://www.bis.org/publ/bcbs233.htm>.

Basel Committee on Banking Supervision. *International Convergence of Capital Measurement and Capital Standards*. Rep. Basel: Bank for International Settlements, 1988. Web. 18 Mar. 2014. <http://www.bis.org/publ/bcbs04a.pdf>.

Basel Committee on Banking Supervision. *Principles for Sound Liquidity Risk Management and Supervision*. Rep. Basel: Bank for International Settlements, 2008. Web. 12 Feb. 2015. <http://www.bis.org/publ/bcbs144.htm>.

Beard, A.J. and Thomas, R.M. *Trade Finance Handbook*. Mason, OH: Thomson, 2006.

Bennett, M. "Banking Deregulation in Indonesia." *Journal of International Business, University of Pennsylvannia* 16.3 (1995): 443–81. Web. 02 Feb. 2015. <www.law.upenn.edu/journals/jil/articles/volume16/issue3/Bennett16U.Pa.J.Int'lBus.L.443(1995).pdf>

Bergstresser, D., Rose, C. and Lane, D. *The Tip of the Iceberg: JPMorgan Chase and Bear Stearns*. B2. Cambridge, MA: Harvard Business Publishing, 2009.

Bergström, C., Thorell, P. and Englund, P. "SECURUM and the Way out of the Swedish Banking Crisis." Report. Stockholm School of Economics Center for Business and Policy Studies, May 2003.

Berkowitz, D., Hoekstra, M. and Schoors, K. "Bank Privatization, Finance, and Growth." *Journal of Development Economics*. 110 (Sept. 2014): 93–106. doi:10.1016/j.jdeveco.2014.05.005

Bernanke, B.S. and Mihov, I. *What Does the Bundesbank Target?* Working paper no. NBER Working Paper No. 5764. National Bureau of Economic Research, 1996. Web. 11 Feb. 2013. <http://www.nber.org/papers/w5764>.

Binham, C. "Lowball Tenders Aimed to Present Rosy Picture." *Financial Times*. 19 Dec. 2012. Web. 28 Feb 2015. <http://www.ft.com/cms/s/0/c43c92fe-49c7-11e2-a7b1-00144feab49a.html#axzz3T2fM1Sjt>.

Blundell-Wignall, A. and Slovik, P. "The EU Stress Test and Sovereign Debt Exposures." *OECD Working Papers on Finance, Insurance and Private Pensions, No. 4*, OECD Financial Affairs Division. August 2010. Web. 15 March 2013 <http://www.oecd.org/finance/financial-markets/45820698.pdf>.

Bonin, H. "Fashion Trends in Banking Business Models since the 1850s." *Business and Economic History Online*. 2009. Web. 07 Jan. 2014. <http://www.thebhc.org/sites/default/files/bonin.pdf>.

Bordo, M., Eichengreen, B., Klingebiel, D. and Martinez-Peria, M.S. "Is the Crisis Problem Growing More Severe?" *Economic Policy* 16, no. 32 (2001): 51–82. Web. 30 January 30, 2014. doi:10.1111/1468-0327.00070.

Boyd, R. "The Last Days of Bear Stearns", *Fortune Magazine*, 31 March 2008.

Bruck, C. *The Predators' Ball: The inside Story of Drexel Burnham and the Rise of the Junk Bond Raiders*. New York: Penguin Books, 1989.

Braudel, F. *Civilisation and Capitalism, 15th-18th Century, Volume 1: The Structures of Everyday Life*. New York: Harper & Row, 1979.

Braudel, F. *Civilisation and Capitalism, 15th–18th Century, Volume 3: The Perspective of the World*. New York: Harper & Row, 1982.

Brush, S. and Leising, M. "*JPMorgan Among 65 to Register as Swap Dealers Under Dodd-Frank*", *Bloomberg*. N.pag. 2 Jan 2013. Web. 02 Feb. 2015. <http://www.bloomberg.com/news/2013-01-02/jpmorgan-to-barclays-register-as-swap-dealers-under-dodd-frank.html)>.

Buck, T. "Spain". *Financial Times*. 23 Oct. 2013. Web. 3 March 2015. <http://www.ft.com/cms/s/0/fd8a20ca-3b3a-11e3-a7ec-00144feab7de.html#axzz3TL3xAKUj>.

Bussière, E. *Paribas 1872–1992: L'Europe et le Monde*. Anvers (Belgique): Fonds Mercator, 1992.

Caprio, G., Klingebiel, D., Laeven, L. and Noguera, G. *Banking Crises Database*. October 2003. Raw data. The World Bank Group, Washington, D.C.

Chiodo, A.J. and Owyang, M.T. "A Case Study of a Currency Crisis: The Russian Default of 1998." *Federal Reserve Bank of St. Louis Review* 84.6 (2002): 7–17. Web. 17 Sept. 2013. <https://research.stlouisfed.org/publications/review/02/11/ChiodoOwyang.pdf>.

Cohan, W.D. "The Tame Truth About the Wolves of Wall Street." *New York Times*. N.p., 15 Feb. 2014. Web. 15 Feb. 2014. <http://www.nytimes.com/2014/02/16/opinion/sunday/the-tame-truth-about-the-wolves-of-wall-street.html>.

Collyns, C. and Senhadji, A. *Lending Booms, Real Estate Bubbles and The Asian Crisis*. Working paper no. WP/02/20. IMF, Jan. 2002. Web. 7 Sept. 2013. <http://www.imf.org/external/pubs/ft/wp/2002/wp0220.pdf>.

Commodity Futures Trading Commission. "United States Of America Before The Commodity Futures Trading Commission." *Order: CFTC v. Barclays PLC, et al.*, 27 June 2012. Web. 23 November 2012. <http://www.cftc.gov/ucm/groups/public/@lrenforcementactions/documents/legalpleading/enfbarclaysorder062712.pdf>.

Connor, G. and Woo, M. "An Introduction to Hedge Funds." (2003): n. pag. Web. 14 Sept. 2013. <http://www.kantakji.com/media/174620/file1374.pdf>.

Coy, P., Wooley, S., Spiro, L.N. and Glasgall, W. "Failed Wizards of Wall Street." *Business Week* [New York] 21 Sept. 1998: n. pag. Web. 28 Sept. 2013. <http://www.businessweek.com/1998/38/b3596001.htm>.

Crosse, H.D. and Hempel, G.H. *Management Policies for Commercial Banks*. Englewood Cliffs, NJ: Prentice-Hall, 1973.

Davidson, K. and Prior, J. "BNP Paribas Accepts $8.9 Billion Penalty." *Politico*. 30 June 2014. Web. 18 Feb. 2015. <http://www.politico.com/story/2014/06/bnp-paribas-to-plead-guilty-sudan-sanctions-108438.html>.

Deane, M. and Pringle, R. *The Central Banks*. New York: Viking, 1994.

Deen, M. "BNP Fine Shows Need to be Wary of U.S. Rule Changes, Noyer Says". *BloombergBusiness*. 23 May 2014. Web. 28 Feb. 2015. <http://www.bloomberg.com/news/articles/2014-05-23/bnp-fine-shows-need-to-be-wary-of-u-s-rule-changes-noyer-says>.

Dermine, J. "European Banking Integration: Don't Put the Cart before the Horse." *Financial Markets, Institutions and Instruments* 15, no. 2 (2006): 57–106. doi:10.1111/j.0963-8008.2006.00114.x.

Dermine, J. "European Banking: Past, Present and Future." In *The Transformation of the European Financial System*. Proceedings of Second ECB Central Banking Conference, Frankfurt Am Main. 24–5 Oct. 2002. N.p. Web. 18 Feb. 2015. <https://www.ecb.europa.eu/events/pdf/conferences/dermine_comp.pdf>.

Dimon, J. "2012 Annual Report Letter to Shareholders." Letter. 10 Apr. 2013. N.p. Web. 18 Feb. 2014. <http://read.jpmorgan.com/i/281164/10>.

Dimon, J. *JPMorgan Chase & Co. 2012 Annual Report*. Rep. N.p.: n.pag. *Letter to Shareholder*. 10 Apr. 2013. Web. 18 Feb. 2014. <http://read.jpmorgan.com/i/281164/10>.

DiVanna, J.A. *The Future of Retail Banking: Delivering Value to Global Customers*. New York: Palgrave Macmillan, 2004.

Drees, B. and Pazarbasioglu, C. *The Nordic Banking Crisis: Pitfalls in Financial Liberalization*. Washington, D.C.: International Monetary Fund, 1998.

DuChene, C. "Remarks by Carolyn G. DuChene, Deputy Comptroller for Operational Risk." N.p. American Bankers Association Risk Management Forum, Baltimore, April 25, 2013.

Eichengreen, B. and Mathieson, D. "Hedge Funds: What Do We Really Know?" *Economic Issues* No. 19 (1999): n. pag. Web. 24 Sept. 2013. <http://www.imf.org/external/pubs/ft/issues/issues19/>.

Engels, A. *Landesbanken Zwischen Marktsteuerung Und Marktwirtschaft: Staatliche Praäsenz Im Bankenwesen in Zeiten Der Finanzmarktkrise.* Baden-Baden: Nomos, 2010.

Enright, M.J., Newton, J. and Tran, E. *Japanese Banking: Crisis and Reform. Case Study.* Cambridge, MA: Harvard Business Publishing, 2005.

Ewing, J. "Deutsche Bank Vows to Focus on Clients with a New Culture of Ethics." *New York Times.* 19 May 2014. Web. 19 May 2014. <http://dealbook.nytimes.com/2014/05/19/deutsche-bank-vows-to-focus-on-clients-with-a-new-culture-of-ethics/?_r=0>.

European Commission. "Crédit Lyonnais: Commission Approves the French Government's Aid Plan in Return for a Serious 'Slimming Cure'". Press release. 26 July 1995. Web. 18 Dec. 2013. <http://europa.eu/rapid/press-release_IP-95-829_en.htm?locale=en>.

European Commission. "Single Supervisory Mechanism". N.pag. 12. Sept. 2012. Web. 02. Feb. 2015. <http://ec.europa.eu/finance/general-policy/banking-union/single-supervisory-mechanism/index_en.htm>

Fallon, P., Adam, N. and Allard, W. "The Great Deregulation Explosion." *Euromoney*, October 1984, 55–9.

Farrell, G. "New York Regulator Lawsky Settles Cases on His Terms." *Bloomberg.* N.p., 14 Sept. 2014. Web. 14 Sept. 2014. <http://www.bloomberg.com/news/2014-09-14/new-york-regulator-1lawsky-settles-cases-on-his-terms.html>.

Fay, S. *The Collapse of Barings.* London: Norton, 1996.

Federal Reserve Bank of New York. "What We Do – Federal Reserve Bank of New York." N.d. Web. 03 Apr. 2014. <http://www.ny.frb.org/aboutthefed/whatwedo.html>.

Ferguson, N. *The Cash Nexus: Money and Power in the Modern World, 1700–2000.* New York: Basic Books, 2001.

Fight, A. *Syndicated Lending.* Oxford: Elsevier Butterworth-Heinemann, 2004.

Financial Crimes Enforcement Network. *Annual Report Fiscal Year 2004.* Washington, D.C.: Financial Crimes Enforcement Network, 2005.

Financial Crisis Inquiry Report: Final Report of the National Commission on the Causes of the Financial and Economic Crisis in the United States. New York: Perseus Books Group, 2011.

Financial Stability Board. "2013 Update of Group of Global Systemically Important Banks (G-SIBs)". 11 Nov. 2013. Web. 2 March 2015. <http://www.financialstabilityboard.org/wp-content/uploads/r_131111.pdf>.

Financial Stability Board, *Strengthening the Oversight and Regulation of Shadow Banking Progress Report to G20 Ministers and Governors.* Basel: Financial Stability Board, 2012. Web. 02 Feb 2015. <http://www.financialstabilityboard.org/publications/r_120420c.pdf>.

Finel-Honigman, I. *A Cultural History of Finance.* Abingdon, Oxon: Routledge, 2010.

Fink, G., Haiss, P., Orlowski, L. and Salvatore, D. "Central European Banks and Stock Exchanges: Capacity Building and Institutional Development". *European Management Journal*, 1998. 16 (4): 431–46.

Fitschen, J. and Jain, A. "Restoring the bond of trust with society is a top priority – for the banking industry and for Deutsche Bank." Deutsche Bank Strategy. March 2014. Web. 28 Feb. 2015. https://www.db.com/cr/en/strategy/fitschen-jain-on-responsibility.htm

Fisher, S. "The IMF and the Asian Crisis." Lecture. N.p. Forum Funds Lecture, UCLA, Los Angeles, March 20, 1998.

Fitch Ratings. *Country Report: Russian Banking System and Prudential Regulation*. Report. New York and London: Fitch Ratings, 2007.

Fitch Ratings. "Credit Suisse Settlement Sets Precedent for Others." *Fitch Wire*. 21 May 2014. Web. 3 June 2014. <https://www.fitchratings.com/gws/en/fitchwire/fitchwirearticle/Credit-Suisse-Settlement?pr_id=831115>.

Fitzpatrick, D. "J.P. Morgan Settles Its Madoff Tab." *Wall Street Journal*. N.p., 7 Jan. 2014. Web. 7 Jan. 2014. <http://online.wsj.com/news/articles/SB10001424052702304887104579306323011059460>.

Galbraith, J.K. *The Great Crash 1929*. (1988) New York: Penguin, 1954.

Gasparino, C. *Blood on the Street: The Sensational inside Story of How Wall Street Analysts Duped a Generation of Investors*. New York: Free Press, 2005.

Gerdesmeier, D., Mongelli, F.P. and Roffia, B. "The Eurosystem, the U.S. Federal Reserve, and the Bank of Japan: Similarities and Differences." *Journal of Money, Credit and Banking* 39(7) (2007): 1785–1819. doi: 10.1111/j.1538-4616.2007.00087.x

Glover, J. "Stanley Ross Eluded Nazi Bombs to Transform World Bond Markets." *Bloomberg.com*. N.p., 25 June 2013. Web. 25 June 2013. <http://www.bloomberg.com/news/2013-06-25/stanley-ross-eluded-nazi-bombs-to-transform-world-bond-markets.html>.

Goeltom, M. *Indonesia's Banking Industry: Progress to Date*. BIS Papers no. 28, part 15, August 2006. 243–7. Web. 02 Feb. 2015. <http://www.bis.org/publ/bppdf/bispap28o.pdf>.

Goethe, J.W. Von (1879) *Faust Part II*; trans. B. Taylor, New York: Crowell-Collier Co.

Goldfajn, I., Hennings, K. and Mori, H. *Working Paper Series ISSN 1518-3548 Brazil's Financial System: Resilience to Shocks, No Currency Substitution, But Struggling to Promote Growth*. Working paper. Brasilia: Banco Central Do Brasil, 2003.

Gordon, A. *A Modern History of Japan: From Tokugawa times to the Present*. New York: Oxford UP, 2003.

Greenville, S. *The IMF and the Indonesian Crisis*, IEO Background Paper, International Monetary Fund, BP/04/3, May 2004. Web. 02 Feb. 2015. <http://www.ieo-imf.org/ieo/files/completedevaluations/BP043.pdf>.

Hancock, D. "'An Undiscovered Ocean of Commerce Laid Open': India, Wine and the Emerging Atlantic Economy, 1703–1813." *The Worlds of the East India Company*. Ed. Bowen, H.V., Lincoln, M. and Rigby, N. Martlesham: Boydell & Brewer, 2002. 153–68.

Hernández-Murillo, R. "Experiments in Financial Liberalization: The Mexican Banking Sector", *Federal Reserve Bank of St. Louis Review*, 89.5 (Sep/Oct 2007): 415–32. Web. 02 Feb. 2015. <https://research.stlouisfed.org/publications/review/07/09/HernandezMurillo.pdf>.

Holder, E. "Too Big to Jail." Senate Judiciary Committee. Washington, D.C. 6 March 2013. Web. 1 Sept. 2014. <http://www.americanbanker.com/issues/178_45/transcript-attorney-general-eric-holder-on-too-big-to-jail-1057295-1.html>.

HSBC. *"HSBC to Sell its Card and Retail Services Business in the US."* Press release. 10 August 2011. Web. 23 Feb. 2014. <http://www.us.hsbc.com/1/2/home/about/press-room/2011/news_08102011_card_sale>.

HSBC. *HSBC Holdings Plc Annual Results 2012*. Rep. N.p., 4 Mar. 2013. Web. 02 Feb. 2014. <http://www.hsbc.com/news-and-insight/2013/hsbc-annual-results>.

Hughes, J.E. and MacDonald, S.B. *International Banking: Text and Cases*. Boston, MA: Addison Wesley, 2002.

Independent Commission on Banking. *Final Report. Recommendations*. London: ICB. Web. 12 Feb. 2015. <http://webarchive.nationalarchives.gov.uk/20131003105424/https://hmt-sanctions.s3.amazonaws.com/ICB%20final%20report/ICB%2520Final%2520Report%5B1%5D.pdf>.

ING Groep. *ING Group Annual Report 2013*. Report. March 2014. Web. 15 May 2014. <http://www.ing.com/About-us/Annual-Reports.htm>.

International Finance Corporation, *Emerging Stock Markets Factbook*. Washington, D.C.: International Finance, 1997.

International Monetary Fund, "Lending by the IMF". Web. 21 Jan. 2014. <http://www.imf.org/external/about/lending.htm>.

International Monetary Fund, *IMF Approves Third and Fourth Turkey Reviews and US$ 7.5 Billion, Supplemental Reserve Facility Credit*, Press Release No. 00/80, December 21, 2000. Web. 2 Feb. 2015. <https://www.imf.org/external/np/sec/pr/2000/pr0080.htm>.

International Monetary Fund. *Indonesia: Financial Sector Assessment Program*, IMF Country Report No. 12/335, December 2012. Web. 2 Feb. 2015. <https://www.imf.org/external/pubs/ft/scr/2012/cr12335.pdf>.

International Monetary Fund, *Mexico: Financial System Stability Assessment*, IMF Country Report No. 12/65, March 2012. Web. 2 Feb. 2015. <http://www.imf.org/external/pubs/ft/scr/2012/cr1265.pdf>.

International Monetary Fund, *People's Republic of China: Financial System Stability Assessment*, IMF Country Report No. 11/321, November 2011. Web. 2 Feb. 2015. <http://www.imf.org/external/pubs/ft/scr/2011/cr11321.pdf>.

International Monetary Fund, *Russian Federation: Financial System Stability Assessment*, IMF Country Report No. 11/291, September 2011. Web. 2 Feb. 2015. <http://www.imf.org/external/pubs/ft/scr/2011/cr11291.pdf>.

International Monetary Fund. *South Africa: Detailed Assessment of Compliance on Basel Core Principles for Effective Banking Supervision*, IMF Country Report No. 10/353, December 2010. Web. 2 Feb. 2012. <http://www.imf.org/external/pubs/ft/scr/2010/cr10353.pdf>.

International Monetary Fund. *Sovereign Debt Restructuring – Recent Developments and Implications for the Fund's Legal and Policy Framework*. Rep. N.p., 26 Apr. 2013. Web. 20 Nov. 2013. <http://www.imf.org/external/np/pp/eng/2013/042613.pdf>.

International Monetary Fund, *Turkey: Financial System Stability Assessment*, IMF Country Report No. 12/261, September 2012. Web. 2 Feb. 2015. <http://www.imf.org/external/pubs/ft/scr/2012/cr12261.pdf>.

Jabaily, R. "Bank Holiday of 1933." *100 Years: Federal Reserve System*. N.p., n.d. Web. 4 June 2013. <http://www.federalreservehistory.org/Events/DetailView/22>.

Jeanneney, J-N. *L'Argent Caché*. Paris: Fayard, 1981.

Jenkins, P., Goff, S. and Mathurin, P. "Bank Ties across EU Carry Risk Concerns." *Financial Times*. N.p., 1 Dec. 2010. Web. 24 Oct. 2013. <http://www.ft.com/intl/cms/s/0/db36d854-fd82-11df-a049-00144feab49a.html#axzz3Eqxi0huz>.

Jonung, L. *The Swedish Model for Resolving the Banking Crisis of 1991–93 Seven Reasons Why it was Successful*. Brussels: European Commission. Feb. 2009. Web. 12 December 2013. <http://ec.europa.eu/economy_finance/publications/publication14134_en.pdf>.

Jordan, P. and Jeffs, L. "LSE, TMX Abort Their Merger, Leaving Both in Play." Reuters. 29 June 2011. Web. 9 May 2014. <http://www.reuters.com/article/2011/06/29/us-tmx-halt-idUSTRE75S5KL20110629>.

Kamm, T. "Alarm Grows as Credit Lyonnais Smolders Amid Heavy Criticism." *Wall Street Journal*, 4 October 1996.

Kaufman, G.G. and Kroszner, R. *How Should Financial Institutions and Markets be Structured?* Washington, D.C.: Inter-American Development Bank, 1997.

Kerry, J. and Brown, H. "The BCCI Affair: A Report to the Committee on Foreign Relations United States Senate." Report. December 1992. N.p. Web. 28 Feb. 2015. <https://info.publicintelligence.net/The-BCCI-Affair.pdf>.

Kindleberger, C.P. *A Financial History of Western Europe*. London: Routledge, 1985.

Kindleberger, C.P. *A Financial History of Western Europe*. 2nd ed. Oxford: Oxford University Press, 1993.

Kindleberger, C.P. and Aliber, R.Z. *Manias, Panics, and Crashes: A History of Financial Crises*. Hoboken, NJ: John Wiley & Sons, 2011.

Kobrak, C. *Banking on Global Markets: Deutsche Bank and the United States, 1870 to the Present*. Cambridge: Cambridge UP, 2008.

Landes, D.S. *The Wealth and Poverty of Nations: Why Some Are so Rich and Some so Poor*. New York: W.W. Norton, 1998.

Liikanen, E. *et al*. *High Level Expert Group on Reforming the Structure of the EU Banking Sector: Final Report*. October 2012. Web. 12 Feb. 2015. <http://ec.europa.eu/internal_market/bank/docs/high-level_expert_group/report_en.pdfc.eur>.

Mandell, L. *The Credit Card Industry: A History*. Boston, MA: Twayne Publishers, 1990.

Mayer, M. *The Bankers: The Next Generation*. New York: Truman Talley Books, 1997.

Mays, E. *Credit Scoring for Risk Managers: The Handbook for Lenders*. Mason, OH: Thomson/South-Western, 2004.

Maude, D. *Global Private Banking and Wealth Management: The New Realities*. Chichester, West Sussex, England: J. Wiley & Sons, 2006.

de la Merced, M.J. "Santander Mexican's Unit Sells U.S. Shares at $12.18 in Dual Listing". *DealBook, New York Times*. 25 September 2012. Web. 28 Feb. 2015. <dealbook.nytimes.com/2012/09/25/santanders-mexican-arm-said-to-price-its-i-p-o-at-12-18/>.

Mihm, S. *A Nation of Counterfeiters: Capitalists, Con Men, and the Making of the United States*. Cambridge, MA: Harvard University Press, 2007.

Miller, R.B. *Citicorp, the Story of a Bank in Crisis*. New York: McGraw Hill, 1993.

Mongelli, F.P., Gerdesmeier, D. and Roffia, B. "The Fed, the Eurosystem, and the Bank of Japan: More Similarities or Differences?" *VOX*. N.p., 7 Feb. 2009. Web. 13 Mar. 2014. <http://www.voxeu.org>.

Mongelli, P., Gerdesmeier, D. and Roffia, B. "The Fed, the Eurosystem, and the Bank of Japan: More Similarities or Differences?" N.p., 7 Feb. 2009. Web. 3 June 2014. <http://www.voxeu.org/article/fed-eurosystem-and-bank-japan-similarities-and-differences>.

Mundell, R. "The Case for the Euro." *The Wall Street Journal* 24–25 Mar. 1998: n. pag.

Myers, M.G. *A Financial History of the United States*. New York: Columbia UP, 1970.

Nash, N.C. "Treasury Now Favors Creation Of Huge Banks." *The New York Times*, June 7, 1987, n.pag.

Northern Rock Plc. *Northern Rock Annual Report and Accounts 2006*. Report. 2006. Web. 27 Feb. 2015. <http://www.n-ram.co.uk/~/media/Files/N/NRAM-PLC/documents/corporate-reports/res2006pr-annualreportandaccounts.pdf>.

Norris, F. "JPMorgan Lost Madoff in a Blizzard of Paper." *New York Times* 10 Jan. 2014, B1 sec.: n. pag.

Norris, F. "Masked by Gibberish, the Risks Run Amok." *New York Times* 22 Mar. 2013, B1 sec.: n. pag. Web. 1 Sept. 2014. <http://www.nytimes.com/2013/03/22/business/behind-the-derivatives-gibberish-risks-run-amok.html?pagewanted=all>.

Office of the Comptroller of the Currency. *Annual Report Fiscal Year 1927*. Report. Washington D.C.: Office of the Comptroller of the Currency, 1928.

Office of the Comptroller of the Currency. *Annual Report Fiscal Year 1928*. Report. Washington D.C.: Office of the Comptroller of the Currency, 1929.

Office of the Comptroller of the Currency. *Annual Report Fiscal Year 1929*. Report. Washington D.C.: Office of the Comptroller of the Currency, 1930.

Office of the Comptroller of the Currency. *Annual Report Fiscal Year 2007*. Report. Washington D.C.: Office of the Comptroller of the Currency, 2008.

Penty, C. and Burton, K. "Santander Offers $1.8 Billion to End Madoff Claims (Update 1)." Bloomberg.com. 28 Jan. 2009. Web. 21 April 2014. <http://www.bloomberg.com/apps/news?pid=newsarchive&sid=afbawNhFQex0>.

""Ponzi" Schemes." *SEC.gov*. N.p., n.d. Web. 01 May 2014. <http://www.sec.gov/answers/ponzi.htm>.

Portes, R. "Debt and the Banks: East Europe's Debt to the West: Interdependence is a Two-Way Street." *Foreign Affairs* 55.4 (1977): 751–82. Web. 13 Sept. 2014. <http://www.foreignaffairs.com/articles/27893/richard-portes/debt-and-the-banks-east-europes-debt-to-the-west-interdependence>.

Pyle, K.B. *The Making of Modern Japan*. Lexington, MA; Toronto: D. C. Heath, 1996.

Rabobank. "The Russian Crisis 1998." *Economic Report* (2013): n. pag. Web. 28 Sept. 2013. <https://economics.rabobank.com/publications/2013/september/the-russian-crisis-1998/>.

Rathbone, J.P. "Money Laundering: Taken to the Cleaners." *Financial Times*. N.p., 20 July 2012. Web. 20 Feb. 2014. <http://www.ft.com/intl/cms/s/0/702a64a6-d25e-11e1-ac21-00144feabdc0.html>.

Regling, K. and Watson, M. *A Preliminary Report on The Sources of Ireland's Banking Crisis*. Report. Claremorris: Government Publications, 2010.

Reinhart, C.M. and Rogoff, K.S. *This Time Is Different: Eight Centuries of Financial Folly*. Princeton: Princeton UP, 2009.

Reuters. "Banco Santander's Brazil Unit Raises $8 billion in I.P.O". *New York Times*. 7 Oct. 2009. Web. 28 Feb. 2015. <http://www.nytimes.com/2009/10/08/business/global/08santander.html>.

Rhodes, W.R. *Banker to the World: Leadership Lessons From the Front Lines of Global Finance*. New York: Mc Graw Hill, 2011.

Roscini, D., Schlefer, J. and Dimitriou, K. "The Greek Crisis: Tragedy or Opportunity?" Harvard Business School Case 711-088, April 2011. (Revised September 2011.)

Rose, C.S. and Sesia, A. *Barclays and the LIBOR Scandal*. Publication no. 9-313-075. 22nd ed. Vol. May. Boston: Harvard Business School, 2013. Print. Ser. 2013.

Rosenberg, M. "Audit Says Kabul Bank Began as 'Ponzi' Scheme". *New York Times*. 26 Nov. 2012. Web. 28 Feb. 2015. <http://www.nytimes.com/2012/11/27/world/asia/kabul-bank-audit-details-extent-of-fraud.html?pagewanted=all&_r=0>.

Rudé, G. *The History of London*. London: Secker & Warburg, 1971.

Ryback, W. *Case Study on Bear Stearns*. Report. Toronto: Toronto Leadership Center. N.d. Web. 7 Dec. 2013. <http://siteresources.worldbank.org/FINANCIALSECTOR/Resources/02BearStearnsCaseStudy.pdf>.

Saltmarsh, M. "Swiss Near Tax Treaties with Germany and Britain". *New York Times*. N.pag. 9 August 2011. Web. 02 Feb. 2015. <http://www.nytimes.com/2011/08/10/business/global/switzerland-moves-to-squeeze-tax-evaders.html?pagewabted+all&_r=2&>

Sawaya, A.J. "Financing Latin America's Low-income Consumers." *The McKinsey Quarterly, 2007 Special Edition: Shaping a New Agenda for Latin America*. 1 Mar. 2007, 58–69. Web. 27 Feb. 2015. <http://www.mckinsey.it/idee/mckinsey_quarterly/financing-latin-americas-low-income-consumers.view>.

Schaede, U. *The 1995 Financial Crisis in Japan*. Working paper no. 85. UC Berkeley: BRIE (Berkeley Roundtable on the International Economy), 1996.

"Shaking Up Europe's Banks." *The Financial Times* (London). Editorial: n. pag. 24 August 1999.

Shull, B. *The Fourth Branch: The Federal Reserve's Unlikely Rise to Power and Influence.* Westport, CT: Praeger, 2005.

Singer, M. *Funny Money.* New York: Knopf, 1985.

Sinkey, J.F. *Commercial Bank Financial Management in the Financial-services Industry.* Upper Saddle River, NJ: Prentice Hall, 1998.

Smith, A. *The Wealth of Nations.* London: W. Strahan and T. Cadell, 1776.

Smith, B.M. *The Equity Culture: The Story of the Global Stock Market.* New York: Farrar, Straus and Giroux, 2003.

Smith, J. "Britain's Labour Party Plans a Post-Thatcher Government." *The International Economy* (1990): n. pag. Web. 21 Jan. 2014.

Sotelino, F. "The Financial Services Industry", in *The Brazilian State; Debate and Agenda.* Eds M. Font and L. Randall. New York: Lexington Books, 2011.

Sotelino, F. and Bermudez, R. "Universal Banking Post Crisis." N.p. 6th IFABS Conference on Alternative Futures for Global Banking, Lisbon, June 2014.

Sotelino, F. and Gustafson, M., "Tailoring the Financing Decision to Project Economics", in *Finance for the Minerals Industry.* Baltimore, MD: Society of Mining Engineers, 1985.

South African Reserve Bank. "History of South African Banknotes 1782 to 1920." N.d. Web. 9 Sept. 2013. <https://www.resbank.co.za/BanknotesandCoin/SouthAfricanCurrency/BankNotes/Pages/HistoryofSouthAfricanbanknotes1782To1920.aspx>.

Spruk, R. "Iceland's Financial and Economic Crisis: Causes, Consequences and Implications." 25 February 2010. Web. 9 March 2010. <http://papers.ssrn.com/sol3/papers.cfm?abstract_id=1574296>.

Standard & Poor's. *Sovereign Government Rating Methodology And Assumptions.* Rep. N.p., 30 June 2011. Web. 14 May 2013. <http://www.standardandpoors.com/spf/upload/Ratings_EMEA/2011-06-30_CBEvent_CriteriaGovSovRatingMethodologyAndAssumptions.pdf>.

Steil, B. *The Battle of Bretton Woods: John Maynard Keynes, Harry Dexter White, and the Making of a New World Order.* Princeton: Princeton University Press, 2013.

Stewart, J.B. *Den of Thieves.* New York: Simon & Schuster, 1991.

Strouse, J. *Morgan: American Financier.* New York: Random House, 1999.

Swagel, P. "Why Lehman Wasn't Rescued", Economix, *The New York Times.* N.pag. September 13, 2013. Web. 03 Feb. 2015 <http://economix.blogs.nytimes.com/2013/09/13/why-lehman-wasnt-rescued/?_r=0>.

The Economist. "Called to Account." N.p., 28 Feb. 2009. Web. 01 Sept. 2014. <http://www.economist.com/node/13186205>.

The Economist. "Europe's Adventure Begins" N. pag. 31 Dec. 1988. Web. 10 Oct. 2013. <http://www.economist.com/node/180539?fsrc=scn/fb/wl/tm/1998/europesadventurebegins>.

The Economist. "The Lesson of Credit Lyonnais". 5 July 1997. Web. 27 Feb. 2015. <http://www.economist.com/node/150795>.

The New York Times, "Bankers Discuss Far Eastern Commerce." October 18, 1901.

Third Annual Report of the Trade Promotion Coordinating Committee. Rep. Washington, DC: U.S. Government Printing Office, 1995. Web. 4 Apr. 2014. <https://ia600400.us.archive.org/10/items/thirdannualrepor00unit/thirdannualrepor00unit.pdf>.

Treaty on European Union, The Maastricht Treaty. Luxembourg: Office for Official Publications of the European Communities, 1993.

Truman, E.M. "The Mexican Peso Crisis: Implications for International Finance." *Federal Reserve Bulletin March 1996* (1996): 199–209. *Federal Reserve.* Web. 12 Dec. 2013. <http://www.federalreserve.gov/pubs/bulletin/1996/396lead.pdf>.

Tschoegl, A. *Foreign Ownership in Mexican Banking*. Philadelphia, PA: The Wharton School of the University of Pennsylvania, October 2006.

UBS. *AG Form 20-F 2010*. SEC Filings. 15 March 2011. Web. 21 Jan. 2014. <http://www.ubs.com/global/en/about_ubs/investor_relations/other_filings/sec.html>.

UBS. *AG Form 20-F 2011*. SEC Filings. 15 March 2012. Web. 21 Jan. 2014. <http://www.ubs.com/global/en/about_ubs/investor_relations/other_filings/sec.html>.

UBS. "Transparency Report." Report. October 2010. Web. 11 Feb. 2014. <http://www.ubs.com/global/en/about_ubs/transparencyreport.html>.

Ugeux, G. *The Betrayal of Finance*. New York: Galileo Global Institute, 2012.

Unicredit Group. "Listen, understand, respond." 2013 Consolidated Reports and Accounts. N.d. Web. 28 August 2014. <www.unicreditgroup.eu/content/dam/unicreditgroup/documents/en/investors/financial-reports/2013/2013-Consolidated-Reports-and Accounts.pdf>.

United States Department of Justice. "Credit Suisse Pleads Guilty to Conspiracy to Aid and Assist U.S. Taxpayers in Filing False Returns". Press Release. 19 May 2014. Web. 20 May 2014. <http://www.justice.gov/opa/pr/credit-suisse-pleads-guilty-conspiracy-aid-and-assist-us-taxpayers-filing-false-returns>.

de la Vega, J.P. *Confusion De Confusiones*. Amsterdam, 1688.

Vogl, F. *Waging War on Corruption: Inside the Movement Fighting the Abuse of Power*. Lanham, MD: Rowman & Littlefield Publishers, 2012.

Waersted, G. "Wealth Management Presentation." Nordea. 26 Oct. 2011. Web. 21 Jan. 2014. <http://www.nordea.com/sitemod/upload/Root/www.nordea.com%20-%20uk/Investorrelations/presentations/2011/111026_CMD_Wealth_Management.pdf>.

Weber, B. and Alfen, H.W. *Infrastructure as an Asset Class: Investment Strategies, Project Finance and PPP*. Chichester, West Sussex, U.K.: Wiley, 2010.

Werker, E., Fisman, R. J. and Weber, L. *Hermitage's Russian Quandary A*. April 25, 2011. Harvard Business School BGIE Unit Case No. 711-054, n.d.

Wilkins, M. *The History of Foreign Investment in the United States to 1914*. Cambridge, MA: Harvard University Press, 1989.

Wolf, M. "Banks are on a Eurozone Knife-edge". *Financial Times*. 24 April 2012. Web. 3 March 2015. <http://www.ft.com/cms/s/0/035c1b2e-8d37-11e1-8b49-00144feab49a.html#axzz3TL3xAKUj>.

World Bank. "The World Bank in Russia. Russia Economic Report. No. 22. June 2010. Web. 3 March 3015. <http://siteresources.worldbank.org/INTRUSSIANFEDERATION/Resources/305499-1245838520910/rer_22_eng.pdf>.

Yago, K. *The Financial History of the Bank for International Settlements*. Hoboken: Taylor and Francis, 2012.

Index